LEGAL PERSPECTIVES ON SUSTAINABILITY

Edited by
Margherita Pieraccini and Tonia Novitz

BRISTOL
UNIVERSITY
PRESS

First published in Great Britain in 2020 by

Bristol University Press
University of Bristol
1-9 Old Park Hill
Bristol
BS2 8BB
UK
t: +44 (0)117 954 5940
www.bristoluniversitypress.co.uk

North America office:
Bristol University Press
c/o The University of Chicago Press
1427 East 60th Street
Chicago, IL 60637, USA
t: +1 773 702 7700
f: +1 773 702 9756
sales@press.uchicago.edu
www.press.uchicago.edu

British Library Cataloguing in Publication Data
A catalogue record for this book is available from the British Library.

Library of Congress Cataloging-in-Publication Data
A catalog record for this book has been requested.

ISBN 978-1-5292-0100-0 hardback
ISBN 978-1-5292-0102-4 ePub
ISBN 978-1-5292-0101-7 ePDF

Cover design by blu inc
Front cover: Getty Images/Steven Robinson Pictures
Printed and bound in Great Britain by CPI Group (UK) Ltd, Croydon, CR0 4YY
Bristol University Press uses environmentally responsible print partners

FSC www.fsc.org MIX Paper from responsible sources FSC® C013604

Contents

PART IV: Places

Notes on Contributors

Nina Boeger is a qualified solicitor and Reader in Law at the University of Bristol Law School. Her research considers sustainable forms of corporate governance, with a particular interest in the development of social and cooperative enterprises. She is co-director of the Law School's Centre for Law and Enterprise.

Clair Gammage is Senior Lecturer in Law at the University of Bristol Law School. Her research interests lie at the intersection between international trade and investment and sustainable development.

Tonia Novitz is Professor of Labour Law at the University of Bristol. Her research interests focus predominantly on labour law, trade law and the protection of human rights.

Margherita Pieraccini is Reader in Law at the University of Bristol. She conducts socio-legal research in environmental matters with a special focus on nature conservation law, marine policy and the commons.

Georgina Tsagas is Senior Lecturer in Private and Commercial Law at Brunel University London Law School and a practising solicitor qualified in England and Wales. Her expertise lies in the areas of mergers and acquisitions law, corporate law and corporate governance. Through her participation in EU-funded research groups that focus on business and sustainability, she conducts research on the role of law in supporting sustainable business practices.

Charlotte Villiers is Professor of Company Law and Corporate Governance at the University of Bristol and is a qualified solicitor. Her publications include *European Company Law – Towards Democracy* (Ashgate, 1998) and *Corporate Reporting and Company Law* (Cambridge University Press, 2006). Her current research focuses on company law and sustainability, including reporting, and on boardroom structures, cultures and worker participation.

Chris Willmore is a qualified barrister and Emeritus Professor of Sustainability and Law at Bristol University. Her research focuses on sustainability and land use, and the innovative pedagogies associated with sustainability.

Introduction

Margherita Pierracini and Tonia Novitz

Sustainability has dominated the policy discourse for at least five decades, with its most popular articulation to be found in the Brundtland report in 1987 (World Commission on Environment and Development, 1987). Today, Agenda 2030 and the Sustainable Development Goals (SDGs) (UN, 2015) have renewed concern with legal perspectives on sustainability, for, at the European and domestic levels, sustainability and sustainable development are prominent in policy, and also in legally binding instruments. Examples include Article 3 of the Treaty on EU, which makes sustainable development a goal for the Union, and the environmental integration principle in Article 11 of the Treaty on the Functioning of the European Union. Sustainable development was mainstreamed into the Europe 2020 strategy in 2010 (EU, 2010), it is included in the 7th Environmental Action Programme and more recently a Communication from the Commission considers the steps for a sustainable European future integrating the SDGs in the European policy framework (European Commission, 2016). At the domestic level, in the UK sustainable development was introduced as the main aim of the Environment Agency with the Environment Act 1995 and today there are a number of statutes incorporating sustainable development as an aim or duty (such as the Marine and Coastal Access Act 2009 and the Well-being of Future Generations (Wales) Act 2015).

Although the policy roots of sustainability date back over 50 years and the sustainability rhetoric today is more visible than ever in the SDGs, the meaning of sustainability and its relationship with law remain highly contested and complex. Indeed, the mainstreaming of sustainable development has not meant homologation. Distinct legal fields, permeated by sustainability, engage with sustainability differently. This book reflects on the multiple intersections of law and sustainability in a variety of fields. Only by considering sustainability through different legal sources and fields is it possible to provide a more comprehensive analysis of the way in which sustainability discourses push certain legal boundaries and the way in which the law itself pushes sustainability in multiple directions. The relationship between law and sustainability is not only a positive one of mutual constitution but can also cause frictions when established legal norms are diluted or legal benchmarks lowered by the SDGs or, alternatively, where the law dichotomises and simplifies sustainability, reducing it to a trade-off between economic and social-economic issues. Such complex entanglements have serious implications for both procedural and substantive justice issues for present and future generations and for the possible sustainable futures. This book explores some of these implications, with a special, though not exclusive, focus on procedural issues regarding inclusion in sustainability decision making and with critical reflections on different visions of sustainability, their conflicts and possible reconciliations.

The book brings together University of Bristol Law School academics with different expertise who research, write and teach in the field of sustainability to provide a critical exploration of sustainability from a variety of legal perspectives. The book stems from a workshop conducted at the University of Bristol in November 2018, where the contributors, together with a number of invited discussants from sustainability studies, offered their reflections on how sustainability had entered their legal field. The speakers, who had also contributed to the teaching of a postgraduate sustainability law module at the University of Bristol Law School, were selected as experts in different legal fields, since the aim was to investigate how sustainability was affecting diverse legal sectors in multiple ways. The book mirrors that diversity, examining sustainability in three broad thematic areas: in corporate governance, in international trade and in places (land and sea). The different contributions examine these themes at a variety of jurisdictional levels (international, European and domestic laws).

Including multiple jurisdictional levels and different thematic areas enables the authors to provide a multifaceted picture of the relationship between law and sustainability, thereby offering reflections not only on different legal sectors' relations with sustainability but also on the ways in which sustainability is interpreted and reinterpreted at different scales. The book aims to move debates beyond a familiar 'pillar approach' to sustainability, taking seriously, yet critically, the holistic aspirations of Agenda 2030. By adopting a broad critical legal perspective on sustainability the book provides an important addition to the academic literature in the area, taking the reader on a journey that goes from the international to the local, from corporate governance to trade issues and from land to sea.

The book is divided into four parts. The chapters in Part I, respectively on the history of sustainability and on the SDGs, provide the co-editors' analysis of the legal and policy foundations of sustainability, informed by critical legal theory. Chapter 1, in tracing the historical legal and policy development of sustainability discourse, discusses the role of sustainability as a directing principle of post-modern law, drawing on de Sadeleer (2002), and in doing so shows how sustainability operates at the borders between the political, legal and ethical fields. This chapter also questions some recurrent assumptions such as sustainability's anthropocentrism and the call for integrating three ontologically separated pillars. In doing so it pushes for a rethinking of sustainability based on a relational approach and on critical debate and inclusion. The subject of inclusion is investigated further in Chapter 2, which focuses on the current framing of sustainability under Agenda 2030 and the SDGs.Chapter 2 follows a threefold structure that looks at the drafting of the SDGs, their content and their supervision through the High-Level Political Forum. The (dis)continuities between SDGs and established international legal norms are discussed, together with the voices that are shaping the sustainability discourse.

Part II presents two contributions on the first broad theme, corporate governance. The two chapters can be read in a continuum. Indeed, Chapter 3 engages with a key issue in debates on sustainability and corporate governance, namely sustainability accounting. In this chapter Villiers and Tsagas present a sophisticated critique of climate accounting at both the international level and the UK level, discussing the shortcoming of UK company law on reporting requirements and enforcement. The chapter then focuses on the issue of risk, arguing that the way it is interpreted matters for the way in which corporations account for their climate change impact. Two types of risks are introduced, with the first narrowly defined as risk to profit maximisation, the second as wider risk to planet and people. As Villiers and Tsagas argue, it is the first type of risk that permeates the corporate response to sustainability reporting in UK company law, and steps are then proposed to move to a less-growth orientated sustainability reporting. The growth-oriented view on sustainability is one of the two main perspectives identified by Boeger in Chapter 4. For Boeger, a thinner perspective, articulated by the author as 'trimming', is centred on sustainable capitalism and does not question the objective of sustainable economic growth. A stronger perspective, articulated by the author as 'sowing', centres on sustainable living and sustainable systems, insisting that more fundamental changes and systemic revisions, including of the growth objective itself, are necessary. As Boeger argues, the two perspectives do not stand necessarily in contradiction to each other but can be complementary, as evidenced by recent moves in UK corporate governance. This view accords with the argument proposed in Chapter 1 on the pluralisation of sustainability, against a unified and single sustainable future.

Not dissimilarly, Part III opens with a contribution by Gammage (Chapter 5) on World Trade Organization (WTO) law and food security, which considers tensions between the liberal view of the international trade system oriented towards economic freedom and rights-based understandings of food security. In this context, she addresses the scope of SDG 2, which aims to 'end hunger, achieve food security and improved nutrition, and promote sustainable agriculture', alongside SDG 17, which envisages an important role for the WTO in reforming global markets sustainably. Her finding is that food security remains the site of contestation for WTO members, with tensions between developing countries in the global South and so-called developed states remaining (as yet) unresolved. She also points to the problems inherent in excluding civil society from engagement with these issues, which are dealt with at a technical level oriented only towards state engagement. Gammage's argument, ultimately, is for 'the reimagination of the trading system as an institutional setting of collective responsibility that seeks to redress the harmful effects of the trade rules'.

Trade issues are also explored in Chapter 6 by Novitz, this time in the context of labour law. Novitz examines both the International Labour Organization (ILO) and the EU conceptualisations of the link between sustainability and labour objectives, noting differences and developments in the level and type of engagement with trade-related issues. In so doing she reflects on ways in which trade and policy coherence objectives in SDG 17 may be achieved with future evolutions of both ILO and EU approaches. For Novitz, attention should be focused on SDG 16 to facilitate the much-needed dialogues to forge connections and solutions.

Finally, Part IV engages with the connections between sustainability and law in different 'places'. Places are understood as a coming together of social-ecological practices and norms in two selected geographical spaces, namely land and sea. Chapter 7 focuses on land and the connections between property rights, regulation and sustainability. Willmore argues in this chapter that the best way to facilitate constructive connections between landowners, state and sustainability is not necessarily through an abdication of responsibility to state regulation or a complete change in the focus and distribution of property rights, but through a pluriversal understanding of the role of land in creating sustainable futures. Such pluriversality, which recalls the discussions in Chapter 1, is theoretically anchored in the relational approach to property envisaged by Radin (1982; 1993). For Willmore there is still a role for property law in the realisation of sustainable land use if pluriversality is welcome.

Chapter 8 moves to the sea to explore, from the context of SDG 14.5, the extent to which EU marine conservation law is indicative of a relational and inclusive approach to sustainability. Drawing on the theoretical insights developed in Chapters 1 and 2, Pieraccini argues that the holism envisaged by Agenda 2030 should be understood not as an attempt to integrate separate pre-existing pillars (environmental and socio-economic) and unify all voices and perspectives into a single whole, but in terms of relational ontology and the ability to bring in plural perspectives on conservation to decision-making fora so as to achieve further inclusivity. Three main sustainability criteria are extrapolated from the theoretically informed reading of SDG 14.5, namely (1) substantive socio-ecological inter-pillar relationality, (2) intra-pillar relationality, unpacking the 'environmental' pillar and (3) procedural inclusion through participatory decision making. This purposive reading of SDG 14.5 is juxtaposed with the approach to sustainability inherent in current EU marine conservation law. Focusing on Council Directive 92/43/EEC (the 'Habitats Directive'), the cornerstone of conservation law in the EU, Pieraccini argues that this Directive falls short of meeting the three sustainability criteria identified.

From this brief introduction, it is evident how the many connections between the chapters cut across the different parts of the book. For instance, the relational view of sustainability emerges in Chapter 1, in Chapter 7 and Chapter 8. The conceptualisation of sustainability as a directing principle, borrowed from de Sadeleer and redefined in specific contexts, is another common ground between Chapter 1 and Chapter 4. Chapter 5 explores the idea of 'global partnership', while Chapter 6 points to the importance of SDG 16 in facilitating the inclusion needed to pluralise sustainability. What all the chapters have in common is an interest with issues of inclusion and pluralisation, demonstrating in different ways how sometimes divergent, sometimes complementary perspectives exist in the conceptualisation of sustainability, and reflecting on how these are internalised by different legal systems in distinct fields. As a whole, the book seeks to reach beyond standard assumptions permeating the sustainability discourse relating to the dominance of the economic sphere in corporate governance and the trade sphere, and the dominance of the 'environment' in marine governance and property law. In doing so, the book considers how legal mechanisms can facilitate or overlook participatory engagement with diverse voices and scope for dissent. In this way, we interrogate the role of law in questioning or reproducing the ontological foundations at the basis of sustainability.

References

de Sadeleer, N. (2002) *Environmental principles: From political slogans to legal rules* (Oxford: Oxford University Press).

European Commission (2016). Commission Communication, '*Proposal for a new European consensus on development: "Our world, our dignity, our future"*' Brussels, Strasbourg, 22.11.2016 COM(2016) 740 final.

Radin, M. (1982) 'Property and Personhood', 34 *Stanford Law Review*, 957.

Radin, M. (1993) 'Lacking a Transformative Social Theory: A Response', 45 *Stanford Law Review*, 409.

UN (United Nations) (2015) *Transforming Our World: The 2030 Agenda for Sustainable Development*, UNGA Res. 70/1.

World Commission on Environment and Development (1987) *Our Common Future* (Oxford: Oxford University Press).

PART I

Sustainability through History

1

Sustainability and Law: A Historical and Theoretical Overview

Margherita Pieraccini and Tonia Novitz

Introduction

This chapter points to the ways in which discussions regarding sustainability and sustainable development have shifted over time and proposes theoretically informed ways forward. Our historical timeline begins in the 1970s with what looks like the emergence of discrete atomistic strands of concern. One focus of attention for the international community was economic 'development', namely the prevention of poverty, in the context of integration into a global capitalist economy. The other policy initiative concerned the environment and acknowledged the need for international cooperation to prevent pollution and preserve biodiversity and ecosystems, evolving into current efforts to also tackle climate change. We address the evolution of these different trajectories regarding sustainable development and how they interact.

However, we see the historical narrative as going beyond a simple tale of tension and reconciliation. For to argue that sustainability or sustainable 'development' is all about economic objectives or even environmental aims is problematic. What may be more accurate is that we have witnessed a growing acknowledgement that both economic and environmental development need to be 'sustainable', that is, durable and long lasting. Tracing this change, we see an emerging recognition that social policy is vital to the achievement of both economic and environmental goals; hence the arrival of what came to be described as 'three pillars' of sustainability: economic, environmental and social. For critical environmental lawyers, this may seem a modernist and still fractured approach to sustainability, which would ideally be viewed as more holistic. For those engaged in social policy, such as labour lawyers, there has been frustration that labour standards and other aspects of social policy are then viewed by many as protected in a sustainability frame only to the extent that they are seen to connect to (and are subsumed by) the dominant strands of economic and environmental sustainability. Holism then has its dangers if it obscures the prioritisation of some objectives over others.

We argue that a historical account can offer more than a tired rehearsal of the various international and European debates that have occurred over the years and the concrete legal instruments they generate. Instead, we identify in the non-linear and controversial historical shifts the emergence of sustainability as a 'directing' principle of post-modern law (de Sadeleer, 2002), which offers an advantage in encompassing a multitude of perspectives in debate and the flexibility necessary for the further development and refinement of ideas. In this sense the vagueness of sustainability and sustainable development and uncertainty over the meaning of such terms provides opportunities.

Rejecting the problematic modernist division between the environmental and the social, we consider the scope for dissensus and a more relational analysis. Tracing legal histories, we find that the relationship between people, their environment and their economic and social capabilities is reaching a new stage of engagement and contestation. This suggests that not only substantive but procedural issues are vital to the longevity of the planet, its economies and societies. It is on this basis that the contributors to this book offer very different legal perspectives on sustainability.

Questions of terminology

In mapping a history, how we use key terms is vital. Sustainability and sustainable development are buzzwords that have been at the core of both policy and academic debates for decades. However, their individual meanings and the relationship between the terms are vague and contested, not only in the academic literature but also on legal and policy grounds (Waas et al, 2011). Some scholars make a distinction between sustainability and sustainable development, arguing that the former is the goal and the latter is the process to achieve sustainability (see for example Reid, 1995; Bagheri and Hjorth, 2007; Lozano,

2007). The difficulty is that such a distinction indicates that there is an end goal to be reached and this is problematic in many respects, not least because it is unclear who decides what such goal should be and because such conceptualisation is often underpinned by a linear, Western-centric view of the world's development.

On the plus side, sustainability is not always accompanied by the heavy and controversial connotations of the word 'development', though many policy and law instruments use the two terms interchangeably and often refer to sustainable development as an objective. As this chapter is focused on the history of legal and policy shifts at the international and European Union (EU) levels, it needs to engage with both terms. Concentrating only on sustainability would leave out much of the crucial history, given that legal and policy conversations are often framed in sustainable development terms. In such legal and policy discussions, sustainable development is at some times interpreted as a goal and at other times as a process, rendering the distinction between sustainability and sustainable development outlined earlier less tenable.

Whether sustainable development is a goal or a process, it can be understood in any case, following de Sadeleer (2002), as a directing principle of post-modern law. De Sadeleer makes a distinction between 'general principles of law' developed by the judicial activism of the courts to fill legal gaps and 'directing principles' such as environmental principles that are permeated by values rather than precise legal rules, bringing ethical and other social and political concerns into play (2002: 252). General principles of law are stabilising in character and are the product of modern law, characterised as a neutral, autonomous system made up of general rules, hierarchy, coherence and precision. Directing principles, to the contrary, set forth by policy makers and legislators, cannot be distinguished so clearly from morality and other non-legal rules, hence they are an instance of post-modern law, embodying the uncertainties and hybridity of the post-modern condition. Directing principles assume a symbolic function as they are set forth in new regimes as legitimating factors and they fulfil a quasi-pedagogic function in that they are reforming rather than stabilising, as they 'announce the law of tomorrow' (2002: 258–9). They are also strategic because their vagueness is easily agreed on and they are functional in a post-modern context aimed at flexibility, adaptability and pluralism (200: 258–9). As Scotford argues (2017: 35), vagueness is what gives principles 'widespread currency in international policy', as sustainability is easy to agree to politically and can cross jurisdictions and appeal to popular sentiments about the status of society and the planet.

Thus, calling sustainable development a principle of post-modern law points at its ethical and political imbrications, which are to be explored in this chapter. At the same time, it must be said from the outset that attributing to sustainable development the characteristics of a post-modern principle does not imply that its legal and policy interpretations and implementations break with modernist assumptions. As the chapter will show, the current articulations of sustainable development often carry with them very modern connotations, namely (1) underlying (capitalist) orientation towards economic growth, (2) the search for a single, unified version of sustainability with references to pillars' integration and holism, (3) anthropocentric foundations. Environmental legal scholarship on sustainable development has argued that an ecocentric reorientation is what is needed for sustainable development to overcome some of these shortcomings. We argue that, although this argument has some merit, an ecocentric reorientation is not necessarily the preferred solution. We argue that, for the Sustainable Development Agenda 2030 (UN, 2015) to be truly emancipatory, emphasis could be put on shifts towards ontological and epistemological pluralism and the recovery of silenced sustainabilities. In this way we see the history of sustainability as one of a gradual opening of space for a multitude of perspectives on environmental, economic and social, as well as cultural, issues, the realisation of which we consider critically in Chapter 2 on Agenda 2030 and the Sustainable Development Goals (SDGs). As explained later, pluralising sustainability and recovering silenced voices can be approached from and supported by different theoretical angles, ranging from theories of deliberative democracy to post-modern critiques on development and politics. Here, we opt for post-development theory and critical legal theory, including Ranciere's notion of dissensus. This proves to be very useful for interpreting inclusivity not as an attempt to reach a single, Habermasian intersubjective truth and unified conceptualisation of sustainability but as a way to disrupt existing boundaries between what is considered inside and outside the acceptable sustainability discourse and practice (see Habermas, 1996).

The chapter is broadly divided into three further substantive sections: the next section provides a historical overview of the sustainability agenda, focusing on the international and EU levels, highlighting tensions between developmental and environmental aspects of sustainability over time and the ways in which tensions have arisen and been resolved. It is followed by a reflection on connections of sustainable development with ethical and political issues, which render it a post-modern principle of law in the de Sadeleer sense but, simultaneously, also rooted in modernist assumptions. We consider the significance of diverse human (and social) engagements with sustainability objectives, which may be preferred to elite capture of policy making. The final section provides initial reflections on how to move beyond the modernist assumptions underlying sustainable development, rethinking the ontology and epistemology of sustainability, bringing forth its pluralist emancipatory potential. We are not convinced that this can be achieved in a post-developmentalist way in practice (Escobar, 1995; Rahnema and Bawtree, 1997), given how deeply economic development remains entrenched within global capitalism and contemporary sustainability legal frameworks. Nevertheless, there is scope to challenge conventional assumptions regarding the need for further development and, even if this is conceded, what its established constitutive elements should be (Mignolo and Escobar, 2013). We suggest that such challenges could be manifested in space created for resistance alongside procedural mechanisms for inclusive dialogue.

A brief history of sustainable development

This section offers a brief history of international and European initiatives related to sustainable development. The employment of the terms sustainability and sustainable development in international policy is reviewed. We map the exploration of sustainability concerns from Stockholm (UN, 1972) to a definition of sustainable development more focused on temporal and spatial distributive justice in the Brundtland Report (World Commission on Environment and Development, 1987). We then find more emphasis on the pillars of sustainable development (social, economic and environmental) in the World Summit on Sustainable Development 2002. The latest policy articulation of sustainability is of course to be found in Agenda 2030 in connection to the 2015 SDGs, which is discussed in the Chapter 2.

This part of the chapter also demonstrates how the vagueness of the meaning of sustainability has implications for its legal status. Indeed, sustainability occupies an ambiguous legal space. It has not been recognised by the International Court of Justice (ICJ) as a customary principle of international law, but it has been used as an interpretative aid by courts and other tribunals, as demonstrated by Barral (2012). At the EU level, sustainable development is not only an important part of the policy discourse but today occupies a central place in the Treaties. However, it is conceptualised more as a guiding principle than as a precise legal tool. It is also recurrent in EU environmental Directives. Sustainability therefore sits at the interface between law and policy and can be seen as a bridge between the two. It is connected to binding norms, yet it is not recognised to date as a binding norm itself. Its imprecision, hybrid status and softness are what guarantee its longevity and its colonisation of fields other than the environmental one (in the context of labour law see van den Putte and Orbie, 2015, and regarding human rights in trade see Gammage, 2019). It is precisely because of this hybrid nature that de Sadeleer (2002) calls it a directing principle of post-modern law.

Declaratory initiatives and other legal instruments

The most straightforward account of sustainability that can be provided consists of a historical tour through the various international and European instruments. We argue that these do not necessarily take a linear path. More probing debates arise in 1972, in Stockholm, relating to economic development and its implications for the environment than do later in Johannesburg in 2002 or even in Rio+20 in 2012. Throughout, concerns regarding the economy loom large, often eclipsing environmental or social issues, or merely viewing these as some minor (and secondary) justifiable constraints on economic operations. The human dominates in terms of the justification for environmental action, but also in more positive ways sparks participatory engagement, the significance of which we return to later in the chapter.

The UN Stockholm Declaration and Report 1972

The roots of sustainable development can be found in the Stockholm Conference on Environment and Development and the resultant 1972 Declaration of Principles for the Preservation and Enhancement of the Human Environment, in which the relations between environmental and development concerns were first considered at the international level. Sweden led on the conference, and this is quite telling as it was often Scandinavian countries that led on environmental initiatives, given their strong sense of environmental protection (Ivanova, 2007: 341). The Declaration is primarily focused on the relationship between the environment and development. Principle 1 links environmental protection to human rights norms, stating that 'man' has a right 'to freedom, equality and adequate conditions of life in an environment of a quality that permits a life of dignity and well-being' and has a duty 'to protect and improve the environment for present and future generations'. This is linked to socio-political considerations: 'in this respect, policies promoting or perpetuating apartheid, racial segregation, discrimination, colonial and other forms of oppression and foreign domination stand condemned and must be eliminated'. The Stockholm Declaration is very much phrased in terms of human interests, as the protection of the environment is for the welfare of humans. For example, principle 2 states that the resources of the Earth are to be safeguarded for present and future generations. This anthropocentrism is recurrent in much of the history of sustainability and will be problematised later in the chapter.

Further, the connections between environmental, economic and social issues are elaborated. Paragraph 4 of the Preamble observes that: 'In the developing countries most of the environmental problems are caused by under-development. Therefore, the developing countries must direct their efforts to development, bearing in mind their priorities and the need to safeguard and improve the environment. For the same purpose, the industrialized countries should make efforts to reduce the gap between themselves and the developing countries.' This can be linked to the assertion in principle 8 that '[e]conomic and social development is essential for ensuring a favorable living and working environment for man and for creating conditions on earth that are necessary for the improvement of the quality of life'; also to the redistributive transfer of 'substantial quantities of financial and technological assistance' envisaged in principle 9. This finding is consistent with acknowledgements, in the context of world trade, that non-reciprocal redistributive measures were needed to assist economic development for so-called developing countries (see Part IV of the General Agreement on Tariffs and Trade (GATT) adopted in 1965 and also the Enabling Clause: *Differential and More Favourable Treatment Reciprocity and Fuller Participation of Developing Countries* 1971 and 1979).

Nevertheless, there is little explicit consideration of the ways in which environmental, economic and social concerns are to be reconciled. Principle 14 offers only a public reason, liberal-type approach, indicating that '[r]ational planning constitutes an essential tool for reconciling any conflict between the needs of development and the need to protect and improve the environment'. In this way, the modernist view of progress found in the notion of development is placed alongside another modernist concept of the carrying capacity of the Earth. As Glacken (1967) argued a long time ago, connecting the idea of progress with that of environmental limits is a necessary development of a post-Enlightenment time. Such a modernist view is not at odds with the previous assertion that sustainable development is a directing principle of post-modern law. Indeed, as de Sadeleer himself argues, there is no rupture as such between modernity and post-modernity because that would underestimate the heritage of modernity (2002: 61).

The Stockholm Declaration does not use the words 'sustainable development', but there is reference in the UN Report to the accepted need for 'a better balance among the major elements that determined the level and quality of life … and its distribution, available resources and their exploitation, and pressures placed on the life systems that *sustained* it' (UN, 1972: 45). Although the outcome of the Stockholm conference was a Declaration, hence not of a legally binding nature under international law, it exerted a positive influence on regional policies, with the European Economic Community for instance developing its 1st Environmental Action Programme in 1973 (Bell et al, 2017: 177). The first definition of sustainable development emerged in the following decade.

The World Conservation Strategy 1980

The International Union for the Conservation of Nature (IUCN, 1980), in the *World Conservation Strategy*, states that for 'development to be sustainable it must take account of social and ecological factors, as well as economic ones; of the living and non-living resource base; and of the long term as well as the short-term advantages and disadvantages of alternative actions'. In this challenge to the dominance of economic considerations it might seem that conservation becomes a goal in and of itself and therefore the strategy seems to depart from the anthropocentrism of Stockholm. However, paragraph 5 does state that: 'Conservation, like development, is for people; while development aims to achieve human goals largely through use of the biosphere, conservation aims to achieve them by ensuring that such use can continue' (IUCN, 1980). In this way, the social dimension provides a justificatory foundation for economic development and environmental conservation, although its content is under-explored. Conservation's value seems to lie here in what today we call ecosystem services (see Millennium Ecosystem Assessment, 2005 for a definition of ecosystem services), not in the protection of nature on its own and for its own sake.

The Brundtland Report 1987

The 1980s witnessed also the establishment of the World Commission on Environment and Development (WCED) in 1983, chaired by the former Norwegian prime minister Gro Harlem Brundtland, again therefore seeing Scandinavian countries taking the lead in the shaping of the sustainability agenda. In 1987 the WCED produced *Our Common Future*, also known as the Brundtland Report, which contains the most popular definition of sustainable development to this day. The definition states that 'sustainable development is development that meets the need of the present without compromising the ability of future generations to meet their own needs' (World Commission on Environment and Development, 1987: 51). The key aspects of that definition are spatial and temporal distributive justice concerns. Sustainable development is about fair allocation of resources to ensure both intra-generational justice (especially between developing and developed nations, but also the poorer and wealthier within these countries) and inter-generational justice (between present and future generations, whose environment should also be nurtured and preserved). The Brundtland Report's focus seems to be purely anthropocentric. It is concerned with ensuring progress for (human) generations and this can be achieved if ecological limits are not exceeded.

It is also interesting to note that the term 'needs', rather than 'rights', is used in the Brundtland Report, hence the choice of language seems not to be underpinned by an empowerment logic but by a green development design decided top-down. However, the report also goes beyond the notion of needs, stating that 'sustainable development requires ... extending to all the opportunity to satisfy their aspirations for a better life' (World Commission on Environment and Development, 1987: 44). Nevertheless, the language of rights, which was present in the Stockholm declaration, is lost in Brundtland. Instead, that rights discourse can be found in attempts to tame the economic development agenda during the same period.

The UN Declaration on the Right to Development 1986

The *UN Declaration on the Right to Development 1986* (UN, 1986) begins with the powerful statement that '[t]he right to development is an inalienable human right by virtue of which every human person and all peoples are entitled to participate in, contribute to, and enjoy economic, social, cultural and political development, in which all human rights and fundamental freedoms can be fully realized'. The Declaration as a whole is powerful in that it pushes for a procedural understanding of justice: a right to development is not only a right to distributive justice but also a right to participate in what justice means (Articles 2 and 8). However, the Declaration does not take into account either environmental considerations or inter-generational concerns. The economic development agenda and the environmental sustainability agenda proceeded in this way along apparently separate trajectories.

The Rio Declaration 1992

Connections between development and environmental agendas were forged in the Rio Declaration 1992 (UN, 1992a), one of the outcomes of the United Nations Conference on Environment and Development (UNCED), with Article 3 on the right to development for present and future generations, emphasising the inter-generational aspect, complemented by Article 6 on intra-generational justice. Article 4 on environmental protection is stated to be integral to the development project. Further, Article 10 stresses the importance of participation in environmental decision making (in a manner comparable to the 1987 UN Declaration on the Right to Development): 'environmental issues are best handled with the participation of all concerned citizens'; and a commitment was made that at the national level each individual should be given access to environmental information held by public authorities, the opportunity to participate in environmental decision making and access to justice.

It was also at Rio that the institutional structure for pursuing protection of sustainable development at the global level was developed. The Commission on Sustainable Development (CSD) was established in 1992 by the UN General Assembly (UNGA) in its resolution 47/191 (UN, 1993) as a commission attached to the Economic and Social Council. The CSD's aim was to ensure the effective follow-up of the UNCED and promote dialogue and partnerships for sustainable development with governments, the international community and 'major groups', including women, indigenous people, workers and trade unions, NGOs, business, the scientific community and farmers. Participation, following Rio+5 in 1997, was facilitated by a two-day, multi-stakeholder dialogue session with the major groups as key participants. The dialogue was then integrated into the CSD official deliberations (Adams and Pingeot, 2013).

Principle 10 of Rio was further translated into law with the advent of the United Nations Economic Commission for Europe (UNECE) Convention on Access to Information, Public Participation in Decision-Making and Access to Justice in Environmental Matters (the Aarhus Convention 1998). This instrument, employing the language of rights, sets out three pillars of procedural environmental justice: access to environmental information, participation in environmental decision making and access to justice in environmental matters. A Compliance Committee was established under Article 15 of the Aarhus Convention in 2002, to which members of the public can bring communications related to non-compliance by a Party. Although in various respects imperfect (Lee and Abbott, 2003), the Aarhus Convention has constituted an important step towards more inclusive environmental decision making globally and also in the EU.[1] This instrument can arguably be considered an important precursor to SDG 16, especially targets 16.3 and 16.7, which restate these principles of democracy and procedural justice in relation not just to environmental sustainability, but also as concerns other economic and social sustainability considerations. We return to this issue in Chapter 2.

The Millennium Development Goals 2000

By way of contrast, the adoption of the Millennium Development Goals (MDGs) by UNGA (UN, 2000) has been criticised for its top-down imposition of social, economic and environmental standards without scope for extensive participatory engagement or reflection. Eight MDGs were identified, namely to: eradicate extreme poverty and hunger; achieve universal primary education; promote gender equality and empower women; reduce child mortality; improve maternal health; combat HIV/AIDS, malaria and other diseases; ensure environmental sustainability; develop a global partnership for development. Each goal was accompanied by more concrete targets and indicators to be achieved by 2015. It is interesting that, unlike the UN Declaration on the Right to Development, environmental sustainability is included explicitly as a development goal, but consists only of four targets and is not necessarily taken as a concern which might impact on the other goals (Castello et al, 2010). Concerns were raised by commentators that the targets had been set by experts top-down, regardless of local priorities (Satterthwaite, 2003; Saith, 2006). Even one of the original architects of this ambitious project, Vandemoortele (2009), voiced concerns that there had been capture of the MDG process, such that money-metric and donor-centric views of development had become too prominent. He saw a need for multi-level social partnership if the MDGs were to be achieved (Vandemoortele 2008). Arguably, we see a repeat of this methodology (consisting of goals, targets and indicators) in the SDGs discussed in Chapter 2, but also more interest in inclusive participation in SDG 16 and the global partnership provisions in SDG 17.

The Johannesburg Declaration 2002

The participatory ethos of the CSD and the Aarhus Convention arguably also seemed to have little influence at the World Summit on Sustainable Development (WSSD), in Johannesburg in 2002. For example, the dialogue session was severely shortened, and its importance was reduced so that it lost its role as an official input into the outcome document (Waas et al, 2011). Johannesburg did not get rid of the participatory discourse altogether, creating so-called 'Type II partnerships', which are projects allowing civil society and private companies to contribute to the implementation of sustainable development in partnership with governments and international organisations. Their formation was justified by the argument that sustainable development required broad-based participation. However, such partnerships also attracted criticism for privatising the implementation of the Rio commitments and diminishing transparency and accountability as a way for governments to avoid negotiating effective and legally binding solutions (Witte, Streck and Benner, 2003).

The Johannesburg conference also produced mixed results in relation to the implementation of sustainable development (Hens and Nath, 2003). Its outcome, the Johannesburg Plan of Implementation (JPI) (UN, 2002b), with the aim of speeding up the implementation of Agenda 21 of the Rio conference (UN, 1992b), pushed for a view of sustainable development based on the now well-established three pillars approach (economic, social and environmental), downplaying the inter-generational justice dimensions and environmental matters that had been at the core of the sustainability agenda at its origin. Although new commitments were absent in Johannesburg, it is fair to say that the JPI began to place social concerns on an equal footing with more familiar environmental and economic aims.

The 'green economy' at Rio+20 and in the EU

The second follow-up to the UNCED conference in 2012, Rio+20, in proposing the theme of the green economy, (re-)narrowed down sustainable development to the economic/environmental nexus (UN, 2012). Although green economy was not to be understood as a replacement to sustainable development but as a tool of sustainable development, as Jacobs wonders, 'why then invent a whole new discourse around it?' (2012: 5). The concept of green economy had also gained traction at the EU level, becoming one of the objectives of the 7th Environmental Action Programme (EAP) and the core of the Europe 2020 Strategy. The Europe 2020 Strategy stresses that environmental protection does not need to be a challenge to economic growth; indeed, this is implicit in the package term of 'the green economy' (European Commission, 2010). This is a weaker approach than enabling sustainable development to place legitimate limits on growth, as was envisaged in the Stockholm UN Report (UN, 1972) and the World Conservation Strategy in 1980 (IUCN, 1980, para 1.2). To that extent, the UN notion of the 'green economy' and the 7th EAP, which speaks in terms of 'natural capital' and aims to turn the EU into a resource-efficient, green and competitive low-carbon economy, seem regressive by way of comparison with earlier, more probing conversations.

European Commission policy documents, for example, stress the importance of sustainability throughout, but this is primarily referred to in economic terms (for example, see European Commission, 2010). Much reference is made to the 'business environment' – less to environmental protection or social sustainability, with training for workers prioritised at the expense of intra-generational justice in the form of improved labour standards (Novitz, 2015). This could be read as retreat to the more limited constructions of sustainability in the Maastricht Treaty 1992, Article 2, which referred to 'development of economic activities, sustainable and non-inflationary growth respecting the environment' and the reference in the Treaty of Amsterdam 1997, Article 2 to 'sustainable development of economic activities'. While in these two instruments, the economic dimension of 'sustainable growth' in the EU seemed paramount, the Treaty of Lisbon 2009 had recognised sustainable development as an objective on its own and stressed the three-dimensional character of sustainable development (see Treaty on the European Union [TEU] Article 3(3)). The 2010 Commission policy documents seemed to revert to older assumptions.

Both at the international and EU levels, then, the introduction of the concept of the green economy in policy instruments risked diluting the other pillars of sustainability and returning to a more narrow, economic-driven definition of sustainability. More recently, though, the EU Policy Coherence for Development has led to some social issues being reclaimed, framing development in the SDGs' language. Chapter 2 will discuss this in more detail.

At Rio+20 the institutional architecture of sustainable development was also rethought by introducing the High Level Political Forum (HLPF), formally adopted by UNGA resolution 67/290 (UN, 2013a). The HLPF replaced the CSD in 2012. The CSD had attracted criticism in the later years of its operation for a number of reasons: lack of integration of the three pillars of sustainable development, given the predominance of environmental ministers; weak engagement of non-State actors in implementation projects; weak transparency and accountability mechanisms (UNGA, 2013b). The HLPF attempts to overcome those criticisms while also building on the participatory modalities of the CSD. The HLPF is now tasked with implementing the new Agenda 2030 and the SDGs. In doing so, the HLPF aims at enhancing the integration of the three dimensions of sustainable development in a holistic and cross-sectoral manner (UNGA, 2013a: para 2). This is delivered, for instance, by making sure that the meetings of the forum shall have a thematic focus reflecting the integration of the three pillars (UNGA, 2013a: para 7(c)). The forum conducts annual reviews on the implementation, although these are voluntary (UNGA, 2013a: para 8 (a)), hence of dubious value in increasing accountability. Major groups are invited to actively participate in reviews of implementation (UNGA, 2013a: para 8) and they have the right to intervene in meetings and can contribute to setting the agenda (UNGA, 2013a: para 22), thereby increasing participation. Chapter 2 will provide a more in-depth discussion of the HLPF in the context of the SDGs.

The evolution of a broad sustainability principle and its status in litigation

Moving from the evolution of policy to the question of litigation, it is unsurprising that sustainable development has not achieved the status of what can be described in technical terms as a customary principle of international law. Its conceptual vagueness and hybridity militate against such a finding. However, as we shall see, the courts have invoked sustainable development more (in a post-modern way) as a 'directing principle', often to address the policy background to a legal dispute, especially in the context of environmental concerns.

The seminal case in this respect is the *Gabcikovo-Nagymaros* Case 1997, in which the concept of sustainable development was invoked by the ICJ in order to interpret environmental obligations. However, as is well known, the Court did not endorse Judge Weeramantry's separate opinion pushing for the recognition of sustainable development as a customary principle of international law. Further, the WTO Appellate Body, in the Shrimp/Turtle case (WTO, 1998), noted that sustainable development was acknowledged in the Preamble to the WTO Agreement and therefore had to be recognised as giving 'colour, texture and shading to our interpretation of the agreements annexed to the WTO Agreement, in this case the GATT 1994' (para 153), but again stopped short of any statement on the status of the principle under customary international law.

The arbitral tribunal in the *Iron Rhine Arbitration* 2005 went a step further in stating that 'where development may cause significant harm to the environment there is a duty to prevent, or at least, mitigate such harm. This duty, in the opinion of the Tribunal, has now become a principle of general international law.' This points to the importance of the integration of environmental considerations in the design and implementation of economic development activities in international law. This arbitral finding has yet to be replicated in the ICJ.

In *Pulp Mills on the River Uruguay* 2010, the ICJ held that the use of a river was not equitable if the interests of other riparian states were not taken into account and sustainable development was an important objective, against which Article 27 of the Statute of the River Uruguay was to be measured for consistency. However, once again sustainable development was not recognised as a customary principle of international law (para 177).

As Barral (2012) argues, although sustainable development has not been granted formal customary legal status by the courts, it has fulfilled various legal functions, being used as an interpretive tool by the courts and as an objective against which legal provisions are to be measured. It also operates as an obligation of means, meaning that it requires 'only the deployment of all possible means to achieve the result, without promising to achieve it' and therefore differs from an obligation of result (Barral, 2012: 390). In other words, it offers directional influence rather than determination of a straightforward end result.

Sustainability can also be found in a number of Multilateral Environmental Agreements (MEA), often as an objective rather than a concrete legal obligation. For example, Article 1 of the Convention on Biological Diversity (CBD) states that 'the objectives of this Convention … are … the conservation of biological diversity and the sustainable use of its components' and Article 2 of the United Nations Framework Convention on Climate Change (UNFCCC) states that the aim of the treaty is to stabilise greenhouse gases' concentration, allowing 'economic development to proceed in a sustainable manner'. It also appears as a right in Article 3 of the UNFCCC, stating that 'the parties have a right to, and should, promote sustainable development'.

There is an inflationary use of the term 'sustainable development' at the EU law level too. Treaty provisions put sustainable development at the core of both internal (Article 3(3))[2] and external relations (Articles 3(5)[3] and 21(2)(d) and (f)[4]). It is also encapsulated in Article 11 of the Treaty on the Functioning of the European Union[5] and Article 37 of the Charter of Fundamental Rights[6] in relation to the environmental integration principle. Sustainable development is also present in secondary legislation although the approach, as de Sadeleer argues, is 'somewhat patchy' (2015: 54).

Many environmental Directives and policies refer to sustainability, sometimes as an adjective for the use of natural resources, sometimes as a factor to be taken into account in the implementation of obligations. For instance, Article 2(1) of Regulation (EU) No 1380/2013 on the Common Fisheries Policy (CFP) states: 'The CFP shall ensure that fishing and aquaculture activities are environmentally sustainable in the long-term and are managed in a way that is consistent with the objectives of achieving economic, social and employment benefits, and of contributing to the availability of food supplies.' Article 1(b) of the Water Framework Directive states that water management must promote 'sustainable water use based on a long-term protection of available water resources'. Article 3(5) of the Marine Strategy Framework Directive defines the core concept of the Directive, that is, 'good environmental status', by reference, inter alia, to the sustainable use of the marine environment 'to safeguard the potential for uses and activities by current and future generations', and sustainable development needs to be given due consideration when Member States draw up programmes of measure to achieve or maintain good ecological status under Article 12.

However, sustainable development is not defined in EU law and, not too dissimilarly from the international context, when invoked by the courts sustainable development has been called a 'concept' (C-371/98 *ex parte First Corporate Shipping*) and an 'objective' of the EU (C-277/02 *EU-Wood-Trading;* C-36/98 *Spain v Council*), rather than a binding norm or principle. Advocate-Generals engaging with sustainable development have not always been consistent in their articulation of the term (for an analysis of this inconsistency, see Scotford, 2017: 192–8). It is also interesting to note that the articulation of sustainable development as an objective that is recurrent in international and EU law and policy also led to discussion of the definitional differentiation made by some scholars between sustainable development (as a process) and sustainability (as an objective), highlighted in the introduction to this chapter.

Reflections on ethics, politics and modernity

The historical excursus described earlier has been unavoidably selective but remains illustrative of the way in which sustainable development has been at the core of both international and EU policy and law for over 50 years without achieving straightforward consensus on its meaning and role. If a unifying thread can be found, it is that, at various stages of the history, the economic dimensions of sustainability have predominated over the other pillars, indicating that the concept is rooted in capitalist modernity. This was pointed out already by Gillespie (2001) in his lucid critique of the greening of the development agenda. Gillespie argued that although the development agenda was reconstituted to incorporate social and environmental considerations, there remains a great fracture between rhetoric and theory, and the economic imperatives of growth continued to predominate in the sustainability agenda. Indeed, rather than operating as a conscious response to the limits of social-ecological 'planetary boundaries' (see Rockstrom et al, 2009), sustainable development fits perfectly with the growth imperatives of modernity, with the discourse on the green economy being a recent indication of this. Earth's needs are to be respected not because they are intrinsically valuable but because they are necessary for the (primarily economic) development of current and future human generations. The sustainability agenda can be read as an attempt to preserve the resources necessary to sustain capitalist modes of production and consumption. Therefore, rather than building an alternative route, sustainable development can serve to internalise the negative externalities of industrial modernity, leaving unquestioned the Western mode of development. Also, the linearity that the concept of development presupposes fits perfectly with the modernist narrative of progress. Yet, at the same time sustainable development is open to considerations of justice and other ethical and political concerns, which make it very complex and ambiguous.

Moreover, the split between nature and society embodied by the three-pillars conceptualisation of sustainable development, which differentiates what is environmental from what is social and economic, is indicative of a Cartesian logic. On this understanding, integration and holism are points of arrival in the sustainable development rhetoric, not points of departure. At the same time, a past difficulty has been the ways in which the social dimensions of sustainability have been subsumed under economic and environmental umbrellas. This has also arguably occurred when environmental concerns are obscured by economic objectives in the context of the 'green economy'. For these reasons, a holistic vision is also not unproblematic, so we need to probe beyond any easy rhetorical resolution of divergent needs and interests.

What we do find is a growing openness to ethical and political considerations, coupled with the conceptual vagueness of the term, leading to greater procedural scope for more inclusive dialogue and debate. An example seems to be the institutional attempts at making sustainability open and participatory with the HLPF.

Here, however, we do encounter an inherent tension. On the one hand, both at the international and EU levels, the meaning and role of sustainable development is left open to respond to the uncertainty and pluralism of the post-modern condition; on the other hand, much of the international policy discourse around sustainability, reproduced also at the EU level, conceptualises it anthropocentrically and as a tool for economic progress and human well-being, hence a very modern concept.

Our historical excursus has demonstrated the ways in which a sustainable development agenda has put at its centre human beings (for example, principle 1 of Stockholm and principle 1 of Rio). At least the masculine wording and orientation of the earlier policy documents has disappeared in time, most recently with SDG 5 on gender equality and the empowerment of women and girls. Yet the accusation of anthropocentrism raised in response to the sustainable development agenda is still common in the environmental international law literature. Gillespie (2014), in discussing the anthropocentric character of international environmental law, uses as an example the discourse on the rights of future (human) generations permeating sustainable development. Consequently, it might seem reasonable to argue for an overcoming of anthropocentrism as a first step towards liberating sustainability from the chains of modern capitalism. Many international environmental lawyers indeed push for sustainability to become more ecocentric (Gillespie, 2014; Bosselmann, 2016; Kotze and French, 2018).

However, such a move is not so straightforward, neither is it necessarily advisable. Following the work of critical legal scholars, the binary anthropocentrism/ecocentrism needs to be problematised, first and foremost because both represent humanity and nature as monolithic concepts, while they are not. What is an *Anthropos* and what is *Eco* can vary quite dramatically. The writings of Anna Grear are especially relevant in unpacking the concept of the *Anthropos*. She asks 'who/what, precisely, is the Anthropos of legal anthropocentrism and of the Anthropocene?' (2015: 227; see also Latour, 2014). She argues that discourses on the Anthropocene, as well as critiques of anthropocentrism, are based on a misleading universalistic, species-based talk on 'humankind', concealing the intra-species hierarchies at play (2015, 2017). Discourse on 'Anthropos', she writes, 'reflects the historically persistent centrality of a particular kind of "human"' (2017: 79). This particular kind of human is, following Haraway (2015), the Western rational subject and resource appropriator. A synecdoche is at play, in which the whole of humanity refers to only a part of it, the part linked mostly with a capitalist view of development. That part of humanity gets contraposed to nature or the environment, the *res extensa* on which the rational subject acts.

Therefore, the subject–object dualism is not overcome in critiques of sustainable development based on condemnations of anthropocentrism. As Grear writes, 'such hierarchies are moreover potentially *re-enacted* by uncritical references to terms presupposing the *anthropos* – raising questions concerning patterned in/justice in the distribution of Anthropocene responsibility – whether past, present or future' (2015: 231). What becomes apparent when we probe the history of international and EU instruments relating to sustainability is not only the emphasis on the human but an attempt in many cases to recognise the diversity of human interests and persons. Intra-generational justice prompted by sustainability concerns has encouraged acknowledgement of the differences between developing and developed countries and the need for redistribution; but could as easily lead us to consider the extremes of wealth within states which operate in a myriad of ways (around, for example, class, gender, race, culture, sexuality, age and disability). A more inclusive identification of the *Anthropos* explains the significance of proceduralisation of sustainability-based decision making and the importance of its inclusiveness. This is vital, bearing in mind also the interconnectedness of people and peoples with their environment (as well as their society/ies and economy/ies).

Similarly, De Lucia argues (2017), the concept of ecocentrism does not problematise the unstable and contested concept of nature. When the eco is equated with nature, it re-proposes the Cartesian dichotomy between *res cogitans* and *res extensa*, the thinking human subject outside and above a (commodifiable) nature, which is integral to the project of modernity. Secondly, as De Lucia argues (2017), ecocentrism's legal trajectory remains embedded within modernity because it is often linked to the rights discourse. 'A rights-based strategy risks locking the framework of legal analysis within a cultural and legal horizon premised on a subject–object grammar and maintains an inevitable linkage with human rights and their anthropocentric frame of reference' (De Lucia, 2017: 190). Thirdly, De Lucia argues, following

Philippopolous-Mihalopoulos (2013), that both anthropocentrism and ecocentrism reproduce the modern epistemology of the centre. The epistemology of the centre implies that there is only one centre from which to know and no other places, there are no alternatives. Indeed, Philippopolous-Mihalopoulos argues that 'while the ontological debate between "us" and "the environment" only insinuated the need for a centre (habitually assumed by humans), the epistemology of anthropo/ecocentricity plainly states that there is no alternative: however much we battle between extremes, we have no choice but to remain faithful to the soothing idea that there must be a centre' (2013: 857).

Therefore, if an ecocentric move consists in expelling the human from nature to save nature, it becomes extremely problematic for sustainability, in that the modernist understanding of the human as an appropriator of nature is left unquestioned. However, even if the eco in ecocentric is interpreted more widely as ecosystem, that again masks more than it reveals, given 'competing narratives' in the articulation of the ecosystem approach (De Lucia, 2015). This means that ecocentrism may not be that radical shift required for rethinking the sustainability agenda and de-rooting it from its modernist foundations. The next and last substantive section of this chapter discusses possible alternatives.

Moving forward: a call towards pluralising sustainability

Given that both *Anthropos* and *Eco* have a plurality of meanings that are lost in the anthropocentric/ecocentric binary, sustainability policy and law need to incorporate such plurality and multiplicity, thereby pushing beyond binaries by opening spaces for a discussion of multiple views and enactments of sustainability. Drawing on the work of post-development scholars on the pluriverse as well as that of Rancière on dissensus, we argue that the emancipatory potential of sustainability is found in rendering visible and available different worldviews and reclaiming difference.

One of the critiques identified in regard to the binary anthropocentrism/ecocentrism is that they are both permeated by the ideology of the centre. This centre is inhabited by a particularistic human subject (anthropocentrism) or particularistic natural subject (ecocentrism) and it is only around this centre that the others, whether human or non-human persons, struggle for recognition. Such centrist ideology is not far from what Rancière has called the 'police' (2010). In 'Ten theses on politics', Rancière distinguishes between the police and politics, arguing that the political/emancipatory moment happens where the boundary separating the public sphere and the realm of social and economic necessity is broken down. Such breaking down is called by Rancière 'the political' as opposed to the 'police', to be interpreted as the status quo and the freezing of particular structures of power. Rancière's aim is to overcome Arendt's idea of the existence of a political sphere of public action separated from the realm of economic and social necessity (Arendt, 1958). If we follow Arendt's separation, power remains in the hands of those who have already a disposition to rule, who are within the political sphere of public action, hence it is not truly emancipatory. Emancipation for Rancière happens only when what is considered to be outside the political sphere becomes viewed as political by some. Hence politics happens where there is a 'dissensus' regarding the boundaries between what is known as the political sphere and the sphere of social and economic necessity and there is an attempt at 're-partioning'. Politics for Rancière happens in places that are assumed to be a-political, it happens out of place. Politics is about the displacement of allocated places and categories, and it is not just a way to redistribute positions of power in a given centre, but it constitutes a break with the assumption that there are dispositions specific to these positions. Such insights are useful in decentring the policy discourse of sustainability from its anthropocentric foundations and its standard international and EU legal formulations. They also enable liberation of the scholarly discourse on sustainability from ecocentric normative goals, searching for other actors and other, less official fora, in sustainability decision making and practice.

We argue that the holism of sustainability should be interpreted not as an integration between distinguished pillars but as a move towards relational ontology, helping to overcome Western ontological dualisms, such as that between nature and society and also the epistemological binarism between anthropocentrism and ecocentrism, and also between the social and the economic, acknowledging different possibilities within each frame. Holism therefore should consist not in a movement towards the suppression, marginalisation of difference in the search for a unified, single sustainability but in a movement towards the recognition of relationality.

Following this line of thinking, the notion of the pluriverse derived from post-development studies (Escobar, 1995; Escobar, 2018; Kothari et al (eds), 2019) can be a useful starting point. The concept of the pluriverse is used by post-development studies to propose alternatives to the dominant policy view of (sustainable) development, to question its structural roots in modernity and its dualisms, its unidirectionality and its homogenising tendencies. According to the proponents of the pluriverse (see Kothari et al (eds), 2019), there are many ways of being in the world and many ways of knowing. The pluriverse implies multiple ontologies and multiple worlds to be known, not only multiple perspectives on one world. There is no linear, unidirectional path on which we all should be moving at different speeds, but there are various directions depending on the types of the encounters and practices undertaken. There are many possible realities, the products of intersubjective practices of human and non-human agents. In the perspective of relational ontology, embraced by proponents of the pluriverse, difference is needed for individual entities to become possible. Reclaiming difference and engagement of the invisible, which is also what Rancière argues for through the notion of 'dissensus', is a useful empowerment tool, because it points to the myriad of possibilities to understand and enact sustainability. The points of departure are not the individual units to be united in a holistic vision. On the contrary, the point of departure is the acknowledgement of relationality and the various entanglements that may be formed in the course of interactions, as developed in a post-developmentalism agenda (Demaria and Kothari, 2017). Such 'post-dualist theory' and 'interbeing' practices point towards the pluriverse, described by the Zapatista as 'a world where many worlds fit' (Escobar, 2011: 139). Following Mignolo (2018), there is no ontological pluriverse without epistemological pluriversity. Mignolo writes: 'pluriversality as a universal project means that the universal cannot have one single owner: the universal can only be pluriversal' (2018: x).

A transition from universe to pluriverse and from epistemological centrisms to pluriversity is needed in sustainability thinking. If the universe privileges homogenisation following universal principles, unidirectionality of growth, single notions of the human, nature and the future, the latter advocates for different forms of communication. The issue for policy and law is how to acknowledge such ontological relationality and epistemological decentring and to listen to the voice to the periphery, to those spheres that have been located outside accepted institutions and discourses of sustainability.

Conclusion

This chapter has argued that the sustainable development agenda is historically bound by very modern principles, such as a unidirectional approach to economic growth and anthropocentrism. However, our historical study also reveals a trend towards inclusive participatory proceduralism which has the potential to challenge earlier underlying assumptions. The overarching principle of sustainability (or sustainable development) emerges as in some ways vague, creating scope for disputation around ethical and political considerations, rendering it a directing principle of post-modern law as defined by de Sadeleer (2002). While environmental legal literature on sustainable development has argued for a move towards ecocentrism in order to overcome the anthropocentrism associated with the sustainable development agenda, we seek a richer vision informed by conflicting and more dissonant voices. Drawing on critical legal scholarship we have pointed out the limitations of a simple ecocentric solution and have argued for an ontological and epistemological pluralisation of sustainability (in its diverse manifestations from different perspectives). Chapter 2 considers the role of the SDGs in allowing a reference point for critical engagement and debate that engages diverse actors and relational rethinking. The remainder of the book seeks to challenge existing assumptions regarding legal perspectives on sustainability. The contributors seek to reach beyond standard assumptions relating to the dominance of the economic in corporate governance and the trade sphere, and to embrace diverse concerns in the marine and land environments. In so doing, they consider how legal mechanisms engage with or overlook participatory engagement with diverse voices and scope for dissent.

Notes

1 At the EU level the first two pillars of the Aarhus Convention were implemented by Directives 2003/4/EC and 2003/35/EC. The Directive on access to justice never materialised, being a matter considered best left at state level.

2 'The Union ... shall work for the sustainable development of Europe based on balanced economic growth and price stability, a highly competitive social market economy, aiming at full employment and social progress, and a high level of protection and improvement of the quality of the environment. It shall promote scientific and technological advance.'

3 'The Union shall define and pursue common policies and actions, and shall work for a high degree of cooperation in all fields of international relations, in order to: ... foster the sustainable economic, social and environmental development of developing countries, with the primary aim of eradicating poverty.'

4 'The Union shall define and pursue common policies and actions, and shall work for a high degree of cooperation in all fields of international relations, in order to: [...] (d) foster the sustainable economic, social and environmental development of developing countries, with the primary aim of eradicating poverty; (f) help develop international measures to preserve and improve the quality of the environment and the sustainable management of global natural resources, in order to ensure sustainable development.'

5 Integration of environmental protection requirements into EU policies and activities must be done 'in particular with a view to promoting sustainable development'.

6 'A high level of environmental protection and the improvement of the quality of the environment must be integrated into the policies of the Union and ensured in accordance with the principle of sustainable development.'

References

Adams, B. and Pingeot, L. (2013) *Strengthening Public Participation at the United Nations for Sustainable Development: Dialogue, Debate, Dissent, Deliberation*. Study for UN DESA/DSD Major Group Programme: www.globalpolicy.org/images/pdfs/images/pdfs/UNDESA_MGs__Report.pdf

Arendt, H. (1958), *The Human Condition*, Chicago: University of Chicago Press.

Bagheri, A. and Hjorth, P. (2006) 'Planning for sustainable development: a paradigm shift towards a process-based approach', *Sustainable Development* 15: 83–96.

Barral, V. (2012) 'Sustainable development in international law: nature and operation of an evolutive legal norm', *The European Journal of International Law* 23(2): 377–400.

Bell, S., McGillivray, D., Pedersen, O.W., Lees, E. and Stokes, E. (2017) *Environmental Law* (9th edn), Oxford: Oxford University Press.

Bosselmann, K. (2016) *The Principle of Sustainability: Transforming Law and Governance* (2nd edn), London: Routledge.

Case C-371/98 *The Queen v Secretary of State for the Environment, Transport and the Regions, ex parte First Corporate Shipping Ltd, interveners: World Wide Fund for Nature UK (WWF) and Avon Wildlife Trust* [2000] ECR I-09235, ECLI:EU:C:2000:600.

Case C-36/98 *Kingdom of Spain v Council of the European Union* [2001], ECR I-00779, ECLI:EU:C:2001:64.

Case C-277/02 *EU-Wood-Trading GmbH v Sonderabfall-Management-Gesellschaft Rheinland-Pfalz mbH* [2004] ECR I-11957, ECLI:EU:C:2004:810.

Castello, L.D., Gil-Gonzalez, D., Diaz, C.A.D. and Hernández-Aguado, I. (2010) 'The environmental Millennium Development Goal: progress and barriers to its achievement', *Environmental Science & Policy* 13(2), 154–63.

Charter of Fundamental Rights of the European Union, OJ C 326/391.

Convention on Biological Diversity (Rio de Janeiro) 5 June 1992, in force 29 December 1993, 31 ILM 822 (CBD 1992).

Convention on Access to Information, Public Participation and Decision-Making and Access to Justice in Environmental Matters (Aarhus) 25 June 1998, in force 30 October 2001, 38 ILM 517 (Aarhus Convention 1998).

Decision No 1386/2013/EU of the European Parliament and of the Council of 20 November 2013 on a General Union Environment Action Programme to 2020 'Living well, within the limits of our planet'. Text with EEA relevance (7th Environmental Action Programme).

Declaration of the Council of the European Communities and of the representatives of the Governments of the Member States meeting in the Council of 22 November 1973 on the programme of action of the European Communities on the environment, OC J 112/1 (1st Environmental Action Programme).

De Lucia, V. (2015) 'Competing narratives and complex genealogies: the ecosystem approach in international environmental law', *Journal of Environmental Law* 27(1): 91–117.

De Lucia, V. (2017) 'Beyond anthropocentrism and ecocentrism: a biopolitical reading of environmental law', *Journal of Human Rights and the Environment* 8(2): 181–202.

Demaria, F. and Kothari, A. (2017) 'The Post-Development Dictionary agenda: paths to the pluriverse', *Third World Quarterly* 38(12): 2588–99.

de Sadeleer, N. (2002) *Environmental Principles – From Political Slogans to Legal Rules*, Oxford: Oxford University Press.

Differential and More Favourable Treatment, Reciprocity and Fuller Participation of Developing Countries – Decision of 28 November 1979 (Enabling Clause – L/4903).

Directive 2000/60/EC of the European Parliament and of the Council of 23 October 2000 establishing a framework for Community action in the field of water policy, OJ L 327/1.

Directive 2003/4/EC of the European Parliament and of the Council of 28 January 2003 on public access to environmental information and repealing Council Directive 90/313/EEC, OJ L 41/26.

Directive 2003/35/EC of the European Parliament and of the Council of 26 May 2003 providing for public participation in respect of the drawing up of certain plans and programmes relating to the environment and amending with regard to public participation and access to justice Council Directives 85/337/EEC and 96/61/EC – Statement by the Commission, OJ L 156/17.

Escobar, A. (1995). *Encountering Development: The Making and Unmaking of the Third World*, Princeton: Princeton University Press.

Escobar, A. (2011) 'Sustainability: design for the pluriverse', *Development* 54(2): 137–40.

Escobar, A. (2018) 'Transition discourses and the politics of rationality: toward designs for the pluriverse', in Reiter, B. (ed), *Constructing the Pluriverse: The Geopolitics of Knowledge*, Durham, NC and London: Duke University Press, pp 63–89.

European Commission (2010) Commission Communication, *'EUROPE 2020: A strategy for smart, sustainable and inclusive growth'* Brussels, 3.3.2010 COM (2010) 2020 final.

Gabcikovo-Nagymaros Project (Hungary/Slovakia) (1997), Judgment, ICJ Reports, p. 7.

Gammage, C. (2019) 'Social norms in EU-free trade agreements: justiciable or not?', in Gammage, C. and Novitz, T. (eds), *Sustainable Trade, Investment and Finance: Toward Responsible And Coherent Regulatory Frameworks*, Cheltenham: Edward Elgar.

General Agreement on Tariffs and Trade (GATT) (1948) as amended.

Gillespie, A. (2001) *The Illusion of Progress: Unsustainable Development in International Law and Policy*, Abingdon: Earthscan.

Gillespie, A. (2014) *International Environmental Law, Policy, and Ethics* (2nd edn), Oxford: Oxford University Press.

Glacken, C.J. (1967) *Traces on the Rhodian Shore: Nature and Culture in Western Thought from Ancient Times to the End of the Eighteenth Century*, Berkeley and Los Angeles, CA: University of California Press.

Grear, A. (2015) 'Deconstructing anthropos: a critical legal reflection on "anthropocentric" law and anthropocene "humanity"', *Law and Critique* 26(3): 225–49.

Grear, A. (2017) '"Anthropocene, capitalocene, chthulucene": re-encountering environmental law and its "subject" with Haraway and New Materialism', in Kotze, L.J. (ed), *Environmental Law and Governance for the Anthropocene,* Oxford: Hart, pp 77–96.

Habermas, J. (1996) *Between Facts and Norms: Contributions to a Discourse Theory of Law and Democracy*, London: Polity Press.

Haraway, D. (2015) 'Anthropocene, capitalocene, plantationocene, chthulucene: making kin', *Environmental Humanities* 6: 159–65.

Hens, L. and Nath, B. (2003) 'The Johannesburg Conference', *Environment, Development and Sustainability* 5(1–2): 7–39.

Iron Rhine Arbitration (Belgium/Netherlands) (2005), PCA Case 2003-02, Final Award 24 May.

IUCN (1980) *The World Conservation Strategy: Living Resource Conservation for Sustainable Development*, Gland, Switzerland: IUCN-UNEP-WWF.

Ivanova, M. (2007) 'Moving forward by looking back: learning from UNEP's history', in Swart, L. and Perry, E. (eds), *Global Environmental Governance: Perspectives on the Current Debate*, New York: Center for UN Reform Education, pp 26–47.

Jacobs, M. (2012) *Green Growth: Economic Theory and Political Discourse*, Centre for Climate Change Economics and Policy Working Paper No 108, Grantham Research Institute on Climate Change and the Environment Working Paper No 92., Available from: www.lse.ac.uk/GranthamInstitute/wp-content/uploads/2012/10/WP92-green-growth-economic-theory-political-discourse.pdf

Kothari, A., Salleh, A., Escobar, A., Demaria, F. And Acosta, A. (eds) (2019) *Pluriverse: A Post-Development Dictionary*, New York: Columbia University Press.

Kotze, L.J. and French, D. (2018) 'The anthropocentric ontology of international environmental law and the sustainable development goals: towards an ecocentric rule of law in the anthropocene', *Global Journal of Comparative Law* 7(1): 5–36.

Latour, B. (2014) 'Agency at the time of the anthropocene', *New Literary History* 45: 1–18.

Lee, M. and Abbott, C. (2003) 'The usual suspects? Public participation under the Aarhus Convention', *Modern Law Review* 66(1): 80–108.

Lozano R. (2007) 'Collaboration as a pathway for sustainability', *Sustainable Development* 16(6): 370–81.

Mignolo, W.D. (2018) 'Foreword: On pluriversality and multipolarity', in Reiter, B. (ed), *Constructing the Pluriverse: The Geopolitics of Knowledge*, Durham, NC and London: Duke University Press.

Mignolo, W.D. and Escobar, A. (eds) (2013) *Globalization and the Decolonial Option*, Abingdon: Routledge.

Millennium Ecosystem Assessment (2005) *Ecosystems and Human Well-being: Synthesis*, Washington, DC: Island Press.

Novitz, T. (2015) 'The paradigm of sustainability in a European social context: collective participation in protection of future interests?', *The International Journal of Comparative Labour Law and Industrial Relations*, 31(3): 243–62.

Philippopoulos-Mihalopoulos, A. (2013) 'Actors or spectators? Vulnerability and critical environmental law', *Oñati Socio-Legal Series* 3(5): 854–76.

Pulp Mills on the River Uruguay (Argentina v. Uruguay) (2010), Judgment, ICJ Reports, p. 14.

Rahnema, M. and Bawtree, V. (eds) (1997) *The Post-development Reader*, London: Zed Books.

Rancière, J. (2010) 'Ten theses on politics', in Corcoran (ed and trans) *Dissensus on Politics and Aesthetics*, London: Continuum International Publishing Group, pp 27–44.

Regulation (EU) No 1380/2013 of the European Parliament and of the Council of 11 December 2013 on the Common Fisheries Policy, amending Council Regulations (EC) No 1954/2003 and (EC) No 1224/2009 and repealing Council Regulations (EC) No 2371/2002 and (EC) No 639/2004 and Council Decision 2004/585/EC, OJ L354/22 (Common Fisheries Policy).

Reid, D. (1995) *Sustainable Development. An Introductory Guide*, London: Earthscan Publications Ltd.

Rockstrom, J. et al (2009) 'Planetary boundaries: exploring the safe operating space for humanity', *Ecology and Society* 14(2).

Saith, A. (2006) 'From universal values to Millennium Development Goals: lost in translation', *Development and Change* 37(6): 1167–99.

Satterthwaite, D. (2003) 'The Millennium Development Goals and urban poverty reduction: great expectations and nonsense statistics', *Environment and Urbanization*, 15(2): 179–90.

Scotford, E. (2017) *Environmental Principles and the Evolution of Environmental Law*, Oxford: Hart.

Treaty on European Union (Maastricht) 7 February 1992, in force 1 November 1993 (Maastricht Treaty).

Treaty of Amsterdam amending the Treaty on European Union, the Treaties establishing the European Communities and certain related acts, (Amsterdam) 2 October 1997, in force 1 May 1999 (Amsterdam Treaty).

Treaty on the Functioning of the European Union, OJ L 326/47 (Treaty of the Functioning of the European Union), (Lisbon) 13 December 2007, in force 1 December 2009.

UN (United Nations) (1972) *Declaration of the United Nations Conference on the Human Environment*, UN Doc A/Conf.48/14.

UN (1986) *UN Declaration on the Right to Development 1986*, UNGA RES/41/128.

UN (1992a) *Rio Declaration on Environment and Development*, UN Doc A/CONF.151/26.

UN (1992b) *Agenda 21: Programme of Action for Sustainable Development*, UN Doc A/Conf.151/26.

UN (1993) *Institutional Arrangements to Follow up the United Nations Conference on Environment and Development*, UNGA RES/47/19.

UN (2000) *Resolution on the United Nations Millennium Declaration*, UNGA RES/55/2.

UN (2002a) *The Johannesburg Declaration on Sustainable Development*, UN Doc A/CONF.199/20.

UN (2002b) *Plan of Implementation of the World Summit on Sustainable Development*, UN Doc A/CONF.199/20.

UN (2012) *Rio+20 Summit. The Future We Want*, UNGA RES/66/288.

UN (2013a) *Format and organizational aspects of the high-level political forum on sustainable development*, UNGA RES/67/290.

UN (2013b) *Lessons learned from the Commission on Sustainable Development*, UN Doc A/67/757.

UN (2015) *Transforming our world: the 2030 Agenda for Sustainable Development*, UNGA RES/70/1.

United Nations Framework Convention on Climate Change (New York) 9 May 1992, in force 24 March 1994, 1771 UNTS 107 (UNFCCC 1992).

Vandemoortele, J. (2009) 'The MDG conundrum: meeting the targets without missing the point', *Development Policy Review* 27(4): 355–71.

Van den Putte, L. and Orbie, J. (2015) 'EU bilateral trade agreements and the surprising rise of labour provisions', *International Journal of Comparative Labour Law and Industrial Relations*, 31(3): 263–83.

Waas, T., Huge J., Verbruggen, A. and Wright, T. (2011), 'Sustainable development: a bird's eye view', *Sustainability* 3(10): 1637–61.

Witte, J.M., Streck, C. and Benner, T. (2003) 'The road from Johannesburg: what future for partnerships in global governance?', in Witte, J.M., Streck, C. and Benner, T. (eds), *Progress or Peril? Partnerships and Networks in Global Environmental Governance: The Post-Johannesburg Agenda*, New Haven, CT: Yale University Press, pp 59–84.

World Commission on Environment and Development (1987) *Our Common Future*, Oxford: Oxford University Press.

WTO (1998) United States: Import Prohibition of Certain Shrimp and Shrimp Products – Report of the Appellate Body (12 October) WT/DS58/AB/R.

2

Agenda 2030 and the Sustainable Development Goals: 'Responsive, Inclusive, Participatory and Representative Decision-Making'?

Tonia Novitz and Margherita Pieraccini

Introduction

This chapter focuses on the contemporary framing of sustainability in the context of the adoption by the UN General Assembly (UNGA) on 25 September 2015 of Agenda 2030 and the Sustainable Development Goals (SDGs). Agenda 2030 offers an opportunity to examine the shift from the distinct itemisation of the 'pillars' of sustainable development to a more holistic vision of interdependent policies and objectives and, potentially, to a more inclusive understanding of sustainability (see Chapter 1, penultimate section). In this setting we will consider the potential coherence and tensions between attempts to protect 'people' and the 'planet' while promoting 'prosperity', 'peace' and 'partnership'. This demands examination of processes of decision making underpinning (a) goal-setting, (b) the content of SDGs and (c) supervision of their implementation at the UN level. It is beyond the scope of this chapter to investigate more fully the processes of decision making operating at national or regional levels. In particular, we consider how sustainable development still operates as a 'directing principle' (de Sadeleer, 2002), as discussed in Chapter 1 and whether, in the words of SDG target 16.7, there has been and will be 'responsive, inclusive, participatory and representative decision-making at all levels'.

Indeed, it is the idea of inclusion that drives our analysis in this chapter. We begin by attending to who the drafters were and their intentions, as are revealed by debates surrounding the preparatory documentation and processes. We then consider the SDGs themselves together with the scope for debate (and even conflict) regarding their content and their interaction. For example, we are alert to the dangers of subsuming the environmental within economic objectives, as well as obscuring social concerns (including human rights norms) behind these two more dominant aims (see Chapter 1). We also find continuities with previous legal and policy instruments concerned with sustainable development, such as the emphasis placed on poverty in SDG 1 and redistributive justice in SDG 10, together with notable enhancement of certain standards, such as that relating to gender in SDG 5 and work in SDG8. Further, we see the environmental pillar unpacked following a sectoral approach categorised under five different goals (SGD 7 on energy, SDG 13 on climate, SDG 14 on marine life, SDG 15 on terrestrial life and SDG 6 on fresh water). What is evident is that the particular wording of each SDG was the outcome of careful negotiation ending in a 'fine balance of competing interests' (Chasek et al, 2016: 5), which means that there is sometimes a discontinuity with what have been regarded as established legal norms on particular issues. While some conflicts may be resolved by implementation plans of regional actors (such as the European Union) and of individual states, there are potential risks of normative fragmentation here that require attention, not least because they beg the question as to the identity of the actors which will address those risks and resolve such conflict. SDG 16 would seem to enable inclusive dialogue with diverse participants offering alternative knowledge bases for policy development. The crucial question is whether that objective can be realised.

Certainly, the efficacy of Agenda 2030 and the SDG framework is likely to depend on the credibility of international supervisory mechanisms, which demands investigation of the role played by the High Level Political Forum (HLPF). We consider here the participatory potential of the HLPF, and the extent to which it embraces previously unheard voices while enabling critical engagement and promoting accountability. We note that SDG 17 prompts cooperation between different international organisations and UN agencies of arguably differential status, which has the potential to harness powerful forces for sustainability objectives. Yet, we also observe simultaneously that there is a risk that those same powerful institutions can act to obscure inconvenient concerns and silence dissent. These critiques have obvious relevance for the development of legal norms and doctrine discussed in Parts II to IV of this book, where we outline a variety of legal perspectives on sustainability.

Analysing Agenda 2030 and the SDGs from an inclusive and participatory perspective

From a legal viewpoint, the 17 SDGs set out in the Resolution *Transforming our world: the 2030 Agenda for Sustainable Development* (UN, 2015) marked a turning point in contemporary debates regarding both development and the idea of sustainability. As observed in Chapter 1, international instruments recognising 'sustainability' and/or 'development' had often taken a declaratory form, see-sawing between concern with economic growth (in the context of world trade), the environment (such as the Brundtland Report and the 1992 Rio Declaration) and more social objectives (such as the 1986 Declaration on the Right to Development). In these settings, we have observed potential tension between ecological and human-focused (anthropocentric) objectives, alongside concern that the latter subordinated environmental to economic concerns (Ross-Robertson, 2003).

The attempt to achieve a form of fusion in the Millennium Development Goals (MDGs) proved in various respects unsuccessful, in part because of the limited scope of its vision, confined to eight simplified objectives and tangible, measurable targets, underpinned by a reductionist quantification logic (See Chapter 1; Fukuda-Parr, 2016). Further, they were more directed by the global North to developing countries in the global South rather than to the globe as a whole (Kanie et al, 2017: 10–11; Fukuda-Parr, 2016: 44). The SDGs offer a new set of challenges, being as ambitious in length as the Rio Declaration and its subsequent re-elaborations but more exciting in terms of their addition of qualitative elements and a re-contextualisation of global connections between what had been previously seen as the three 'pillars' of sustainability: economic, environmental and social. Arguably, a fourth, cultural, pillar has been brought into the frame by pledging to foster 'intercultural understanding, tolerance, mutual respect and an ethic of global citizenship and shared responsibility', recognising that 'that all cultures and civilizations' can 'contribute to, and are crucial enablers of, sustainable development' (UN, 2015: para 36).

That acknowledgement of divergent cultural perspectives has the potential to enable engagement with divergent voices and offer diverse ontological possibilities regarding interpretation and application of the SDGs. On the one hand, there is the need to take seriously the findings of experts on ecological and other issues. On the other hand, in order for the assessment of evidence and operationalisation of sustainability to work in practice, local communities and other forms of social governance need to be engaged so as to generate the commitment and effective planning for their achievement. Moreover, this is not only an instrumental or operational concern, but is also vital to giving the norms meaning to those whom they are intended to benefit. Further, inclusive processes offer opportunities to challenge established barriers and boundaries inherent in the status quo, such that the partitions of the sensible are challenged by those considered previously to have no qualifications to rule (Ranciere, 2001). When those traditionally policed and excluded can gain access to decision making and actually voice their dissent in meaningful ways, this can have potentially disruptive but also creative consequences (Van Poeck and Vandenabeele, 2012; Boano and Kelling, 2013). This thinking is in line with Mouffe's understanding of radical democracy, whereby the objective is not to create a universal consensus by means of rational argumentation, denying the antagonist character of politics, but by bringing forth the disruptive, not always-rational arguments to decision making. For Mouffe, the question for democratic politics is not arrival at a rational consensus reached without exclusion, at the establishment of an us without a matching them.

> This is impossible because there cannot exist an 'us' without a 'them'. This question, pace the rationalists, is not how to arrive at a rational consensus reached without exclusion, or in other words how to establish an 'us' which would not have a corresponding 'them'. This is impossible because there cannot exist an 'us' without a 'them'. What is at stake is how to establish this 'us – them' discrimination in a way that is compatible with pluralist democracy. In the realm of politics, this presupposes that the 'other' is no longer seen as an enemy to be destroyed, but as an 'adversary', somebody with whose ideas we are going to struggle, but whose right to defend those ideas we will not put into question. We could say that the aim of democratic politics is to transform an 'antagonism' into an 'agonism'. (1995: 263)

In this way, difference can be reclaimed and those often excluded from political spheres can be empowered, as would be the ideal in a post-developmentalism agenda (Demaria and Kothari, 2017).

Such an inclusive ethos is consistent with a more pluriversal vision which entails relational ontologies without a clear, linear, unidirectional path. Through such lenses we can consider the scope for various understandings of sustainability, or rather, sustainabilities, and consider their viability. In this way we can evaluate not just the substantive goals, targets and indicators now presented to us but the procedural mechanisms appropriate to their application, and supervisory procedures that could facilitate their monitoring and assessment.

Accordingly, the third section of the chapter will examine the processes by which the SDGs and the broader Agenda 2030 were devised, evaluating the extent to which they seem (with hindsight) to be inclusive and representative. The fourth section will explore the potential for contestation over the content of and relationship between the SDGs, as well as their connection with other international legal sustainability and human rights norms. We will also consider in this context the ways in which the SDGs themselves give guidance regarding inclusive decision making, suggesting that this extends beyond SDG 16 to, for example, SDGs 5 and 10. Finally, we will consider the supervisory processes originally envisaged and how the HLPF is working in practice from the perspective of the normative position taken in the SDGs.

Inclusion in goal and agenda setting

We begin by considering the extent to which diverse voices and interests were included in the process of goal (and, indeed, agenda) setting, which tells us something about the SDGs' purpose and legitimacy. Previously, the MDGs set goals and targets from on high, informed by expert opinion, regardless of local priorities (Satterthwaite, 2003; Saith, 2006, Vandemoortele, 2009).

Rio+20 did not seem likely to offer much more from a participatory perspective. As we have noted in Chapter 1, the 'green economy' emerged as one its two main foci (next to institutional reform), so that suspicions that the economic would take precedence over the environmental and social aspects of sustainability were reawakened (Jacobs, 2012: 5). Ultimately, Rio+20 was seen as voicing some important environmental objectives on the world stage and promoting the voices of developing countries and their concern with making eradication of poverty a key focus, which remains prominent in Agenda 2030 (Clemenson, 2012). However, the final Rio+20 declaration lacked some of the international commitments that might make a difference: 'such as phasing out of fossil fuel subsidies, an agreement on managing global oceans, creating a World Environmental Organization, or breaking the deadlock on climate change negotiations' (Barbier, 2012: 887). Nor did the G20 meeting that same year offer any 'concrete actions or policies for achieving "inclusive green growth"' (Barbier, 2012: 887).

Goodman and Salleh (2013) saw the 2012 UN Resolution as the culmination of a 'green economy' idea that 'took shape during a 20-year debate, which reflected the rise of neoliberal ecologism, with "ecological" sustainability translated first into "economic" sustainability, and then into "free markets"'. The question was whether this then could be a helpful starting point for the shift from the MDGs to SDGs proposed at the conclusion of the conference.

It was clear from *The Future We Want* (UN, 2012: para 6) that 'people are at the centre of sustainable development' and that this is to be broadly defined, but ecological issues were given more prominence than others. Curiously, trade was tackled in two brief paragraphs towards the end, which was problematic because its centrality to sustainability outcomes was clear but seemingly too controversial to be readily addressed in depth. Certainly, *The Future We Want* did not, as a document, achieve the integration it advocated. It was a complex task to tame the objectives in that document and arrive at the extant 17 SDGs. That process has also to be understood in terms of the limited inclusivity of the 'Open Working Group' (OWG) established in its wake and the creation of the HLPF in 2013.

Certainly, the European Union (EU) sought to promote a scientific expert-led approach to the design of the SDGs, while governments from developing countries sought inclusion of their own appointed 'experts' (Kanie et al, 2017: 15). Ultimately, there was agreement on an OWG that would (UN, 2012: para 76):

> (a) Promote the balanced integration of the three dimensions of sustainable development;
> ...
> (c) Underscore the importance of interlinkages among key issues and challenges and the need for a systematic approach to them at all relevant levels;
> (d) Enhance coherence, reduce fragmentation and overlap and increase effectiveness, efficiency and transparency, while reinforcing coordination and cooperation ...

The OWG was to do so via 'fair, equitable and balanced representation', namely the standard UN geographical distribution into five regional groups with 30 representatives nominated by governments. Of these representatives, Kanie et al (2017) reported that a few spoke for other countries, while others spoke only on their own behalf. They estimated that approximately 70 countries were represented in ways that were to 'ease traditional North–South confrontations' (Kanie et al 2017: 16). This process was achieved by the appointment and intervention of Co-Chairs (Chasek et al, 2016: 11–12). The first session of the OWG was heavily reliant on expert advice, but later drew on more widespread consultation.

The OWG responded to initiatives taken by UN Secretary-General Ban Ki-moon, including reports produced by his 'Sustainable Development Solutions Network' and the 'High-Level Panel of Eminent Persons on the Post-2015 Development Agenda'. Account was also taken of studies 'from civil society, business, think tanks, colloquia and conferences' (Nanda, 2016: 403). The Report of the OWG in 2014 (UN, 2014) proposed 17 SDGs accompanied by 169 targets, with further indicators to be identified.

Pogge and Sengupta (2015) wrote a lobbying article suggesting that the SDGs (as drafted by the OWG) were a 'nice idea' poorly executed. They expressed concern at three 'failings' in the 2014 draft (2015: 573): first, 'failing to call for transformative change in the international institutional order'; second, 'failing to include human rights language'; and third, 'failing to provide objective and precise measures to track progress'. With similar concerns, 27 civil society groups sent a letter to the UN Secretary-General and the President of the UNGA seeking 'to ensure human rights accountability of all development actors' in a way which would align the SDGs with all human rights standards (Nanda, 2016: 404). As we shall see later, there are indications of a closer alignment with human rights provisions (such as freedom from forced labour) than we have previously seen in a sustainable development instrument, but at the same time there is no simple mapping across to more established international human rights norms. In January 2015 the UNGA began the negotiating process for Agenda 2030, and again extensive input from all sectors came within the consultative scope of the final push for adoption of the SDGs.

There has been praise for the involvement of 'business and industry' (such as Paul Polman from Unilever) in this process 'alongside groups representing indigenous peoples, women, children and youth, and farmers' (reported by Scheyvens, Banks and Hughes, 2016: 374). Others have noted that the scope of engagement for different actors was 'uneven'. Pingeot (2014), in particular, observed that a preponderance of corporate involvement hailed from Europe and the

United States, but also that mining/oil and gas companies were over-represented. He suspected that this led to an emphasis on economic growth and the treatment of that objective as readily reconcilable with other sustainability objectives (Pingeot, 2014: 17). He also described how corporate sustainability became a focus of policy making in this way alongside defence of corporate interests. Pogge and Sengupta (2015: 574–5) gave as an example the decision to move from a stand-alone target for global cooperation to reduce international tax evasion in an earlier OWG draft, which now in the SDGs seeks only reduction of 'illicit financial and arms flows' (target 16.4) and asks for cooperation toward improving poor countries' capacity for tax and revenue collection (target 17.1). Arguably 'big business' can be a true 'partner' in sustainable development (alongside governments and civil society) only if there is acknowledgement of its power and its prior preparedness to use that power to the disadvantage of these other actors (Scheyvens, Banks and Hughes, 2016).

Scope for conflict and proposals for inclusion embedded in the SDGs

In this section we focus on the content of the SDGs themselves and their relational ontology. We reject the accusation that they merely dilute previous protections and risk the principle of sustainable development becoming over broad and even more uncertain (Smith and Farley, 2013; Dernbach and Cheever, 2015). However, we acknowledge that there remain unresolved questions regarding the ways in which they interact, the priority to be given to the different pillars and, indeed, whether the pillars are self-standing and the extent to which certain SDGs have cross-cutting operational effects. Their relationship with existing human rights standards as already protected within a UN framework is also a matter for concern (MacNaughton, 2018). Some connections between SDGs might be viewed as indicative of a new form of holistic unity, but we would prefer to see these as relational interactions offering potentially a wider range of perspectives and possibilities than were envisaged by the MDGs. Additionally, we examine connections (and dissonance) between SDGs and other international legal norms.

We recognise that the SDGs are now an obvious focus for disputes and contestation of the substance of sustainability norms and their application. 'The carefully negotiated language of the 17-goal agenda, emphasising intangible qualitative objectives of equitable and sustainable development, has led to a complex language' (Fukuda-Parr, 2016: 50).

Accordingly, it may be that 'sustainability' per se remains something not altogether concrete, but rather a post-modern 'directing' principle or even a plurality of potentially interrelated principles. Indeed, the titles of 'goals' and 'targets' (with subsidiary 'indicators') may be misleading, for many of the statements in each SDG are procedural, more concerned with a process than linear achievement of a simple outcome (although the latter is sometimes the case). We therefore also consider how Agenda 2030 and the SDGs offer guidance on procedures for determination of the content of sustainability norms and their implementation, focusing on those targets which indicate a need for greater inclusiveness and participation.

The substantive content of the Agenda 2030 and the SDGs

The SDGs have been framed around purposive alliteration: People, Planet, Prosperity, Peace and Partnership. These are shared values that are almost incontestable as having merit. What matters, of course, is how they have been operationalised in Agenda 2030. They reflect the outcome of an 'extensive negotiating and consultation process' (Kanie et al, 2017: 3), such that the apparent consensus achieved does not neatly map onto previous international sustainability and other (such as human rights) legal norms. Moreover, their relationship, while said to be integrated and coherent, is indicative of various tensions.

First comes *People*, such that anthropocentrism arguably remains central to a sustainability agenda (Adelman, 2017; Kotze and French, 2018). As discussed in Chapter 1, this is not a notable departure from past international (and European) instruments relating to sustainability. Thus, it is not surprising that the first SDG is 'to end poverty' and the second is to end 'hunger' for humans. Also significant is the phraseology. For example, there is to be water and energy 'for all' (see SDGs 6 and 7); this is a claim that all have by virtue of being human. Indeed, the significance of human dignity, equality and health is repeatedly stressed in Agenda 2030, the last of these certainly (and arguably all of them) having significant links to the well-being of the '*Planet*'.

As one would expect, numerous environmental objectives are highlighted, concerning agriculture (SDG 2), water (SDG 6), climate change (SDG 13), oceans and seas (SDG 14), as well as ecosystems and biodiversity on land (SDG 15) and energy (SDG 7). Not only people but also the planet, then, is to be protected from 'degradation', 'including through sustainable consumption and production, sustainably managing its natural resources and taking urgent action on climate change, so that it can support the needs of the present and future generations' (UN, 2015: 2). In this sense, intra- and inter-generational justice again enter the framework. One might hope that the term 'present and future generations' is inclusive not only of humans but also of all species.

Prosperity might seem to return Agenda 2030 to the achievement of economic objectives that dominated the history of 'sustainability'. For example, SDG 8 is concerned not only with 'decent work' (as promoted by the International Labour Organization (ILO)) but also with 'sustained, inclusive and sustainable economic growth'. In this sense, there are links that can be drawn with an end to poverty, with an emphasis not only on access to participation (and justice) in the formal labour market but also on access to entrepreneurial activity, seeking to 'encourage the formalization and growth of micro-, small- and medium-sized enterprises, including through access to financial services' (target 8.3). On this basis, some commentators see this facet of the SDGs as a potential route towards sustainable investment and longer-term profitability, maintaining and improving global capitalism (Busch, Bauer and Orlitzky, 2016). Others express more concern. For example, Adelman (2017) links the capitalist logic underpinning the sustainable development agenda with anthropocentrism, stating that the SDGs 'reproduce growth fetishism by promoting an intrinsically anthropocentric approach to sustainability that reinforces the longstanding criticism that sustainable development is an oxymoron' (2017: 16). We will see the corporate and financial strands of this approach linked to issues raised in later chapters in this book relating to financial reporting and corporate governance (or the public presentation of the latter).

Peace is arguably concerned with intra-generational distributive justice and can be linked to some over-arching SDGs concerned not only with specific concrete outcomes but also with overcoming barriers to achievement of other SDGs. These may be prevented by gender equality (SDG 5) and addressing 'inequality within and between countries' (SDG 10). The latter can be linked to Anna Grear's observation that 'patterned hierarchies' have led to environmental crises (Grear, 2014). This radical concern with equality, and particularly gender equality, has been identified as 'transformative' (Fredman, Kuosmanen, and Campbell, 2016; Fredman, 2018). Potentially even more significant among these over-arching SDGs in terms of the benefit of 'peace' is SDG 16, which aims to: 'Promote peaceful and inclusive societies for sustainable development, provide access to justice for all and build effective, accountable and inclusive institutions at all levels'. This is concerned with the promotion of inclusive participatory mechanisms for multi-level decision making and also protection from harm through effective judicial and other mechanisms.

Finally, crucial to achievement of all the SDGs is *Partnership*, written into SDG 17, which seeks to: 'Strengthen the means of implementation and revitalize the Global Partnership for Sustainable Development'. This is to be achieved by 'finance', 'technology', 'capacity-building' and 'trade', all of which feature as further targets under this heading. Further, the SDGs end with subheadings (in SDG 17) on 'policy and institutional coherence', 'multi-stakeholder partnerships' and 'data, monitoring and accountability', under each of which further targets are listed.

Both SDGs 16 and 17, highlighting inclusive participation and policy coherence, are reminiscent of Martha Nussbaum's (2011) identification of certain 'central capabilities', and among these are two (affiliation and practical reason) which perform an 'architectonic' role in securing others (2011: 39). For our purposes, 'affiliation' may be the most significant of these (from the perspective of inclusive representation and participation), for Nussbaum envisages this as the ability 'to engage in various forms of social interaction; to be able to imagine the situation of another'. She further explains that protection of 'affiliation' 'means protecting institutions that constitute and nourish such forms of affiliation, and also protecting the freedom of assembly and political speech' (Nussbaum, 2003: 41–2).

It is possible that these SDGs may perhaps offer an even richer sense of what these capabilities may mean in practice. Gupta and Vegelin (2016: 436–9) argue that the social, economic and relational inclusiveness of the SDGs, particularly SDGs 10, 16 and 17, offer hope for reconciliation of potential tensions between the application of different goals. They observe that previously there was overall 'little emphasis on including the knowledge of all, or engaging all, or promoting effective capacity building to enable better participation' (2016: 441). At least the SDGs 'reflect relational criteria by putting pressure on developed countries to take their responsibilities seriously and to work through multilateral institutions …' (2016: 444).

Coherence of the SDGs

In terms of the coherence of these goals, it is already evident that they are connected potentially in a variety of ways. An ILO Report on SDG 8 has, for example, described these as 'dynamic interlinkages' (ILO, 2019: pp 27ff). SDGs 16 and 17 have self-evidently the greatest capacity to affect the interpretation, application and significance of other SDGs.

In terms of what were the separate economic, environmental and social pillars, there is arguably a tension, as has been observed between 'balance' and 'integration' presenting 'a contested normative vision' (Bernstein, 2017: 216–17).

Ecological integrity must be an overarching boundary within which social and economic considerations should be placed and which they cannot violate. In this respect, Barral's conception of sustainability is not uncommon. She considers development as sustainable 'only when both intergenerational (environmental protection) and intra-generational (fair economic and social development) [justice] are guaranteed and this is to be achieved through their integration' (Barral, 2012: 380). As such, it might seem that social and economic objectives have to be linked to environmental objectives in order to be eligible for protection under sustainability principles. This is a view also shared by some environmental commentators, who consider that the environmental pillar should be encompassing of the other two (Bosselmann, 2016).

In this sense, a planetary boundaries approach to sustainability seems entirely sensible, for there can be no economy and no society without a planet (Raworth, 2017). However, this does not necessitate the view that social and economic concerns cannot relate to sustainability unless environmental issues also arise. In the labour standards literature (see Novitz and Mangan, 2011; also Novitz, 2015 and Polomarkakis, 2019) it is argued that (subject to planetary boundaries) the environmental, economic, social and cultural dimensions of sustainability need to be jointly *and severally* enforceable as the component parts of development.

There is arguably some evidence of such an approach in the UN SDGs, which are described as 'integrated' and 'interdependent' (UN, 2015: para 5), but which set out targets and indicators not obviously engaged with the ecological or environmental matters at certain junctures. Bernstein (2017: 216) notes that planetary boundaries are not mentioned in SDG 8. It is also clear from the Agenda 2030 UNGA Resolution that 'equal access to justice' and 'human rights' are themselves vital regarding the pursuit of peace, without merely being instrumental for environmental purposes (see para 35). Perhaps more potently, SDG 16.2 is not concerned directly with the environment but addresses the need to 'end abuse, exploitation, trafficking and all forms of violence against and torture of children'. Children's forced labour cannot be linked necessarily to environmental concerns, but obviously raise issues of both inter- and intra-generational justice, for this practice affects the capacity of those children when adults to contribute to society and affects the distribution of wealth within society at the present time. The SDGs thereby do not just offer a vision of sustainability wherein only environmental or economic issues matter, although environmental and economic concerns will have to be addressed in crafting solutions to social sustainability problems.

The relationship with prior international legal norms

There remains here a risk of trespassing into spheres which have already been the subject of international law and ongoing issues as to the fragmentation of sources of international law (De Schutter, 2015: 2–3). However, in the context of sustainability we are now long used to balancing existing customary international law and treaty provisions and acknowledging difficulties in achieving appropriate outcomes. The challenge is to make such processes explicit. A failing of the MDGs has been said to be the way in which they 'sidestepped rather than aligned with human rights obligations', such as equality and non-discrimination (Frey and MacNaughton, 2016: 5). This question of alignment versus fragmentation, as well as how such tension is managed, is therefore explored later in this chapter.

Certain SDGs incorporate what have become acknowledged to be international human rights, such as non-discrimination between women and men (SDG 5) or protection from child or forced labour (SDG 8). Does this mean that these SDGs (or particular targets and indicators that include them) 'are symmetrical to or a deviation of present obligations set out in law'? (Kotze and French, 2018: 3). What is now to be regarded as the proper reference point for the identification of legal and political norms? There are already significant allegations from various sources that international law is becoming increasingly fragmented (Benvenisti and Downs, 2007; Van Asselt, Sindico and Mehling, 2008). Are the SDGs a reflection of common consensus on the normative foundations of the international community, as Agenda 2030 claims? Or do they give scope for deregulatory effects and detraction from what have been established human rights, labour laws and environmental requirements (international, regional and national)?

As we shall see, it is unclear the extent to which these statements are intended to incorporate the terms of the Convention on the Elimination of Discrimination against Women or the terms of core ILO Conventions (in particular, Forced Labour Convention, 1930 (No. 29), Abolition of Forced Labour Convention, 1957 (No. 105), Minimum Age Convention, 1973 (No. 138), Worst Forms of Child Labour Convention, 1999 (No. 182), and even the Equal Remuneration Convention, 1951 (No. 100) and Discrimination (Employment and Occupation) Convention, 1958 (No. 111)). One might expect that at least the minimum standards in these instruments can be taken as accepted, with scope for further improvements for policy promoted through the aspirational quality of the SDGs (cf Kanie and Biermann, 2017; also Kim, 2016). At a minimum, we would hope that the SDGs are not be regarded as diluting fundamental aspects of international legal instruments and EU Directives relating to social and environmental protection. SDG 16.10 sets out a commitment to 'protect fundamental freedoms, in accordance with national legislation and international agreements'. Notably, the UN Special Rapporteur on the rights to freedom of peaceful assembly and of association has advocated in his Report on implementation of the 2030 Agenda for Sustainable Development that this be taken to entail all the internationally recognised rights relating to freedom of association, including trade union representation, collective bargaining and a right to strike, in compliance with ILO instruments (especially Freedom of Association and Protection of the Right to Organize Convention, 1948 (No. 87) and Right to Organize and Collective Bargaining Convention, 1949 (No. 98)) and the 1966 Covenants (UN, 2018, paras 59–64 and para 87). SDG 16.b requires that states 'promote and enforce non-discriminatory laws and policies for sustainable development', which indicates a desire for consistency with UN and ILO discrimination legal standards rather than any obvious departure. However, SDG target 14.5 on conservation appears to reduce previous international commitments by stripping away established qualitative dimensions of conservation (see the Aichi target 11 discussed in Rees et al, 2018 and by Pieraccini in Chapter 8 of this book).

It should also be acknowledged that in previous contexts where international instruments have adopted declaratory principles, such as the ILO Declaration on Fundamental Principles and Rights at Work 1998, there has been ongoing dispute as to the extent to which the core Conventions inform their content (see Alston 2005). This suggests that the relationship between SDGs and other legal instruments cannot merely be assumed but could be the subject of challenge, which may be played out at the national and regional levels as well as in the context of international law. Of course, not all challenge may be problematic, if participatory inclusion enables new discussions and shifts boundaries in ways that engage those previously excluded from debate (Koskenniemi and Leino, 2002; Young, 2002). However, it seems more likely that there could be deregulatory effects, familiar from the ILO experience, given an international context responsive to corporate power dynamics.

Last, but not least, as noted in Chapter 1, the appropriate mechanisms for enforcement and supervision of sustainability principles have remained in doubt. Can policy objectives set out in the SDGs be given the force of law? This could entail movement from a loose 'directing' principle (which in a post-modern sense is open to divergent manifestations) to a more concrete principle of customary international law. It would not be the first time that a declaratory instrument has come to be understood to contain provisions that constitute *jus cogens*. The most obvious example is the Universal Declaration of Human Rights in 1948, which contains various provisions that have arguably acquired that status (Simma and Alston, 1988). Further, many of the SDGs embody existing human rights and other legal principles, such as environmental legal principles, under international law. However, we are more used to sustainability offering a principle of 'rebalance' within legal proceedings rather than offering a 'trump' in the sense of a human right (cf Dworkin, 1977). There is arguably a strong prompt for legal reform in many of the SDGs. This is sometimes general in form, such as making greater provision for 'special and differential treatment' in SDG target 10.A. It can also be more particular, such as ensuring at the national level effective mechanisms for remittances of pay home by migrant workers under SDG target 10.C, such that there is no more than a 3% transaction cost for doing so. This is a very specific requirement that would have a palpable effect on the savings of migrant workers.

Procedural norms for inclusion

The increased interest in procedural aspects of justice by those advocating the international sustainability agenda is also explicitly embodied by one of the goals itself, namely SDG 16. SDG 16 builds on Principle 10 of the 1992 Rio Declaration of Principles (and the subsequent Aarhus Convention of 1998), which stressed the importance of 'participation of all concerned citizens at the relevant level'. There may be particular promise in the statement in SDG 16.7 which undertakes to: 'Ensure responsive, inclusive, participatory and representative decision-making at all levels'. SDG 16 offers a route towards valuing diverse people in the context of pursuit of protection for the planet and the achievement of prosperity by strengthening the procedural justice dimensions of sustainability, previously overshadowed by distributive concerns regarding intra- and inter-generational justice. The difficulty is that the rhetoric of the Agenda 2030 Resolution, namely that it is 'an Agenda of the people, by the people and for the people' (at para 52), does not acknowledge those distanced from UN processes and the limitations of those processes. This suggests that there may be more rhetorical mileage than transformational potential in the SDGs and Agenda 2030. We have yet to see whether SDG 16 is sufficient for the pluralisation of sustainability. However, this may be part of a longer-term path towards mobilisation around sustainability issues.

The emphasis on inclusion is also present in targets of other SDGs. For example, target 5.5 on ensuring 'women's full and effective participation and equal opportunities for leadership at all levels of decision-making in political and economic and public life', target 10.2 on political inclusion, women's participation and leadership, target 6.b on supporting and strengthening the participation of local communities in improving water and sanitation and management, and target 10.2 on political inclusion to reduce intra-generational inequality.

Perhaps even more significant is the provision in target 10.6 to: 'Ensure enhanced representation and voice for developing countries in decision-making in global international economic and financial institutions in order to deliver more effective, credible, accountable and legitimate institutions'. This flows from ongoing scepticism expressed by developing countries regarding the benefits of so-called 'development' itemised in economic terms by countries from the global North (Abrahamyan et al, 2017: 66). Their concerns are more with 'going beyond the symptoms of poverty, to issues of peace, stability, human rights and good governance' and more local 'inclusive and participatory goal setting' (Abrahamyan et al, 2017: 68). This chimes with the view of Gupta and Vegelin (2016: 444) that the very content of the SDGs has the potential 'to mobilize scholarly communities, communities of practice and social movements around them ...'. However, as implementation of those aspects of the SDGs needs 'significant resources', which are difficult to find domestically, 'access to decision making in international financial institutions is vital' (Abrahamyan et al, 2017: 83).

Inclusion in supervisory processes

The mechanism set up for the supervision of any future SDGs, namely the HLPF, was both to assist in establishing the SDGs and also to 'promote the review and stocktaking of progress in the implementation of all sustainable development commitments, including commitments related to means of implementation' (UN, 2012: para 76). There was a tension at the outset in the HLPF, which was to replace the Commission for Sustainable Development, while also operating in an economically efficient manner: 'The high-level political forum shall follow up on the implementation of sustainable development and should avoid overlap with existing structures, bodies and entities in a cost-effective manner' (UN, 2012: para, 84). Alongside 'political leadership' and a platform for dynamic policy making, the HLPF would 'follow up and review progress', sharing best practice, achievements and lessons learned, while also promoting 'system-wide coherence and coordination of sustainable development policies'. This seems more like Rancière's police disciplining the potential outcomes of dialogue, rather than the enablement of a free-flowing discussion with multiple participants and viewpoints.

The plan was at the outset for the HLPF to 'provide political leadership, guidance and recommendations for sustainable development' (UN, 2013: para 2). Moreover, its remit was ambitious, perhaps overly so. For example, it was intended to follow up and review 'implementation' of 'all the major conferences and summits in the economic, social and environmental fields'(UN, 2013: para 7(d)), while Ban Ki-Moon had envisaged that the HLPF would 'guide the UN system … and hold it accountable' (cited in Bernstein, 2017: 217 and 222, respectively). One wonders how this could possibly be feasible for a relatively recently created body with no ostensible powers of enforcement. The rhetoric seemed bold but unrealistic. Abbott and Bernstein (2015) suggested that this could be achieved by 'orchestration', such that the HLPF would work through intermediary organisations using 'leadership, persuasion, incentives' to guide their actions. Therefore, the HLPF does not exercise a form of command and control, or direct regulation, but is emblematic of a more collaborative form of governance, guiding the various governance actors ('intermediaries') to engage with agreed policy goals targets. Orchestration, differently from delegation, 'cuts the chain of electoral accountability because the orchestrator lacks hard control over intermediaries. Ultimately, intermediaries exercise their authority in an (externally) uncontrolled and unaccountable way. This potentially allows governors to use orchestration to pursue goals 'outside their mandate' (Abbott et al, 2015: 9). Orchestration could be understood as an indirect form of governance with disciplining effects, and potentially as lacking legitimacy.

One might expect this to be a way to secure 'policy coherence for development' in line with the apparently more holistic ambitions of Agenda 2030 and the stated aim of a 'global partnership'. This raises 'systemic issues' highlighted in SDG 17, particularly in targets 17.13 (namely to 'enhance global macroeconomic stability, including through policy coordination and policy coherence') and 17.14 (baldly, to 'enhance policy coherence for sustainable development'). Some clue as to how this is to be done is offered in target 17.15, which indicates respect for state sovereignty. But then target 17.16 stresses global partnership, reallocation of resources and participation of 'developing countries'. What takes the initiative out of the realm of merely state-based governmental control is target 17.16, with its reference to an obligation to 'encourage and promote effective public, public-private and civil society partnerships'. Indeed, at all levels of governance (international, regional and national), and across the private and public spheres, the HLPF was considered to have the mandate to 'take over sustainable development mainstreaming' (Bernstein, 2017: 225). However, that potential does not seem to have been realised.

The current voluntary review procedure of the HLPF in relation to the SDGs

The HLPF, first established in 2013, is now adjusting to a politically more sensitive function in receiving voluntary state reports relating to particular SDGs. States now can comply with the Guidelines for voluntary national review so as to submit reports to the HLPF on their compliance with SDGs and accompanying targets and indicators, which are then published on the HLPF website for all states and interested stakeholders to see.[1] Key UN agencies and other transnational actors also have the capacity to contribute their views (for example, ILO, 2019).

The HLPF meets only annually for eight days, under the umbrella of the UN Economic and Social Council (ECOSOC), and also for two days every four years as Heads of State and Government under the auspices of the UNGA. Moreover, given that there are two organisations (the UNGA and ECOSOC) engaged here, it may be difficult to ensure a coherent treatment of these issues (Desai and Sidhu, 2015). The HLPF is a forum in which all 197 UN Member States can participate, alongside interested UN agencies and other international organisations, as well as non-governmental organisations (NGOs) accredited by ECOSOC and those 'major groups and other stakeholders' (MGOS) registered in advance. In 2019 the dates for sessions were Tuesday, 9 July to Thursday, 18 July, including the three-day ministerial meeting of the forum from Tuesday, 16 July to Thursday, 18 July. In other words, this annual meeting takes place in a relatively short period of time.

Different SDGs are given different priorities for review by the HLPF. For example, SDG 17 falls to be reviewed every year, while SDG 8 (which raises issues of 'decent work') was reviewed for the first time only in 2019, one hundred years after the ILO was created, which is presumably not a coincidence. Also reviewed in 2019 were goals 4, 6, 10, 13 and 16. What is already apparent from the earlier outline is how tightly the participation and timing of review before the HLPF is constructed, making it difficult to see what meaningful discussions can take place within these limits; rather, it is the surrounding dialogue which is less focused which may be of use.

The role of states in the HLPF

Country-based voluntary national reviews are available online. The numbers participating in the HLPF process in July 2019 were 51, consisting of a mixture of developed and developing countries including, for example, Australia, France, New Zealand and the UK alongside Azerbaijan, Cambodia and Cote d'Ivoire. It is interesting that the ten states that have engaged with the process previously are all developing or emergent economies, such as Brazil. China engaged only in 2016 and the United States is notable in its absence. To date, 179 countries have participated. As such, this participatory process is again uneven, but perhaps more inclusive than one might have expected.

However, this does remain a process of inherently partial review, limited in terms of normative references, led by states, and then only some states. According to the revised Voluntary Common Reporting Guidelines, '[a]s national ownership is key to achieving sustainable development, the outcome from national-level processes will be the foundation for reviews at the regional and global levels', not international statistics held on a country.

Tensions between developing states in the global South and developed states in the North have been blamed for the difficulties in achieving coherence and integration of the seventeen SDGs, and also the difficulty of achieving meaningful implementation through the HLPF. Certainly, the sensitivity of many of the issues raised by the SDGs regarding financial and other capabilities suggest that it will be difficult to gain consensus for clear condemnation of certain state practices. Instead, we may expect more of a 'nudge' directed at various actors at all levels to more gently guide behaviour (Bernstein, 2017: 233–4).

Stakeholder engagement with the HLPF

Agenda 2030 envisaged a role for 'the diverse private sector, ranging from micro-enterprises to cooperatives to multinationals, and that of civil society organisations and philanthropic organisations' in its implementation (UN, 2015: para 41). The Guidelines likewise stress the significance of processes that are 'open, inclusive, participatory and transparent for all people and will support reporting by all relevant stakeholders, which will also be 'people-centred, gender-sensitive, respect human rights and have a particular focus on the poorest, most vulnerable and those furthest behind'.[2] Such statements seem to offer scope for Gupta and Vegelin's notion of relational inclusion (2016), thereby evading the potential for Rancière's more disruptive 'dissensus'. However, Gupta and Nilsson (2017: 277) have subsequently sounded a warning regarding the implicit lack of hierarchy amid such a multiplicity of voices: 'Each of these different actors and stakeholders may decide to prioritize or interpret goals in vastly different and possibly inconsistent ways as they try to align them with their own interests.'

In 2017 the HLPF advice sheet for MGOs indicated there were 12 special tickets with a microphone for such members of civil society, as well as seats in the gallery and overflow rooms.[3] However, it is also anticipated that involvement of the MGOS will extend beyond this to:

- have access to all official information and documents;
- submit documents and present written and oral contributions;
- make recommendations;
- and organize side events and round tables, in cooperation with Member States and the Secretariat.[4]

There is annually an extensive 'side events' programme,[5] and numerous inputs from MGOS are made available online,[6] which does indicate that dialogue is being generated even though this is not necessarily before the HLPF itself. In a sense, inclusion and participation are still happening at the borders, but not yet fully within the margins of influence. Moreover, the multiplicity of voices indicates that some messages may be obscured, and it is difficult to detect which those are. It is likely to be those who can exert other more meaningful forms of power, the multinational rather than the cooperative, the international rather than the local NGO, which will be heard. In this context Gupta and Nilsson (2017) advocate an 'action framework' providing both vertical and horizontal coherence, but the HLPF seems some way from achieving this.

That perception of lying on the margins is seemingly reinforced by an instruction in the HLPF Guidelines to the effect that the voluntary review will 'build on existing platforms and processes, where these exist, avoid duplication and respond to national circumstances, capacities, needs and priorities. They will evolve over time, taking into account emerging issues and the development of new methodologies, and will minimize the reporting burden on national administrations'.[7] This does not seem likely to provoke significant changes in established power relations between or within states or, arguably, beyond their borders, although the same Guidelines do mention 'active support of the United Nations system and other multilateral institutions'.

The HLPF annual report

Following each cycle of review before the HLPF, a Report is produced on the session.[8] The 2018 Report highlighted progress in terms of compliance with international legal commitments and disaggregated data collection, but noted how the least-developed countries are lagging behind.

The Report did not encourage departure from existing international instruments through the medium of the SDGs. Arguably, this is not so surprising, for, as other commentators have noted, the HLPF was never in a position to challenge or undermine existing UN and other legal structures: 'the HLPF lacks authority for direct or mandatory control over states, IGOs (Inter-governmental Organisations) or private actors, and lacks the material resources to provide strong incentives for desired actions' (Abbott and Bernstein 2015: 223).

However, it is potentially significant that, despite this weakness, the 2018 HLPF Report (at 3) did focus on distributive issues, raising concerns as regards not only inter- but also intra-generational justice. The Forum also reported from regional meetings, which indicated the divergent concerns of particular geographical areas, limiting dominant forms of Western bias. Country implementation was not focused only on particular statistical indicators but, rather, on new modes of promoting inter-ministerial and stakeholder-led governance: 'At the same time, there are continuing challenges, including the complexity of taking integrated approaches, the need to broadly communicate the Sustainable Development Goals and the means of implementation.' Holism is not yet simply or straightforwardly achieved (cf Nilsson, 2017).

The rest of the Report merely documented the debates at the HLPF (listing at length the actors, the documents submitted and briefly their contributions) and did not offer detailed analysis of the voluntary reports. One has the sense of a 'softly softly' approach in which change is being prompted gradually, incrementally and indirectly. However, this is a far cry from the proposal that the HLPF be 'the orchestrator' promoting effective coordination within a fragmented governance space (cf Bernstein, 2017). At the time of writing there is potential strengthening of the HLPF role when a full UN summit is to be held in September 2019 'to follow up and comprehensively review progress' in the implementation of the SDGs more generally.[9] At present, the pluralising promise of inclusive debate and decision making under (inter alia) SDG 16 seems some way off; nor is it possible to predict with any certainty the likelihood of SDGs not furthering but, rather, undermining existing human rights norms and environmental standards. This is a work in progress.

Conclusion

This chapter has considered the ways in which the SDGs reflect 'responsive, inclusive, participatory and representative decision-making at all levels', which is, after all, the normative target set in SDG 16.7. If sustainable development (or various facets of sustainable development) will continue to operate as a directing principle (as discussed in Chapter 1), then the question arises as to who is engaged in the processes of direction and who is being so directed in the processes leading up to 2015 and beyond the adoption of Agenda 2030.

The first section of this chapter examined the participatory processes leading up to the adoption of the SDGs, highlighting contestation over their content and potential influence. Here we explored the power dynamics inherent in the operation of these procedures and what we can detect regarding their effects, namely the limitations evident in Agenda 2030 and the SDG targets and indicators. The second section considered the result of the elaborate negotiations and consultations which resulted in Agenda 2030 and the SDGs. We found that the scope for disputes continues, over both the content of each separate SDG (and target) and their relationship with one another. We applaud the attempts to achieve integration, but also doubt whether this is ultimately reflected in the text of the UNGA Resolution (UN, 2015). Certainly, there are issues still to be addressed and clarified. There also remain questions regarding the relative interpretative status of the SDGs when compared with previous established legal norms, regarding such matters as environmental standards and international human rights. However, it is possible to identify a UN commitment to inclusion in the interpretation and application of the SDGs and we turned to this issue in the third section of the chapter. Here we outlined the operations of the HLPF and found it less an effective orchestrator of UN and multi-level responses, but rather an institution placed under unreasonable strain, struggling to amalgamate all voices and respond effectively to them. The implications of the architecture established in 2015 and its ongoing effects will be considered further in the remaining, more subject-specific chapters of this book.

Notes

1 See https://sustainabledevelopment.un.org/content/documents/17346Updated_Voluntary_Guidelines.pdf.
2 See https://sustainabledevelopment.un.org/content/documents/17346Updated_Voluntary_Guidelines.pdf.
3 See https://sustainabledevelopment.un.org/content/documents/16077HLPF_Information_note_final_3July.pdf.
4 This additional information is taken from the website, which cites the UN General Assembly Resolution A/RES/67/290, para 15: https://sustainabledevelopment.un.org/majorgroups/hlpf.
5 See, for example, https://sustainabledevelopment.un.org/content/documents/20158Tentative_programme_913_July_v9.pdf.
6 See https://sustainabledevelopment.un.org/inputs/.
7 See https://sustainabledevelopment.un.org/inputs/.
8 See, for example, http://www.un.org/ga/search/view_doc.asp?symbol=E/HLPF/2018/7&Lang=E.
9 See https://sustainabledevelopment.un.org/sdgsummit (accessed 18 June 2019).

References

Abbott, K.W. and Bernstein, S. (2015) 'The High-Level Political Forum on sustainable development: Orchestration by default and design', *Global Policy* 6(3): 222–33.

Abbott, K.W., Genschel, P., Snidal, D. and Zangl, B. (2014) 'Orchestration: global governance through intermediaries', in Abbott, K.W., Genschel, P., Snidal, D. and Zangl, B. (eds), *International Organizations as Orchestrators*, Cambridge: Cambridge University Press.

Abbott, K.W., Genschel, P., Snidal, D. and Zangl, B. (2015) 'Two logics of indirect governance: delegation and orchestration', *British Journal of Political Science* 46(4): 719–29.

Abrahamyan, P., Al-Farsi, O., Te, K., Addo, O., Moussa Niandou, N., Gaber Hamad Mohamed, M., Gracia, T. and Zhamalova, V. (2017) 'SDGs in post-truth: do SDGs matter for developing countries?', in *Economic Integration and Development Partnerships: Southern Perspectives*, Report, New Delhi: Research and Information Systems for Developing Countries (RIS).

Adelman, S. (2017) 'Tropical forests, climate change and neoliberal environmental governmentality', in Tan, C and Faundez, J. (eds), *Natural Resources and Sustainable Development*, Cheltenham: Edward Elgar Publishing.

Alston, P. (2005) 'Facing up to the complexities of the ILO's core labour standards agenda', *European Journal of International Law* 16(3): 467–80.
Barbier, E.B. (2012) 'The green economy post Rio+20', *Science* 338(6109): 887–8.
Barral, V. (2012) 'Sustainable development in international law: nature and operation of an evolutive legal norm', *European Journal of International Law* 23(2): 377–400.
Benvenisti, E. and Downs, G.W. (2007) 'The empire's new clothes: political economy and the fragmentation of international law', 60 *Stanford Law Review*, 595–632.
Bernstein, S. (2017) 'The United Nations and the governance of the Sustainable Development Goals', in Kanie, N. and Biermann, F. (eds), *Governing Through Goals: Sustainable Development Goals as Governance Innovation*, Boston: MIT Press, pp 213–40.
Boano, C. and Kelling, E. (2013) 'Toward an architecture of dissensus: participatory urbanism in South-East Asia', *Footprint* 7(2): 41–62.
Bosselmann, K. (2016) *The Principle of Sustainability: Transforming Law and Governance*, 2nd edn, London: Routledge.
Busch, T., Bauer, R. and Orlitzky, M. (2016) 'Sustainable development and financial markets: old paths and new avenues', *Business and Society* 55(3): 303–29.
Chasek, P.S., Wagner, L.M., Leone, F., Lebada, A-M. and Risse, N. (2016) 'Getting to 2030: negotiating the post-2015 Sustainable Development Agenda', *Review of European Community and International Environmental Law (RECIEL)* 25(1): 5–14.
Clemencon, R. (2012) 'Welcome to the Anthropocene: Rio+20 and the meaning of sustainable development', *Journal of Environment and Development* 21(3): 311–38.
de Sadeleer, N. (2002) *Environmental Principles – from Political Slogans to Legal Rules*, Oxford: Oxford University Press.
De Schutter, O. (2015) *Trade in the Service of Sustainable Development: Linking Trade to Labour Rights and Environmental Standards*, Oxford: Hart/Bloomsbury.
Demaria, F. and Kothari, A. (2017) 'The Post-Development Dictionary agenda: paths to the pluriverse', *Third World Quarterly* 38(12): 2588–99.
Dernbach, J.C. and Cheever, F. (2015) 'Sustainable development and its discontents', *Transnational Environmental Law* 4(2): 247–87.

Desai, B.H. and Sidhu, B.K. (2015) 'Quest for international environmental institutions: transition from the CSD to the HLPF', in Alam, S., Atapattu, S., Gonzalez, C.G. and Razzaque, J. (eds), *International Environmental Law and the Global South*, Cambridge: Cambridge University Press, pp 152–70.

Dworkin, R. (1977) *Taking Rights Seriously*, Cambridge, MA: Harvard University Press.

Fredman, S. (2018) *Working Together: Human Rights, the Sustainable Development Goals and Gender Equality*, London: The British Academy. Available at SSRN: https://ssrn.com/abstract=3295693 or http://dx.doi.org/10.2139/ssrn.3295693

Fredman, S., Kuosmanen, J. and Campbell, M. (2016) 'Transformative equality: making the Sustainable Development Goals work for women', *Ethics & International Affairs*, 30(2): 177–87.

Frey, D.F. and MacNaughton G. (2016) 'A human rights lens on full employment and decent work in the 2030 Sustainable Development Agenda', *Journal of Workplace Rights* 1–13. Available at: https://journals.sagepub.com/doi/pdf/10.1177/2158244016649580

Fukuda-Parr, S. (2016) 'From the Millennium Development Goals to the Sustainable Development Goals: shifts in purpose, concept, and politics of global goal setting for development', *Gender and Development* 24(1): 43–52.

Gammage, C. (2019) 'Social norms in EU-free trade agreements: justiciable or not?', in Gammage, C. and Novitz, T. (eds), *Sustainable Trade, Investment, and Finance: Toward Responsible and Coherent Regulatory Frameworks*, Cheltenham: Edward Elgar, forthcoming.

Gammage, C. and Novitz, T. (2019) 'Trade, investment and corporate sustainability', in Sjåfjell, B. and Bruner, C. (eds), *Cambridge Handbook on Corporate Sustainability*, Cambridge: Cambridge University Press, forthcoming.

Goodman, J. and Salleh, A. (2013) 'The "green economy": class hegemony and counter-hegemony', *Globalizations* 10(3): 411–24.

Grear, A. (2014) 'Towards "climate justice"? A critical reflection on legal subjectivity and climate injustice: warning signs, patterned hierarchies, directions for future law and policy', *Journal of Human Rights and Environment* 5: 103–33.

Gupta, J. and Nilsson, M. (2017) 'Toward a multi-level action framework for Sustainable Development Goals', in Kanie, N. and Biermann, F. (eds), *Governing through Goals: Sustainable Development Goals as Governance Innovation*, Boston: MIT Press, pp 275–94.

Gupta, J. and Vegelin, C. (2016) 'Sustainable development goals and inclusive development', *International Economic Agreements: Politics, Law and Economics* 16(3): 433–48.

ILO (2019) *Time to Act for SDG 8: Integrating Decent Work, Sustained Growth and Environmental Integrity*, Geneva: ILO.

Jacobs, M. (2012) 'Green growth: economic theory and political discourse', Centre for Climate Change Economics and Policy Working Paper No 108, Grantham Research Institute on Climate Change and the Environment Working Paper No 92. Available at: www.lse.ac.uk/GranthamInstitute/wp-content/uploads/2012/10/WP92-green-growth-economic-theory-political-discourse.pdf

Kanie, N., Bernstein, S., Biermann, F. and Haas, P. (2017) 'Global governance through goal setting', in Kanie, N. and Biermann, F. (eds), *Governing through Goals: Sustainable Development Goals as Governance Innovation*, Boston: MIT Press, pp 1–28.

Kim, R. (2016) 'The nexus between international law and the Sustainable Development Goals', *RECIEL* 25(1): 15–26.

Koskenniemi, M. and Leino, P. (2002) 'Fragmentation of international law? Postmodern anxieties', *Leiden Journal of International Law* 15(3): 553–79.

Kotze, L.J. and French, D. (2018) 'The anthropocentric ontology of international environmental law and the Sustainable Development Goals: towards an ecocentric rule of law in the anthropocene', *Global Journal of Comparative Law* 7(1): 5–36.

MacNaughton, G. (2018) 'The mysterious disappearance of human rights in the 2030 Development Agenda', in Srikanth, R. and Halim Chowdhury, E. (eds), *Interdisciplinary Approaches to Human Rights: History, Politics, Practice*, London: Routledge, pp 131–47.

Mouffe, C. (1995) 'Post-Marxism: democracy and identity', *Environmental and Planning D: Society and Space* 13: 259–65.

Nanda, V.P. (2016) 'The journey from the Millennium Development Goals to the Sustainable Development Goals', *Denver Journal of International Law and Policy* 44: 389–412.

Nilsson, M. (2017) *Important Interactions among the Sustainable Development Goals under Review at the High-Level Political Forum 2017*, Stockholm: Stockholm Environment Institute.

Novitz, T. (2015) 'The paradigm of sustainability in a European social context: collective participation in protection of future interests?', *The International Journal of Comparative Labour Law and Industrial Relations* 31(3): 243–62.

Novitz, T. and Mangan, D. (eds) (2011) *The Role of Labour Standards in Development: From Theory to Sustainable Practice?* Oxford: British Academy/Oxford University Press.

Nussbaum, M. (2003) 'Capabilities as fundamental entitlements: Sen and social justice', *Feminist Economics* 9(2–3): 33–59.

Nussbaum, M. (2011) *Creating Capabilities: The Human Development Approach*, Cambridge, MA: Harvard University Press.

Pingeot, L. (2014) *Corporate Influence in the Post-2015 Process*, working paper, Misereor–GPF–Brot fur die Welt. Available at: www.cid.org.nz/assets/Key-issues/Beyond-2015/Corporate-influence-in-the-Post-2015-process.pdf

Pogge, T. and Sengupta, M. (2015) 'The Sustainable Development Goals (SDGs) as drafted: nice idea, poor execution', *Washington International Law Journal* 24(3): 571–87.

Polomarkakis, K. (2019) 'The European Pillar of Social Rights and the Quest for EU Social Sustainability', *Social and Legal Studies.* Available pre-print at: https://journals.sagepub.com/doi/pdf/10.1177/0964663919829199

Rancière, J., Davide Panagia, D. and Rachel Bowlby, R. (2001) 'Ten theses on politics', *Theory & Event* 5.3. Available at: www.after1968.org/app/webroot/uploads/RanciereTHESESONPOLITICS.pdf

Raworth, K. (2017) *Doughnut Economics: Seven Ways to Think Like a 21st Century Economist*, White River Junction, VT: Cornerstone Books, Chelsea Green Publishing.

Rees, S.E., Foster, N.L., Langmead, O., Pittman, S. and Johnson, D.E. (2018) 'Defining the qualitative elements of Aichi Biodiversity Target 11 with regard to the marine and coastal environment in order to strengthen global efforts for marine biodiversity conservation outlined in the United Nations Sustainable Development Goal 14', *Marine Policy* 93: 241–50.

Ross-Robertson, A. (2003) 'Is the environment getting squeezed out of sustainable development?', *Public Law* 2: 249–59.

Saith, A. (2006) 'From universal values to Millennium Development Goals: lost in translation', *Development and Change*, 37(6): 1167–99.

Satterthwaite, D. (2003) 'The Millennium Development Goals and urban poverty reduction: great expectations and nonsense statistics', *Environment and Urbanization* 15(2): 179–90.

Scheyvens, R., Banks, G. and Hughes, E. (2016) 'The private sector and the SDGs: the need to move beyond "business as usual"', *Sustainable Development* 24(6): 371–82.

Simma, B. and Alston, P. (1988) 'The sources of human rights law: custom, jus cogens, and general principles', *Australian Yearbook of International Law* 12: 82.

Smith, Z.A. and Farley, H.M. (2013) *Sustainability: If It's Everything, Is It Nothing?* London: Routledge.

UN (United Nations) (2012) GA Resolution *The Future We Want*, 27 July 2012, UNGA A/RES/66/288.

UN (2013) GA Resolution *Format and organizational aspects of the high-level political forum on sustainable development*, 9 July 2013 A/RES.67/290.

UN (2014) GA Report of the Open Working Group of the General Assembly on Sustainable Development Group, UN Doc A/68/970, 12 August 2014.

UN (2015) GA Resolution *Transforming our world: the 2030 Agenda for Sustainable Development*, 25 September 2015 A/Res/70/1. Available at: https://sustainabledevelopment.un.org/post2015/transformingourworld/publication

UN (2018) GA Report of the Special Rapporteur on the rights to freedom of peaceful assembly and of association A/73/279.

Van Poeck, K. and Vandenabeele, J. (2012) 'Learning from sustainable development: education in the light of public issues', *Environmental Education Research* 18(4): 541–52.

Van Asselt, H., Sindico, F. and Mehling, M.A. (2008) 'Global climate change and the fragmentation of international law', *Law & Policy* 30(4): 423–49.

Vandemoortele, J. (2009) 'The MDG conundrum: meeting the targets without missing the point', *Development Policy Review* 27(4): 355–71.

Young, I.M. (2002) *Inclusion and Democracy*, Oxford: Oxford University Press.

PART II

Corporate Governance

3

Accounting for Climate Change: Rethinking the Chaotic Corporate Reporting Landscape and Its Purpose, with the UK's Failure as a Case Study

Charlotte Villiers and Georgina Tsagas

Introduction

Climate change is a global crisis, largely resulting from human action, that threatens the continued existence of human, animal and plant life on the planet and requires a global solution in response (Vitousek and Mooney, 1997; Spratt and Dunlop, 2018). The *Special Report on Global Warming*, published by the Intergovernmental Panel on Climate Change (IPCC, 2018), highlighted the urgency of the need to reduce carbon emissions by approximately 45%, in order to limit global warming to 1.5°C above pre-industrial levels by 2030, to be cut to zero carbon by 2050. This lends support to the 2030 Agenda for Sustainable Development and the Sustainable Development Goals (SDGs) of 2015, especially SDG 13, on urgent action to combat climate change. SDG 13 highlights the relevance of climate change for sustainability. Indeed, the United Nations (UN) observes that climate change 'presents the single biggest threat to sustainable development everywhere and its widespread, unprecedented impacts disproportionately burden the poorest and most vulnerable'. This observation leads the UN to conclude that 'urgent action to halt climate change and deal with its impacts is integral to the successful implementation of the Sustainable Development Goals' (UN, nd).

That evidence also makes even more imperative acceptance of the message of the Paris Agreement 2015, which came into force in November 2016, calling for an internationally coordinated effort to tackle climate change. Although, as a primarily soft law instrument, it has weaknesses (Rajamani, 2016; Lawrence and Wong, 2017), the contribution of the Paris Agreement is that it highlights the need, urgently, to strengthen the global response to the threat of climate change and to eradicate poverty. The Paris Agreement sets out commitments to hold the increase in the global average temperature to well below 2°C above pre-industrial levels and pursue efforts to limit the temperature increase to 1.5°C above pre-industrial levels, to increase the ability to adapt to the adverse impacts of climate change and to foster climate resilience and low greenhouse gas emissions development. Some scientists suggest that these measures might not be enough to stem the accelerating climate impacts or prevent us passing the critical thresholds that threaten catastrophe (Spratt and Dunlop, 2018: 1), but the Paris Agreement does enable us to appreciate the enormity of the challenge climate change presents.

Wright and Nyberg observe that corporations are the 'principal agents' of greenhouse gas emissions in their production processes and the products they supply (Wright and Nyberg, 2015: 3). A few companies in particular have been identified as responsible for emitting nearly two-thirds of industrial carbon dioxide (CO2), while a small number of carbon producers, as well as 83 producers of coal, oil and natural gas and seven cement manufacturers, are responsible for methane (CH4) emissions, contributing to a rise in atmospheric concentrations of CO2 and CH4, and increases Global Mean Surface Temperature and global sea level (Heede, 2014; Ekwurzel et al, 2017). This significant corporate contribution to climate change has led policy makers to target corporations in their efforts to reduce global warming and carbon emissions. As is suggested by the chief executive of the Carbon Trust, 'business will do the heavy lifting in the transition to a sustainable future' (Carbon Trust, nd). Considering that corporations are at the centre of the problem, one would expect that company law and corporate governance would provide an effective means of tackling it. However, it is suggested that the framework of company law and corporate governance is, on the contrary, worsening the problem of climate change by enabling corporations to operate freely without being fully accountable for the impacts of their activities. This chapter explores the role of company law and corporate governance within the context of climate change by focusing on the inadequacy of the reporting requirements to produce a meaningful response to the urgent and existential risks posed by climate change.

Multiple efforts at national and international levels aim to reduce corporations' climate-related impacts. The chapter considers whether company law and corporate governance-related initiatives provide effective mechanisms for holding corporations to account for their contribution to climate change. A key regulatory device targeted at corporations is disclosure, the goal of which, in this context, is to achieve greater transparency regarding the risks and opportunities connected to climate change. The chapter explores to what extent climate change-related reporting contributes to the efforts towards reducing global warming. It is argued that there a number of significant problems with climate-related reporting in its current state, in so far as there are many different requirements, including standards, codes, guidelines, at industry or sector level as well as at national and international levels; all these combined create a chaotic reporting landscape. Moreover, there is no meaningful link between the disclosures required under company law and initiatives within the area of environmental protection; hence it becomes difficult to identify clearly what the key reporting information is and what the responses and possible legal consequences of any such disclosures should be. Consequently, corporations' accountability for their contribution to climate change is open to question.

The first section presents an overview of climate change-related disclosure initiatives at the international level. The focus in the second section shifts to the UK to demonstrate some of the challenges that arise. In particular, we will focus on the UK's failure adequately to address climate change via corporate reporting in terms of how these issues are reported and the poor formal enforcement processes offered by company law. The third section concentrates on how there is an emphasis in this arena on risks and opportunities, and we suggest that this has significance for potential corporate responses to climate change. We make the point that the risk currently being referred to by corporations is limited in nature and relates to risks to their profit-maximisation objectives rather than to the more critical risks to people and the planet more generally, and that this has unfortunate consequences for the climate change reduction goals. Finally, the chapter proposes some solutions to combat climate change more effectively within the parameters of company law and corporate reporting.

The climate change-related disclosure initiatives

Context and examples from the national and international framework

Disclosure is a conventional regulatory strategy in the business arena and it largely operates as a market discipline tool, by targeting investors as the priority recipient group. With the relevant information, investors can make profitable investment decisions that will help efficient companies to thrive in the market, and punish companies that are not well managed. Financial reporting has been a long-established tool for accountability and a similar approach has also been increasingly adopted for non-financial impacts of corporate activity (Villiers, 2006). The problem of climate change has prompted a response typical in corporate governance, following Anglo-Saxon models, which requires corporations to disclose their carbon emissions and to report on the risks and uncertainties related to climate change. As with other reporting requirements, the primary target audience is investors.

A range of initiatives on carbon and climate change reporting have been developed internationally and nationally. There exist approximately 400 climate-related information disclosure schemes (WBCSD, 2018), promulgated by 'industry groups, NGOs, stock exchanges, regulators, and international organizations' (Task Force on Climate-Related Financial Disclosures, 2016a) and these vary in their (i) status, from laws to voluntary guidance; (ii) scope, from greenhouse gas emissions to broader environmental risks; and (iii) ambition, from simple disclosure to full explanations of mitigation and divestment strategies (Carney, 2015). A 2017 update of a Report entitled *Climate Change Disclosure in G20 Countries* noted that at least 15 countries in the G20 had introduced mandatory climate reporting, but this takes various forms, is implemented by different actors and has numerous objectives, including risk assessment of reporting entities (OECD, 2015; OECD, 2017). The Organisation for Economic Co-operation and Development (OECD) observes that these schemes, in aggregate, require a mix of information including: greenhouse gas (GHG) emissions; consumption of resources and energy that affects climate change (for example, fossil fuels); the strategy and governance practices and policies implemented by companies to mitigate, adapt to and manage climate change impacts, including extreme weather events, resource shortages, changing market conditions and so on; performance (for example, in reducing emissions) against targets; the principal risks and opportunities expected by the company as a result of climate change (for example, demand for new products, regulation related to climate change, increased costs to transition to a low-carbon economy and supply chain resilience). The Carbon Disclosure Project (CDP), a not-for-profit charity, makes information requests and uses the power of information disclosure to drive organisations to measure, manage and reduce their impact on the environment and build resilience, while providing high-quality information to the market. The CDP prompted 5,000 companies globally to respond annually to its climate change questionnaire, with the CDP then relaying this information and identifying three risk categories – risks driven by changes in regulation, risks driven by changes in physical climate parameters and risks driven by changes in other climate-related developments – to stakeholders, including more than 800 institutional-investor signatories (Christophers, 2017: 1114). Also, in 2007, the Climate Disclosure Standards Board, a nonaligned body with similar aims, was established (Christophers, 2017: 1114). The Climate Disclosure Standards Board's – *Framework for reporting environmental information and natural capital* (CDSB, 2015) provides a framework for organisations to prepare and present environmental information in mainstream reports that is consistent, comparable and clear so that investors can use it in decision making. Another initiative is the Coalition for Environmentally Responsible Economies, which, according to Christophers (2017: 1114), has consistently prioritised the disclosure of business risks related to the environment in general and, increasingly, climate change in particular, which led to the adoption of the Global Reporting Initiative (GRI) in 1997 (Christophers, 2017: 1114). According to the UK's Department for Environment, Food and Rural Affairs (Defra), while the relationship is complex, overall emissions reductions and behavioural change are achieved through a combination of drivers (including measuring and reporting of emissions), awareness and action (Defra, 2010: 8).

Defra states that 'emissions reports are used to demonstrate the current situation of the business, to enable targets to be set and to track progress' (Defra, 2010: 7). Such reports are therefore central to the commitment of the company to act. Emissions reports also communicate information to investors, who use this information for research and analysis and as the basis for direct engagement with companies on climate change (Defra, 2010: 7). Defra's report makes it clear that 'reporting in isolation is not enough, but … reporting might be seen as an integral part of wider activities leading to reductions as it plays a major role in the communication of climate change related information' (Defra, 2010: 14). Reporting also facilitates dissemination of information to those who can use it, perhaps for setting emissions targets, for identifying where emissions reduction activities should be targeted or for deciding on strategies to mitigate against liability (Defra, 2010: 15). Ultimately, reporting is seen as a communication tool (see, for example, Bubna-Litic, 2007), both internally to the organisation's board, encouraging further engagement on climate change strategies, and externally for use in brand building or demonstrating market leadership and increasing the value of the business (Defra, 2010: 17).

As we noted at the beginning of this chapter, climate change is an inherent part of sustainability. Thus, while climate change reporting may be seen as a necessary activity in its own right, it might also be viewed as relevant within broader sustainability reporting. Indeed, there are important relationships that might be recognised within sustainability and a company's triple bottom line for which climate action may be relevant. For example, environmental and social dimensions may cover both communities and environment, or environmental activities may have implications for employees' safety (Lozano and Huisingh, 2011: 104–5). As was observed in Chapter 2 of this book, the SDGs cover a range of sustainability-related activities, and the inclusion of SDG 13, on climate action, indicates recognition of the connections that can be made. Sustainability reporting more broadly might therefore also have relevance to a company's climate change actions and vice versa. From this perspective the existence of other initiatives that do not focus on climate change specifically, but include it as part of the objective of supporting sustainable capital and finance, might also be utilised to contribute towards reducing climate change. In general terms, sustainability reporting is intended to prompt organisations to consider their impacts on a wide range of sustainability issues, enabling them to be more transparent about the risks and opportunities they face and to take smart strategic decisions (GRI, nd). A sustainability report provides information about an organisation's economic, environmental and social impacts caused by its production processes and its everyday activities. The organisation also uses the particular report to present its corporate values and governance model, and to show how, through its strategies, it is committed to a sustainable global economy. A corporation's sustainability report also, in theory, provides an opportunity for consumers, the public and communities to become empowered through greater awareness of the corporation's impacts, and this may build greater levels of trust in businesses and governments (GRI, nd). Organisations using the International Integrated Reporting Framework, for example, purport to explain to providers of financial capital how they create value over time, including their response to environmental matters (IIRC, Ernst and Young, 2013). The Financial Accounting Standards Board establishes and improves standards of financial accounting and reporting that foster financial reporting by non-governmental entities to provide decision-useful information to investors and other users of financial reports. The GRI has established Sustainability Reporting Guidelines (currently the G4 version) and G4 Sector Disclosures with the aim of placing pressure on all organisations – regardless of size, sector or location – to report relevant sustainability information. International Financial Reporting Standards provide high-quality, transparent and comparable information for investors through a common language for financial reporting. The International Organization for Standardization, through its ISO 26000, provides guidance on how, in its view, businesses and organisations might operate in a socially responsible manner.

At European Union (EU Level), the EU High Level Expert Group (HLEG) on Sustainable Finance recommended in its interim report in June 2017 that sustainability be integrated into the EU's regulatory and financial policy framework through climate disclosure, accounting, fiduciary duties, corporate reporting and stewardship codes. Among the recommendations in its final report in January 2018, the HLEG advocated upgrading disclosure rules to make climate change risks and opportunities fully transparent. The EU Non-Financial Reporting Directive requires, from 2018, around 6,000 large firms to include *non-financial statements in their annual reports* and to disclose relevant information on environmental and social aspects, including reporting on due diligence processes as well as the risks of environmental and social impacts with regard to an entity's own operations or products, services and business relationships.

There is a growing body of national-level measures specifically focused on climate-related disclosures. For example, in 2015 France introduced Article 173-VI of the Law on Energy Transition for Green Growth, requiring mandatory carbon disclosures for listed companies and for asset owners and investment managers on a comply or explain basis, to disclose climate-related financial risks and to report on how environmental, social and governance (ESG) criteria are considered in their investment decisions.

Examples of key problems and proposed solutions

A number of problems with these multiple initiatives can be identified. The key international initiatives are voluntary, which immediately raises difficulties in terms of enforcement. As voluntary measures, they leave freedom to corporations themselves to decide whether to provide information, what information to provide and how to respond to the information gathered as regards the corporation's targets and strategies around its carbon and climate impacts. These difficulties are compounded by the fact that the initiatives are normally accompanied by many different disclosure guidelines and reporting standards – promulgated by a variety of actors and organisations who, according to Christophers, are not well coordinated (Christophers, 2017: 1114). Thistlethwaite describes the framework as 'an uneven, incomplete patchwork' that 'is highly fragmented and lacks the coordination and enforcement necessary to adequately measure and communicate the impacts of climate change on financial markets' (Thistlethwaite, 2015: 1). Similarly, the OECD, has described these schemes collectively as a 'fragmented and heterogeneous landscape' which 'reduces the usefulness of information for decision-makers, including investors and other financial market participants' (OECD, 2017: 3). This fragmentation might also reflect the contested nature of concepts such as sustainability and climate change, as will be discussed later in this chapter.

According to the Financial Stability Board '[the] ... wide range of existing disclosure schemes' highlights the need for 'consensus on the characteristics of effective disclosures', hence it was considered necessary for a Task Force on Climate-Related Financial Disclosures (TCFD) to be established in order to develop recommendations on 'consistent, comparable, reliable, clear and efficient' disclosures in regard to all types of climate risks (Financial Stability Board, 2015a, and 2015b). The TCFD disclosure requirements cover climate issues related to governance, strategy, risk management and metrics and targets. While the disclosures are voluntary, the TCFD recommends that all financial and non-financial organisations with publicly listed debt or equity implement them as part of their mainstream financial filings. Companies should also disclose the business opportunities arising from climate change as well the risks (TCFD, 2016b). While concern about climate change is evident in these initiatives, they are weakened because they do not offer a universally agreed definition of climate-related information (OECD-CDSB, 2015, 6; Ang and Copeland, 2018), possibly because climate change is a phenomenon that is so multi-layered and multidimensional. However, efforts are being made along these lines, as the Corporate Reporting Dialogue has adopted a new project to align the different initiatives (Corporate Reporting Dialogue, 2019).

Similarly, climate change frequently features as a concept, not in its own right, but as an aspect of sustainability reporting more generally, as mentioned earlier. In this respect, it assists stakeholder engagement by providing information which could also encourage involvement in collective efforts to reduce carbon emissions; and disclosure could contribute to achievement of the SDGs by identifying the company's own positive or negative impacts on the SDG efforts. However, a major challenge in this regard arises because of the multiple and competing possible definitions of sustainability – as was observed in Chapter 1 of this book (and see, for example, Rose and Cachelin, 2018) – and of climate change (Goldman et al, 2018), which entail geographical distinctions (see Chapter 8 of this book) and diverse understandings of sustainable development. The second part of the definition of Sustainable Development provided by the Brundtland Report remains important. It states: 'Sustainable development … contains within it two key concepts: the concept of "needs", in particular, the essential needs of the world's poor, to which overriding priority should be given; and the idea of limitations imposed by the state of technology and social organization on the environment's ability to meet present and future needs' (UN, 1987: 43). The climate change element potentially becomes obfuscated by the broader and varied dimensions of sustainability as a whole, given that there are so many different understandings of sustainability, although SDG 13 arguably confirms the importance of the need to tackle climate change.

These different understandings of sustainability also give rise to a focus on different priorities, leading to a fundamental concern raised in this chapter that relates to identifying risks within the context of the planetary boundaries (Steffen et al, 2015), including environmental, human and social risks. While sustainability reporting, including carbon reporting, tends to emphasise risks and opportunities that arise from climate change, this chapter argues that the emphasis placed on investor-related consideration of risk – financial risk – is unlikely to assist companies in seriously reducing or eliminating their carbon emissions for the purposes of protecting people and the planet in the long term (see further related discussion in Chapter 4 of this book). We shall return to this aspect later. Before doing so, we will explore some of the problems arising from climate change reporting within the UK's company law system that serve as illustrative examples.

Accounting for climate change in the UK

Substantive aspect: climate change-related disclosure requirements

In the UK, quoted companies became subject to compulsory environmental reporting requirements in 2013 with the introduction of Regulations on Strategic Reporting. In 2013 the UK Government introduced compulsory requirements for quoted companies to report their annual GHG emissions in their directors' report (Companies Act 2006 (Strategic and Directors' Reports) Regulations 2013). Carbon reporting was viewed as a first step for companies to make reductions in emissions. By measuring and reporting GHG emissions companies would be able to set targets and put in place carbon-management initiatives to reduce emissions in the future. Defra, the UK Department for Environment, Food and Rural Affairs, estimated that reporting would contribute to saving four million tonnes of CO2 equivalent (CO2e) emissions by 2021 (Defra, 2012). This belief may arise from the claims observed earlier, that reporting would help firms to develop greater understanding of carbon emissions and climate change, and it would force firms to disclose their performance publicly and thereby encourage them to make efforts to improve their performance, leading to positive behavioural change (Tang and Demerrit, 2018). This might be regarded as an example of reflexive law promotion of companies' responsibility with regard to sustainable development (Buhmann, 2010).

In the UK, the statutory requirements for the strategic report in the Companies Act 2006, section 414C(2), require directors of a company to disclose 'the principal risks and uncertainties facing the company', and listed companies to report the 'main trends and factors likely to affect the future development, performance and position of the company's business', as well as information about other matters, including 'environmental matters' (or explain why they have not included such information, per section 414(7)). The 'non-financial information statement' in their strategic report must include information about the impact of the company's activity in relation to various matters, including the environment, and 'a brief description of the company's business model' and 'the principal risks' in relation to these matters (section 414CB(1)–(2). The Regulations that introduced the new strategic report and directors' report requirements include Schedule 7, which specifies the details to be provided on the GHG emissions of quoted companies. Paragraph 15 of the Schedule provides that quoted companies must state the annual quantity of emissions in tonnes of CO2e from activities for which that company is responsible, including: (a) the combustion of fuel; and (b) the operation of any facility. Under this provision, quoted companies must state in their directors' report the annual quantity of emissions in tonnes of CO2e resulting from the purchase of electricity, heat, steam or cooling by the company for its own use. Paragraph 18 provides that such companies (with the exception of the first year for which the directors' report contains the required information) must state in their report also that corresponding information disclosed in the report for the preceding financial year.

Plaza's early research soon after the Regulations were introduced suggested that the Companies Act Regulations would be likely to cause smaller companies to begin CO2e measurement, improve companies' accuracy of CO2e emission source reporting and cause the majority of companies to create an emission-intensity ratio for their emission reporting (Plaza, 2014). In addition, the previously mentioned Regulations appeared to encourage companies to improve the format of emissions reporting in their annual reports, allowing for greater transparency and readability (Plaza, 2014). The Regulations also encouraged companies either to set stronger emission reduction targets or to maintain existing targets (Plaza, 2014).

Despite these positive claims for the Regulations, the resulting outcomes appear not to have been so impressive. A report to Parliament in 2018 notes that during the past ten years in the UK the power sector has managed to reduce its carbon outputs but this progress 'masks a marked failure to decarbonise other sectors' where failure to decarbonise has, in the last five years, 'become more acute, as emissions reductions in these sectors have stalled' (Committee on Climate Change, 2018). Overall, while the UK has enjoyed some success in reducing its carbon emissions, it is not on course to meet the forthcoming legally binding carbon budgets (Committee on Climate Change, 2018: 12). Even beyond company law, there are numerous reasons for this lack-lustre progress, including delays to infrastructure development and lack of consistency with policies for tackling climate change (Committee on Climate Change, 2018: 12). A contributory factor might also be weaknesses in the reporting regime. Indeed, researchers, such as Tang and Demeritt, found limited evidence for the efficacy of carbon reporting in consistently driving emission reductions, leading them to conclude that overall the impacts of carbon reporting seem modest (2018: 455). One problem might be the lack of standardisation and the rather messy reporting landscape that has developed. This is picked up in the Committee on Climate Change's Report. Another possible weakness may be that these reporting requirements are part of a company law and corporate governance framework that offers little support to strengthen their effectiveness.

Company law subjects company directors to a number of duties, now codified in sections 170–7 of the Companies Act 2006 (CA 2006). However, the duties have always, save in special circumstances, been owed to the company as a whole and not to individual shareholders or any stakeholders separately (*Foss v Harbottle* [1843]). A good example is that the previous duty to act bona fide in the interests of the company was substituted by section 172 CA 2006, which imposes on a director the duty to 'act in a way he considers, in good faith, would be most likely to promote the success of the company for the benefit of its members as a whole' and in doing so to have regard to a series of factors listed in the section, one of which is: (d) the impact of the company's operations on the community and the environment. Section 172 requires the promotion of the success of the company not in its own right as a separate legal person, but for the benefit of the shareholder constituency as a default priority. Regard need be had to other constituencies only when considering what promotes shareholders' interests (Kershaw, 2001: 382–4). This is an example of the UK's position which largely gives priority to shareholders' profit-maximising interests.

The reporting requirements of directors fall within their broader duties, and so what they report is also likely to be difficult to challenge, even though, in theory, their reports are the basis for shareholders, and others, to hold them to account for their behaviours. In 2018 the revised version of the Corporate Governance Code incorporated and embraced the wording and rationale of section 172 CA 2006, and now refers to it specifically in its General Principles by emphasising the need for the annual report – particularly the strategic report and other complementary information – to contain information that would allow for shareholders to assess how the directors have performed their duty under section 172 (Principle 1, section 5). We can see here that shareholders are viewed as the primary recipients of these reports but that directors are also expected to take into account the interests of other key stakeholders in their decisions. However, the company law is limited in its supervision of the contents of a company's reports and in how shareholders, stakeholders or any regulatory bodies might be able to respond or to hold directors or corporations to account for their reports. We explore this in the next section.

Enforcement function of the courts, and directors' duties

In order for reporting to be effective in any sphere, including climate change, it needs to be accompanied by a framework, whether formal or informal, that guarantees effective accountability. The true value of reporting for the purposes of effecting change will be evidenced only if: (i) it is taken into account by markets in their assessment of the company's performance; (ii) it is relevant in terms of shareholders' investment choices; (iii) shareholders, stakeholders or the private sector are in a position to rely on the report as a means of enforcement in the case of inaccurate disclosure or failure to disclose; and (iv) a public body exists which is equipped with the necessary powers to penalise companies or responsible persons for misconduct or inaccurate disclosure or failure to disclose.

It is difficult, in practice, to challenge directors when there is a perceived breach of their duties. The proper plaintiff is the company itself, and it is rare for fellow directors, as the organ of the company that collectively represents the company, to challenge each other in court. Minority shareholders are provided with the opportunity of suing on the company's behalf under the statutory derivative claim for a breach of directors' duties under Part 11 of CA 2006. However, this is a cumbersome process to go through to gain permission to proceed with the claim. At a first stage shareholders need to establish that they have a prima facie case to be given leave by the court to pursue the derivate claim on behalf of the company, and then the court must consider whether to grant permission to the shareholder to proceed with the action by reference to a series of factors according to sections 263(2)(a) and 263(3)(b) CA 2006. Case law on the factors that the court takes into account mainly relates to the financial interests of the company vis-à-vis the claim being pursued. The case law on how the court interprets this largely reinforces the point that it is the financial merits of the claim versus the company's interests that the court will take into account. This was seen in the case of *Franbar Holdings Ltd v Patel and others* (2008: [36]), in which the court refused permission to pursue a derivative action relating to a complaint of diversion of business opportunities to a connected person, concluding in part that a hypothetical director, acting in accordance with section 172 CA 2006, would not have continued with the claim on the company's behalf.

If we turn to enforcement of section 172 CA 2006 more specifically, the picture is grim. As Davies and Worthington explain, the subjective test inherent in section 172 CA 2006 means that 'litigation is likely to be relatively uncommon and probably even less often successful' (Davies and Worthington, 2012: 543). They state further: 'This is because it is very difficult to show that the directors have breached this duty of good faith, except in egregious cases or cases where the directors have, obligingly, left a clear record of their thought processes leading up to the challenged decision' (Davies and Worthington, 2012: 543). Case law on section 172 CA 2006 evidences the difficulties in enforcing the duty, even at instances in which a majority shareholder in the company might have a legitimate basis to request compliance with the 'have regard to' factors of the section. In *R (People & Planet) v HM Treasury* (2009) the claimant specifically argued that there was a legitimate expectation engendered 'that when the government [as a shareholder in a corporation] exercises its powers, it does so with a view to preventing public money being spent on projects that have the most obviously detrimental impact on climate change' (para 9). The court in this case, however, found that the company in which the government was a shareholder, Royal Bank of Scotland (RBS), had correctly identified the proper way in which social and environmental considerations are to be taken into account in accordance with the duty (para 34). The court found that HM Treasury, as a shareholder, should not have sought to impose its own policy in relation to combating climate change and promoting human rights on the Board of RBS, contrary to the judgment of the Board. It was found that this would not only conflict with the duties of the Board of RBS as set out in section 172(1) CA 2006 but would also have given a real risk to litigation by minority shareholders complaining that the value of their shares had been affected by the Government seeking to impose its policy on RBS (para 35). The court also made clear that HM Treasury was operating under its common law powers and not legislation, and that the nature of the Green Book is closer to guidelines for the formation of policy, rather than a prescriptive, mandatory set of rules to ensure strict compliance (paras 21–2).

The conclusion that can be drawn in relation to section 172 CA 2006 when discussed through the prism of 'enforceability' and accountability is that although the duty establishes a right, it does not come with a clear remedy, thus making it highly problematic as an accountability mechanism to be used by the company against directors. Hence, the regime of reporting on section 172 CA 2006 and ensuring accountability becomes even more important. However, an additional complication is that the climate-related reporting appears to be bolted on to the general annual report requirements and now appears as part of the strategic reporting framework. Section 172 does not offer an easy way of challenging directors, nor would this be a promising avenue to follow for enforcing the reporting requirements, considering that this job becomes part of the role of the Financial Reporting Council.

The enforcement function of the Financial Reporting Council vis-à-vis reporting

The Financial Reporting Council (FRC) is a quasi-regulatory body that regulates auditors, accountants and actuaries and oversees updates of and compliance with the UK's Corporate Governance and Stewardship Codes. Despite having been delegated a statutory mandate to undertake such tasks, it remains an independent company limited by guarantee and derives its regulatory powers mainly from the Department for Business, Energy and Industrial Strategy and through provisions of its own constitution. The FRC, as a quasi-self-regulatory body, is not subject to oversight by government, Parliament or the public. The Conduct Committee and the Corporate Reporting Review (CRR) team of the FRC specifically seek to ensure that the provision of financial information by public and large private companies complies with relevant reporting requirements, and they specifically review the directors' reports and accounts of public and large private companies for compliance with the Companies Act 2006 ('the 2006 Act') and applicable accounting standards (FRC, nd). The FRC selects reports and accounts for review on a risk basis, and adds to this some random sampling to ensure coverage of all potential companies within the scope of its review powers. The CRR team also investigates complaints received, including from other regulators, in relation to corporate reporting. The FRC supplements its monitoring work with thematic reviews and then shares examples of good-practice reporting and highlights those areas where improvements can be made (Kingman Review, 2018: 33).

If the FRC finds an inconsistency between what has been reported in the annual report, including the strategic report, of a company and the actions of the company, it has the power to make an application to the court alleging that the report has failed to comply with the requirements of the Act. The court can then provide an order requiring the directors to prepare revised accounts or a revised report. However, more typically, any dispute that arises will be dealt with via an agreement with the company involved and within the FRC itself, so that the more formal powers are not exercised, and the court process will not be customarily followed. Where the FRC has started proceedings, these have resulted in a settlement with the company before reaching a court hearing. The FRC's review work is, according to the Kingman Review, 'respected and has real value, though is hindered somewhat by a lack of visibility, low levels of review activity (by international standards) and cumbersome enforcement mechanisms' (Kingman Review, 2018: 33). A further constraint is that while FitzGerald, Director of the Financial Reporting Lab at the FRC, makes clear that calling for companies to be more transparent on how they are addressing climate risk is one of the issues that the regulator is dealing with (Fitzgerald, 2018), the FRC is not a body known for expertise in climate change science, so its reviews of any information related to such matters are bound to be limited. In addition, the lack of transparency relating to FRC investigations – the outcome of any such investigation is disclosed only to the company concerned – may also be problematic for other stakeholders hoping to engage with the process.

The informal enforcement functions of investors

Company law and corporate governance generally prioritise the interests of shareholders, and it is the shareholders who have the ability to instigate legal challenge to the directors for any breach of duties. However, company law is notorious for the limitations of legal challenges through the derivative action or for unfair prejudicial conduct, as already noted. Moreover, the investor community is known for its general apathy in responding to information given in company accounts, or in attending company meetings where it might seek to hold directors to account (Villiers, 2006). Therefore, to rely on investors to take their boardrooms to task on climate-related issues via company reporting and communication might be regarded as wishful thinking. When they do give their attention to these matters it is often limited. For example, Solomon et al (Solomon et al, 2011: 1139) observe that the investor community reacts 'by attempting to quantify and manage the unmanageable and unquantifiable, hiding behind their comfortable financial view of the world where everything can be modelled, estimated and insured'. This observation suggests that institutional investors have limited capacity to make a positive contribution to reducing the emissions of their investee companies. However, their central position gives to investors great potential to exert their power. Perhaps one way forward is to educate them more fully on the connections of their quest for profits with climate impact. Indeed, some investors are pioneering more progressive efforts in this regard. For example, one leading institutional investor, BlackRock, is helping to drive up the quality of climate change disclosure. According to Pip Best, Senior Manager of Climate Change and Sustainability Services, Ernst and Young, 'where BlackRock was a substantial shareholder, the quality of climate risk disclosure was a cut above the rest, on average covering 77% of the TCFD Recommendations; achieving a quality score of 42% (17% higher than the ASX200 average)' (Ernst and Young, 2018: 5).

Shareholders might contribute more informally by campaigning and involvement in policy development. Indeed, there exist collective groups of shareholders who may target specific companies, or they might adopt broader policies encouraging better behaviour from companies more generally. Those investors who have signed up to the UN Principles for Responsible Investment offer a positive contribution, but overall it might be argued that this is too soft in character and does not guarantee to result in any positive impacts (Villiers, 2014). Our review in this section leaves us with an impression that the company law and corporate governance system does not offer a very supportive environment in which to pursue climate-related matters. The reporting requirements are limited, and neither company law nor corporate governance provides any mechanisms that will guarantee useful or compliant reports, let alone a genuine reduction in carbon emissions or any other environmental improvements.

A fundamental problem is that company law and corporate governance seek to facilitate business growth and pursuit of profits by giving generous freedoms to corporate actors to make decisions around their activities without any significant interference. The focus of these actors then becomes one of limiting or reducing risks to their businesses and increasing opportunities for them to grow profitably. The purpose of company law and corporate governance is broadly to support those endeavours, and this leads to a serious challenge for those concerned with a changing climate and the threats that environmental process brings.

Risk

Assessing risk: for whom and why?

Climate change disclosure requirements follow the objective of other corporate disclosures of helping to achieve effective risk management. Indeed, climate change disclosure requirements aim to achieve a varied set of objectives, including risk management, which could include focus on risks to the business or its investors (see Chapter 4 of this book) as well as to the environment, and on risks to people and the planet. Climate disclosure may also help to raise awareness of the risks, as well as to reduce the risks; it may give rise to accountability by owning up to carbon footprint as well as paying for or explaining actions. Hahn et al (2015: 81) suggest that there are many benefits for companies that record and disclose their GHG emissions, including improved financial performance. Alongside other measures, such as developing climate-friendly products, carbon disclosures also contribute to improving a company's image, to improved carbon management and to reduced energy consumption and energy costs. Thus, Hahn et al view carbon accounting as 'the first necessary step toward improved management of GHG emissions' (Hahn et al, 2015: 81).

The risk- and opportunities-oriented approach to reporting on climate change, largely for the purposes of investors' needs, has the result that often the reporting is not very helpful and that, in reality, while companies might signal in their reports that they are proactively managing such risks, they are not necessarily actually really doing what they say. As Cho et al (2015: 79) express it: 'the argument exists that corporations do not walk the sustainability talk, resulting in sustainability reports consisting largely of spurious claims and unmet commitments rather than signalling rational plans and actions that address substantive concerns ... companies engage in social and environmental reporting mainly to secure their own position and private interests'.

Risks and opportunities

The FRC interprets the provisions on the strategic report – and arguably, by extension, the directors' report – as suggesting that 'it is important that entities consider both the trends in the market in which the entity operates and the trends and factors relating to society more generally. For instance, an entity should consider the risks and opportunities arising from factors such as climate change and the environment, and where material, discuss the effect of these trends on the entity's future business model and strategy' (FRC, 2018: 28). The FRC goes on to explain how climate change might present a risk: 'Risks arising from climate change could include the risks and opportunities facing the entity's operations from a transition to a low carbon economy, the physical risks to the entity's operations posed by climate change, for instance direct damage to assets or supply chain disruption, and could also include the risks that the entity's operations contribute to climate change risk. These different types of risk may not be relevant for every entity, but directors should consider each category and report on those that constitute principal risks' (FRC, 2018: 28). Hahn et al (2015: 81) note similarly that 'improved carbon management can help companies deal with natural (e.g., drought, flood) and regulatory risks related to climate change. Moreover, carbon disclosure helps investors estimate a company's regulatory and natural risks related to climate change' (Hahn et al, 2015: 81).

This emphasis on risk can be observed in many of the other disclosure provisions and guidance. For example, in the US, the Securities and

Exchange Commission (SEC) increasingly focuses on disclosure of potential liabilities for global climate change (Hancock, 2004). Thus, companies must disclose the costs of achieving compliance with current laws, as well as liabilities from actual or threatened legal proceedings, with information on how the company might be impacted financially (Hancock, 2004: 235). Item 303 of Regulation S-K, the Management Discussion and Analysis section, contains a general requirement to disclose any known trends, demands, commitments, events or uncertainties that are reasonably likely to have a material effect on the company's bottom line (Regulation S-K, 17 CFR §229.303(a)(ii) 2004). Hancock (2004) predicted a growth in climate change-related litigation that would fuel a risk-based approach to disclosure.

This risk-based approach has been continued into more recent efforts connected with the design of disclosure requirements. Thus, during the UN climate negotiations in Paris in December 2015, the FSB announced the creation of the Task Force on Climate-related Financial Disclosures which was given the task of designing a set of recommendations to encourage climate disclosure by financial and non-financial institutions. Those recommendations were introduced in June 2017 and they contain four broad themes: (1) governance around climate-related risks and opportunities; (2) strategy on the actual and potential impacts of climate-related risks and opportunities on the organisation's businesses, strategy and financial planning; (3) risk management focusing on the processes used by the organisation to identify, assess and manage climate-related risks; and (4) metrics and targets used to assess and manage relevant climate-related risks and opportunities.

Why is risk the main focus?

It might be argued that this focus on risk arises partly because sustainability has not been clearly defined and is an open-ended concept. This open-endedness leads to geographically variable understandings of the term, as noted elsewhere in this book (Pieraccini, Chapter 8). That geographical specificity and variability has to be acknowledged and requires us to recognise differences, conflicts, controversy, dispute and thinking beyond an unhelpful consensus. This has the potential consequence of enabling corporations to invent their own meanings of the term, with the possibility of those corporate definitions being even further removed from global South understandings, even though it is often the countries in the global South that will suffer the worst impacts of climate change and global warming. In effect, this variability highlights to us that sustainability is a word with an unstable consensus on its meaning, and this gives space, as noted in Chapter 3 of this book, for corporations to shape its meaning and the policy agenda – such as in negotiating the SDGs – in ways that are beneficial to their own needs rather than to the planet. Indeed, it is not clear that corporations see sustainability in terms of operating inside planetary boundaries, as many others might view it. Dauverne and Lister (2013), for example, highlight how big brands have taken over the sustainability agenda through their 'eco-business' strategies and activities and, in so doing, have pushed a narrower definition of sustainability that focuses on sustainability of big business rather than on sustainability of people and the planet.

This flexibility around the meaning of sustainability itself gives rise to insecurity and uncertainty about the implications and practical significance of working around it. Solomon et al (2011) point then to the logic that, located within the context of a 'risk society' as identified by Beck (1999) in his account of our transition from an industrial to a risk society, public sustainability reporting has been captured by corporate investors and is largely preoccupied with the business case for decisions on sustainable development. Thus, risk management becomes a predictable and logical focus for corporations when they are responding to sustainability and to the problems of climate change. Indeed, for corporations there is potentially high financial risk connected with sustainability, including the impact and implications of climate change and global warming. Yet, at the same time, narrowing the focus down to financial risk leads to an insular approach being adopted by corporations that concentrates on the relationships that they prioritise and the preservation of their finances. As Solomon et al (2011: 1140) note, the priority is the interests of the corporation's investors, in particular the institutional investors, and in their private reporting to those investors the concerns are financial risk and risk management.

Mark Carney's speech in 2015 to insurers at Lloyd's of London centred on the issue of risk and illustrates well the emphasis on protection against financial risks that arise from climate change and the responses to it. Carney identified the possibility of insuring 'new classes of risk in new parts of the world – from cyber to climate, from space to specie, from Curitiba to Chengdu' (Carney, 2015: 2), and he added that insurers 'need to manage emerging, mega risks' (Carney, 2015: 3). In particular, his speech homed in on financial stability risks, which fall into three categories: physical risks: 'the impacts today on insurance liabilities and the value of financial assets that arise from climate- and weather-related events, such as floods and storms that damage property or disrupt trade'; liability risks: 'the impacts that could arise tomorrow if parties who have suffered loss or damage from the effects of climate change seek compensation from those they hold responsible' and transition risks: 'the financial risks which could result from the process of adjustment towards a lower-carbon economy' (Carney, 2015: 5–6). Carney added in reference to transition risks: 'a wholesale reassessment of prospects, especially if it were to occur suddenly, could potentially destabilise markets, spark a pro-cyclical crystallisation of losses and a persistent tightening of financial conditions' (Carney, 2015 : 11). Other writers identify physical and regulatory risks that 'relate to the potential costs of current and future carbon-related policies and regulations' (Eligido-Ten and Clarkson, 2017: 1067) and business risks that 'encompass legal, reputational and competitive risks' (Labatt and White, 2007; ElijidoTen and Clarkson, 2017: 1067, citing Labatt and White, 2007) Christophers (2017: 110–13), for example, sees physical and non-physical risks, stability risks and policy and legal risks, technology risks, market/economic risk, reputation risk and liability or transition risks being viewed essentially as financial risks. These conceptualisations of risk related to climate change that focus on risks to the business of a company have been 'manufactured' by private, non-state actors who have played a key role in developing the disclosure initiatives as key governance mechanisms (Pattberg, 2012). Hence, initiatives such as the CDP, discussed earlier, that have been developed by private bodies and endorsed by corporations, have helped to establish and embed these narrower risk conceptualisations.

Problems

One result of this financial risk emphasis that arises by the centre-stage position of corporations and their investors is that it leads to a preoccupation with the business case, 'a complete absence of any ethical discourse' and 'a narrow rather than a broad view of accountability' (Solomon et al, 2011: 1140). Consequently, profit orientation and shareholder wealth maximisation remain the priority and an economic, growth-fixated agenda remains central. This serves to add further challenges with regard to climate change. Sullivan and Gouldson (2012), for example, suggest that despite improvements in energy efficiency gains these may then be outstripped by the impact of business growth and further indirect emissions.

From a science and planetary boundaries perspective the corporate approach to risk really misses the point and fails to tackle the central problem. Climate change activists have begun to recognise the climate change risks as existential risks, and so, to them, we 'urgently require a reframing of scientific research within an existential risk-management framework' (Spratt and Dunlop, 2018: 5). Clearly, protecting from financial risk does not protect against the dangers to the planet arising from climate change. Efforts to prevent climate change from occurring as far as possible are required.

Potential for change

Companies might differ in their climate change strategies, and the features of such strategies may be influenced by firm-specific characteristics such as 'corporate size, internationalization, financial performance (e.g. liquidity or profitability), managerial attitude, managerial international experience, strategic direction and attitude, ownership structure, board diversity, and position in the value chain, among others' (Tang and Demerritt, 2018: 452). Firms with managers who are more willing to support and commit to these issues will more likely have the resources to disclose the relevant information. This may require that managers have education and training on climate change and how this relates to the industries in which they are operating. In turn, management within organisations should seek to avoid the development of silos that might not operate in a coordinated way, thereby inhibiting efforts to address climate change.

Reporting is a central feature of company law and corporate governance and it does have potential for raising awareness and for making behavioural and activity changes. Indeed, qualitative research of narrative disclosures by Eligido-Ten and Clarkson (2017) indicates that superior performers provide more detailed description of climate change strategies that go beyond managing climate change risks. At the same time, additional factors might be required to contribute to more positive environmental practices. Researchers have, for example, identified a positive relationship between firms' environmental activities and government regulatory pressure (Christmann, 2004; Lee, 2008), as well as influence of non-governmental organisations on corporate environmental strategy, governance and performance (Guay et al, 2004). The results of another study also indicated that perceived social expectations, organisational support (availability of internal resources) and stakeholder pressure (availability of external resources) might be important antecedents for the adoption of corporate environmental responsibility and green practices (Lee et al, 2018). Indeed, Eligido-Ten and Clarkson observe that 'society's ethical expectations have shifted to the point that there is now a stream of research seeking "to explain the moral or ethical considerations between firms and climate change"'(Eligido-Ten and Clarkson, 2017: 1068; citing Galbreath et al, 2016: 217). We might ask if these developments could lead to different types of law or regulation. The disclosure requirements might be changed to move away from a risk and opportunities approach to requiring that corporations show their policies on reducing emissions and global warming and also show how and to what extent they are achieving their goals and, further, if they are not achieving their goals, explain why not and what they will do to address any such failures. The social and environmental impacts of their climate-related activities need also to be addressed and incorporated into their climate reports. This would arguably be consistent with the broader Agenda 30 and SDGs which indicate the connections between climate change and eradication of hunger and poverty, forest management and biodiversity, clean energy, and sustainable cities and communities (Nachmany et al, 2017: 12). Climate change or sustainability reports should show these connections and their related impacts.

These economic, social and environmental connections need also to be reflected in the risks that are identified in connection with climate change, and if risk management is still to be viewed as the main objective. It is essential to recognise the environmental risks on the basis of scientific evidence as well as the ethical and social risks that come with climate change, not just the financial risks that interest the company and its shareholders (see further, Chapter 4 of this book).

The Carbon Trust highlights the progressive steps taken by the leading companies (Carbon Trust, nd). These include coordination of corporate strategy with sustainability, including engaging with customers about their products. Under this model, companies might start with internal practices and energy use, looking at where energy savings might be made. They might also appoint sustainability officers to audit their internal operations and energy use and to look for where savings can be made. Such companies would seek to educate their workers within the organisation, look for clean energy sources and promote sustainability champions in the organisation. They would work on making products that require less energy use and that have longer life and are able to be repaired easily, or can be recycled easily. In their supply chains they might think about the whole production process, looking upstream and downstream, and have coordinated communications through the whole chain from suppliers and producers through to customers and recyclers. Corporate strategies would establish a balance between growth and carbon efficiency.

A critical change required is to expand the company's horizons beyond the interests of its investors and to recognise fully that its stakeholders are of fundamental importance. The shareholder primacy versus stakeholder debate has become stale within the journals, but a truly sustainable company will accept the relevance of its stakeholder constituents, and this corresponds with observations about inclusivity made in Chapter 1 of this book. Hahn et al (2015: 86) note that 'the varying power of stakeholders influences the urgency of a company's reaction and they argue that stakeholder thinking has contributed to the development of social and ethical accounting, auditing, and reporting'. This must be a sincere step in which we should be asking how reporting and transparency may truly invite and respond positively to the participation of the other stakeholders. A reporting framework that supports and encourages these internal and organisational behaviours is necessary, and this might require a more holistic company law and corporate governance system that does not narrow its emphasis on profit maximisation but which embraces an environmentally and socially responsible ethic. Rather than a handful of companies pursuing a sustainable development agenda, the whole system must encompass such an approach. This also requires a rationalisation and streamlining of the multiplicity of mechanisms currently in use. Positively in this regard, work has begun by the Corporate Reporting Dialogue on a rationalisation of the reporting terrain to align the corporate reporting initiatives, as well as to use such initiatives for addressing and ensuring transparency with regard to the SDGs (Corporate Reporting Dialogue, 2019). This work will be of interest as it develops.

Conclusion

This chapter has demonstrated that corporate reporting on climate change within the existing company law and corporate governance system is inadequate for responding effectively to the existential and catastrophic threats accompanying climate change. It is necessary for companies to reduce their carbon emissions drastically, and so far, in that respect, they are on a trajectory of failure. The climate scientists are extremely concerned, but our company law requirements appear not to reflect the level of urgency of response. The reporting requirements are too soft in their approach, leaving companies free to decide upon what to disclose and their shareholders free to decide how to respond to those disclosures. So much is voluntary. So much is without comparability or any meaningful measurement of the companies' success rates in reducing their emissions. So much is without sufficient enforcement or sanctions that companies themselves feel no threat to their activities.

The disclosure framework that targets corporations and their carbon emissions, prompting them to identify and critically assess the risks and opportunities, places investors in an inappropriately powerful position that is likely to hinder carbon-reduction efforts. The climate-related reporting framework must be redesigned to include holistic disclosure of carbon emissions and tracking of efforts to reduce those emissions, with details of the results of those efforts and further plans to make more reductions across the companies' whole business relations covering investors, suppliers, production, customers and product life and recycling. The risks involved in climate change are much broader than the company law and corporate governance framework would lead us to believe. The involvement of private actors within this territory has led to narrowly constructed approaches to the concepts of sustainability and of climate change, and this has been exacerbated by focusing on a narrow risk perspective. But these concepts are highly contested, leading us to conclude that climate change and the necessary responses to global warming are unlikely to present only financial or business risks. Indeed, not only corporate actors and shareholders are affected by climate change. Rather, the risks are faced by all people and by the planet. The corporate behaviours involved are relevant to those people and the planet also. The legal and regulatory responses must also make space for the participation of those who might be so affected by corporate behaviours and their climate impacts.

The target audiences for such reporting are therefore relevant, for purposes of substance but for enforcement also. Rather than focus on risks and opportunities of interest to existing and potential investors, the information disclosed should include evidentially supported detail related to the company's impact on the climate and ecosphere and to its efforts towards planetary sustainability as well as to the company's socially related impacts on its stakeholders. The information should be provided to a centralised body with expertise to audit and verify that information and hold it in a central register accessible to stakeholders. The company should also supply to customers and consumers information to inform them of how they might be able to use the product efficiently and how the life of the product might be prolonged. These changes will depend on reorienting company boardrooms away from prioritising their investors and towards engagement with their stakeholders, as well as educating those boardrooms more strongly on climate change issues. Hardening up and simplifying the regulatory approach to make clearer the requirements and to provide enforceable demands will also be necessary.

References

Albertini, E. (2013) 'Does environmental management improve financial performance? A meta-analytical review', *Organization & Environment* 26: 431–57.

Ang, G. and Copeland, H. (2018) *Integrating Climate Change-related Factors in Institutional Investment*. Available at: www.oecd.org/sd-roundtable/papersandpublications/Integrating%20Climate%20Change-related%20Factors%20in%20Institutional%20Investment.pdf

Beck, U. (1992) *Risk Society: Towards a New Modernity*, London: Sage.

Beck, U. (1999) *World Risk Society*, Oxford: Blackwell.

Bubna-Litic, K. (2007) 'Environmental reporting as a communications tool: a question of enforcement?', *Journal of Environmental Law* 20(1): 69–85.

Buhmann, K. (2010) *Reflexive Regulation of CSR to Promote Sustainability: Understanding EU Public-Private Regulation on CSR Through the Case of Human Rights*, 18 (University of Oslo Faculty of Law Research Paper Series, Paper No 2010-07). Available at: http://ssrn.com/abstract=1712801

Carbon Trust (nd) Learning from Leaders – Lessons from the Frontline of Corporate Climate Action. Available at: www.carbontrust.com/corporate-sustainability-leadership/new-frontiers-corporate-climate-action/

Carney, M. (2015) *Breaking the Tragedy of the Horizon – Climate Change and Financial Stability*, Speech, Lloyd's of London, 29 September. Available at: www.bankofengland.co.uk/-/media/boe/files/speech/2015/breaking-the-tragedy-of-the-horizon-climate-change-and-financial-stability.pdf?la=en&hash=7C67E785651862457D99511147C7424FF5EA0C1A

Cho, C.H., Laine, M., Roberts, R.W. and Rodrigue, M. (2015) 'Organized hypocrisy, organizational facades, and sustainability', *Accounting, Organizations and Society* 40: 78–94.

Christmann, P. (2004) 'Multinational companies and the natural environment: Determinants of global environmental policy standardization', *Academy of Management Journal* 47(5): 747–60.

Christophers, B. (2017) 'Climate change and financial instability: risk disclosure and the problematics of neoliberal governance', *Annals of the American Association of Geographers* 107(5): 1108–27.

Climate Disclosure Standards Board (2015) *Framework for Reporting Environmental Information and Natural Capital*, June. Available at: www.cdsb.net/sites/cdsbnet/files/cdsb_framework_for_reporting_environmental_information_natural_capital.pdf

Committee on Climate Change (2018) *Reducing UK Emissions*, Progress Report to Parliament. Available at: www.theccc.org.uk/wp-content/uploads/2018/06/CCC-2018-Progress-Report-to-Parliament.pdf

Companies Act 2006 (Strategic and Directors' Reports) Regulations 2013 No. 1970.

Corporate Reporting Dialogue (2019) *The Sustainable Development Goals and the Future of Corporate Reporting*. Available at: http://corporatereportingdialogue.com/wp-content/uploads/2019/02/The-Sustainable-Development-Goals-and-the-future-of-corporate-reporting.pdf

Dauverne, P. and Lister, J. (2013) *Eco-Business: A Big Brand Takeover of Sustainability*, Cambridge, MA: MIT.

Davies, P.L. and Worthington, S. (2012) *Gower and Davies Principles of Modern Company Law* (9th edn), London: Sweet & Maxwell.

Defra (Department for Environment, Food and Rural Affairs) (2010) *The Contribution that Reporting of Greenhouse Gas Emissions Makes to the UK Meeting its Climate Change Objectives. A Review of the Current Evidence*, London: Defra.

Defra (2012) Press release, 'Leading businesses to disclose greenhouse gas emissions', 20 June. Available at: www.gov.uk/government/news/leading-businesses-to-disclose-greenhouse-gas-emissions

Directive on the disclosure of non-financial and diversity information by certain large undertakings and groups Text with EEA relevance (Directive 2014/95/EU) *OJ L* 330, 15.11.2014, p. 1–9.

Ekwurzel, B., Boneham, J., Dalton, M.W., Heede, R., Mera, R.J., Allen, M.R. and Frumhoff, P.C. (2017) 'The rise in global atmospheric CO2, surface temperature, and sea level from emissions traced to major carbon producers', *Climatic Change* 144(4): 579–90.

Elijido-Ten, E.O. and Clarkson, P. (2019) 'Going beyond climate change risk management: insights from the world's largest most sustainable corporations', *Journal of Business Ethics* 157:4: 1067–89.

Ernst and Young (2018) *Carbon Risk Disclosure Barometer*. Available at: www.ey.com/Publication/vwLUAssets/ey-carbon-risk-disclosure-barometer-2018/$File/ey-carbon-risk-disclosure-barometer-2018.pdf

Fitz-Gerald, P. (2018) 'Changing climate: changing reporting', Blog. Available at: www.frc.org.uk/frc-for-you/blogs-and-podcasts/blog-changing-climate-changing-reporting (accessed 17 October 2019).

Foss v Harbottle (1843) 2 Hare 461.

Franbar Holdings Ltd v Patel and others [2008] BCC 885.

FRC (Financial Reporting Council) (nd) Corporate Reporting Review. Available at: www.frc.org.uk/accountants/corporate-reporting-review

FRC (2018) *Revised Guidance on the Strategic Report*, London: FRC.

FSB (Financial Stability Board) (2015a) *FSB to Establish Task Force on Climate-related Financial Disclosures*. Available at: www.fsb.org/wp-content/uploads/Climatechange-task-force-press-release.pdf

FSB (2015b) *Proposal for a Disclosure Task Force on Climate-related Risks*. Available at: www.fsb-tcfd.org/wp-content/ uploads/2016/01/FSB_Disclosure-task-force-on-climaterelated-risks.pdf

Galbreath, J., Charles, D. and Ockzkowski, E. (2016) 'The drivers of climate change innovations: evidence from Australian wine industry', *Journal of Business Ethics* 135(2): 217–31.

Goldman, M.J., Turner, M.D. and Daly, M. (2018) 'A critical political ecology of human dimensions of climate change: epistemology, ontology, and ethics', *Wiley Interdisciplinary Reviews: Climate Change* 9(4): 526.

GRI (Global Reporting Initiative) (nd) *About Sustainability Reporting*. Available at: www.globalreporting.org/information/sustainability-reporting/Pages/default.aspx

GRI (2007/8) *The Sustainability Report*. Available at: www.globalreporting.org/resourcelibrary/GRI-Sustainability-Report-2007-2008.pdf

Guay, T., Doh, J.P. and Sinclair, G. (2004) 'Non-governmental organizations, shareholder activism, and socially responsible investments: ethical, strategic, and governance implications', *Journal of Business Ethics* 52(1):125–39.

Hahn, R., Reimsbach, D. and Schiemann, F. (2015) 'Organizations, climate change, and transparency: reviewing the literature on carbon disclosure', *Organization & Environment* 28(1): 80–102.

Hancock, E. (2004) 'Red dawn, blue thunder, purple rain: corporate risk of liability for global climate change and the SEC disclosure dilemma', *Georgetown International Environmental Law Review* 17: 233.

Heede, R. (2014) 'Tracing anthropogenic carbon dioxide and methane emissions to fossil fuel and cement producers 1854–2010', *Climatic Change* 122: 229–41. Available at: www.businessgreen.com/bg/news/3065789/climate-disclosure-global-reporting-bodies-to-align-around-tcfd-guidelines

IIRC (International Integrated Reporting Council) and Ernst and Young (2013) *Value Creation*. Available at: http://integratedreporting.org/wp-content/uploads/2013/08/Background-Paper-Value-Creation.pdf

IPCC (Intergovernmental Panel on Climate Change) (2018) (UN) *Special Report on Global Warming of 1.5°C (SR15)*. Available at: www.ipcc.ch/report/sr15/

Kershaw, D. (2012) *Company Law in Context* (2nd edn), Oxford: Oxford University Press.

Kingman, J. (2018) *Independent Review of the Financial Reporting Council*, December, London: DBEIS.

Labatt, S. and White, R.R. (2007) *Carbon Finance: The Financial Implications of Climate Change*, Hoboken, NJ: Wiley.

Law no. 2015-992, *Loi sur la Transition Énergétique pour la Croissance Verte – LTECV*, see eg *Forum pour L'Investissement Responsible*, 'Article 173-VI: Understanding the French regulation on investor climate reporting – The ESG-Climate approach: from reporting to strategy, a tool for better investing', October 2016.

Lawrence, P. and Wong, D. (2017) 'Soft law in the Paris Climate Agreement: strength or weakness?', *Review of European, Comparative & International Environmental Law* 26(3): 276–86.

Lee, J.W., Kim, Y.M. and Kim, Y.E. (2018) 'Antecedents of adopting corporate environmental responsibility and green practices', *Journal of Business Ethics* 148(2): 397–409.

Lee, S. (2008) 'Drivers for the participation of small and medium-sized suppliers in green supply chain initiatives', *Supply Chain Management: An International Journal* 13(3): 185–98.

Lozano, R. and Huisingh, D. (2011) 'Inter-linking issues and dimensions in sustainability reporting', *Journal of Cleaner Production* 19(2–3): 99–107.

Matisoff, D.C. (2013) 'Different rays of sunlight: understanding information disclosure and carbon transparency', *Energy Policy* 55: 579–92.

Murray, J. (2018) 'Climate disclosure: global reporting bodies to align around TCFD guidelines', *Business Green*. Available at: www.businessgreen.com/bg/news/3065789/climate-disclosure-global-reporting-bodies-to-align-around-tcfd-guidelines

Nachmany, M., Fankhauser, S., Setzer, J. and Averchenkova, A. (2017) *Global Trends in Climate Change Legislation and Litigation: 2017 Update*, Columbia, NY: Grantham Research Institute on Climate Change and the Environment.

OECD (Organisation for Economic Co-operation and Development) (2015) *Climate Change Disclosure in G20 Countries*. Available at: www.oecd.org/daf/inv/mne/Report-on-Climate-change-disclosure-in-G20-countries.pdf

OECD (2017) *Corporate Climate Disclosure Schemes in G20 Countries After CoP 21*. Available at: www.oecd.org/environment/cc/g20-climate/collapsecontents/Climate-Disclosure-Standards-Board-climate-disclosure.pdf

OECD-CDSB (2015) *Climate Change Disclosure in G20 Countries: Stocktaking of Corporate Reporting Schemes*. Available at: www.oecd.org/daf/inv/mne/Report-on-Climate-change-disclosure-in-G20-countries.pdf

Pattberg, P. (2012) 'How climate change became a business risk: analyzing nonstate agency in global climate politics', *Environment and Planning C: Government and Policy* 30(4): 613–26.

Plaza, C. (2014) 'An analysis of the effectiveness and impact of mandatory company greenhouse gas emission reporting under the Companies Act 2006 (Strategic Report and Directors' Report) Regulations 2013'. Available at: www.era.lib.ed.ac.uk/handle/1842/10407

R (People & Planet) v HM Treasury [2009] EWHC 3020 (Admin) (QBD).

Rajamani, L. (2016) 'Ambition and differentiation in the 2015 Paris Agreement: interpretative possibilities and underlying politics', *International & Comparative Law Quarterly* 65(2): 493–514.

Rose, J. and Cachelin, A. (2018) 'Critical sustainability: incorporating critical theories into contested sustainabilities', *Journal of Environmental Studies and Sciences* 8(4): 518–25.

Simnett, R., Nugent, M. and Huggins, A.L. (2009) 'Developing an international assurance standard on greenhouse gas statements', *Accounting Horizons* 23: 347–63.

Solomon, J., Solomon, A., Norton, S.D. and Joseph, N.L. (2011) 'Private climate change reporting: an emerging discourse of risk and opportunity?', *Accounting, Audit and Accountability Journal* 2(8): 1119–48.

Spratt, D. and Dunlop, I. (2018) *What Lies Beneath: The Understatement of Existential Climate Risk*, Australia: Breakthrough: National Centre for Climate Restoration.

Steffen, W., Richardson, K. et al (2015) 'Planetary boundaries: guiding human development on a changing planet', *Science* 13 February, 347(6223): 1–17.

Sullivan, R. and Gouldson, A. (2012) 'Does voluntary carbon reporting meet investors' needs?', *Journal of Cleaner Production* 36: 60–7.

Tang, S. and Demeritt, D. (2018) 'Climate change and mandatory carbon reporting: Impacts on business process and performance', *Business Strategy and the Environment* 27(4): 437–55.

TCFD (Task Force on Climate-Related Financial Disclosures) (2016a) *Phase I report of the Task Force on Climate-Related Financial Disclosures*. Available at: www.fsb-tcfd.org/wp-content/uploads/2016/03/Phase_I_Re port_v15.pdf

TCFD (2016b) *Recommendations of the Task Force on Climate-related Financial Disclosures*. Available at: www.fsbtcfd.org/wp-content/uploads/2016/12/TCFD-Recommendations-Report-A4-14-Dec-2016.pdf

Thistlethwaite, J. (2015) *The Challenges of Counting Climate Change Risks in Financial Markets*. Available at: www.cigion line.org/sites/default/files/policy_brief_no.62.pdf

UN (United Nations) (nd) *Achieving the Sustainable Development Goals through Climate Action*. Available at: https://unfccc.int/achieving-the-sustainable-development-goals-through-climate-action

UN Documents (1987) *Gathering a Body of Global Agreements Our Common Future*, Chapter 2: Towards Sustainable Development from A/42/427. Our Common Future: Report of the World Commission on Environment and Development. Available at: www.un-documents.net/ocf-02.htm

Villiers, C. (2006) *Corporate Reporting and Company Law*, Cambridge: Cambridge University Press.

Villiers, C. (2014) 'The role of investor networks in transnational corporate governance', in Fenwick, M., Van Uytsel, S. and Wrbka, S. (eds), *Networked Governance, Transnational Business and the Law*, Berlin: Springer, pp 285–313.

Vitousek, P.M., Mooney, H.A., Lubchenco, J. and Melillo, J.M. (1997) 'Human domination of Earth's ecosystems', *Science* 25 July, 277(5325): 494–9.

WBCSD (2018) *Climate Change Deep Dive Analysis 2018 Addendum Report*. Available at: https://docs.wbcsd.org/2018/10/Reporting_Matters_2018_CC.pdf

Wright, C. and Nyberg, D. (2015) *Climate Change, Capitalism, and Corporations*, Cambridge: Cambridge University Press.

4

Sustainable Corporate Governance: Trimming or Sowing?

Nina Boeger

Introduction

This chapter links to other discussions in this book by identifying different interpretations of sustainability and sustainable development, in conversations about economic and political reform, and their relevance for law and legal governance. It considers that sustainability is currently understood in terms of two rather distinct conceptual perspectives: one version centring, broadly speaking, on ensuring sustainable economic growth and on socially embedding global markets (*sustainable-capitalism*); the other insisting that more fundamental changes and systemic revisions, including of the growth objective itself, are necessary (*sustainable-systems*). The purpose of the chapter is to trace these versions of sustainability through current reform proposals in the area of corporate law and governance, which have as their objective to make companies operate more sustainably.

The chapter begins by sketching out the two perspectives on sustainability. Sustainable-capitalism is built fundamentally on an optimistic view of our existing systems and their operating principles, and their ability to address, if appropriately engaged and policed, sustainability challenges. Figuratively speaking, this perspective assumes that, much like we might trim a hedge or tree to adjust it to its environment, so we must trim our established systems to align them with our political concern for sustainable development. In both scenarios, however, while we might trim them, we leave their existing organisms intact. Sustainable-systems, on the other hand, insists that the scope and urgency of sustainability challenges today make a fundamental overhaul of central aspects in our current systems necessary; replacing some of the existing narratives of post-industrial capitalism, and its operating principles, with an alternative set of narratives and principles. Figuratively speaking, rather than trimming a hedge or tree – a process of curbing excess through intervention – this view on sustainability encourages that we should sow, and grow, alternative seeds (operating principles) that will yield alternative organisms (systems).

Based on these sketches, the chapter argues that while express linkages between corporate governance and sustainability are a relatively recent phenomenon, it is clear that these conceptual distinctions do matter in the framing of sustainable corporate governance reform. How we choose to frame sustainability – whether we understand it in the (stylised) terms of a sustainable-capitalism or sustainable-systems perspective – directly influences how we set about shaping a sustainable corporate governance framework. Such a conclusion, however, does not necessarily equate to saying that we must choose between one or the other perspective in this context. While they are conceptually separate in contention, the chapter points out, drawing on some examples in the British context, that there is room for engaging them together to help address political barriers and problems of marginalisation that both perspectives encounter. It also helps to overcome what we may call technical barriers of uncertainty to work out, by way of experimentation, which of these approaches might ultimately be effective in achieving sustainability. This suggestion, then, implies that we should be looking after hedges and seeds, both trimming and sowing – tidying up the garden to make room for a variety of sustainable business organisations. If this sounds a little esoteric now, it is hoped that the following sections will bring some clarity to the idea.

Perspectives on sustainability

There is now a considerable body of commentary, some of it very recent and widely received, that emphasises the power of 'stories' – accessible narratives and patterns – in our desire to explain our history, and our existing systems (Korten, 2015; Lent, 2017). From a range of disciplinary (and political) perspectives, these commentators chart how this power translates into social paradigms and systemic behaviour (Meadows, 2009; Capra and Luisi, 2016). They also explain its relevance for change: how, through the development of *counter*-stories that challenge traditional narratives, we can identify and formulate responses to problematic but systemic patterns and path-dependencies (Monbiot, 2017; Raworth, 2017; Reich, 2019). As Korten puts it, when 'dealing with a self-destructive system supported by a false story, the only solution is a different system grounded in a different story' (Korten, 2015: 29).

Sustainability provides such a counter-story; one that encourages changes to our legal, political and economic institutions to take account of our concerns for sustaining life on Earth and its future. It is not fundamentally a complex concept. The narrative is essentially about nurturing our 'ability to continue a defined behaviour indefinitely' (Thwink, 2019) by maintaining certain social, economic and environmental standards, and it builds on the simple observation that our survival and well-being as individuals, communities and societies are fundamentally connected to our political and physical environment. Nor are sustainability or sustainable development particularly new concerns. Historical accounts of their origins trace ideas of sustainable organising back to pre-modernity. Throughout modernity, these ideas survived, constructing a counter-narrative to the major thought-stories we associate with the Enlightenment and Industrial Revolution, including our commitments to prosperity as economic growth, to individual human development and to the operation of competitive markets (Du Pisani, 2006; Caradonna, 2014).

And yet, the modern sustainability movement has never defined uniformly what story to tell, nor precisely what practices or systems to support (Ratner, 2004). As others in this book have set out more fully, socially ambitious debates in the 1970s were followed by a period of ambiguity that turned on economic prosperity first and foremost, before the advent of the Sustainable Development Goals breathed some new life into the earlier debates. To some extent, these ambiguities are encouraged by design and are necessary for sustainability to operate as a general directing principle, 'creating scope for disputation around ethical and political considerations' (Pieraccini and Novitz, Chapter 1 in this book; citing de Sadeleer, 2002). They are also, in part, the result of the movement's growth and its increasing institutional diversity. Environmentalists and labour lawyers, for example, while sharing an overarching concern for sustainability, will still have distinct primary (disciplinary) concerns and, accordingly, might not always share the same expectations of how the principle might be engaged (Pieraccini and Novitz, Chapter 1; Novitz, Chapter 6; Willmore, Chapter 7; Pieraccini, Chapter 8 in this book).

However, while it might not offer a 'unidirectional path' (Pieraccini and Novitz, Chapter 1) towards change, sustainability is not as vague and fractured as some might, in this context, suggest. It does offer a set of normatively coherent narratives that enable those invested in change to mobilise towards an agreed direction – narratives that, broadly speaking, tend to follow two rather distinct conceptual perspectives, described often as 'weak' and 'strong' versions of sustainability (Ekins et al, 2003; Neumayer, 2013; Pelenc et al, 2015). The following discussion presents these perspectives by incorporating some of the same ideas, but without embracing the conceptual labels of 'weak' and 'strong'. The aim is not only to avoid the normative implications of these labels and replace them with more neutral language; more substantively, this account is intended to build on the importance of narratives or 'stories' for human development. It presents these perspectives as two different ways of framing counter-narratives to the historical thought-stories of post-industrial capitalism; counter-stories that present a more or less radical departure from the currently prevailing narratives of growth, individualism and competition, the rise of financial wealth and, more generally, a conception of human development as a predominantly linear process.

Trimming: sustainable capitalism

The first perspective insists on developing a system of sustainable economic growth or, more broadly conceived, sustainable capitalism (Ikerd, 2005). Its proponents continue to accept, even as they acknowledge rising concern for sustainability, the traditional narratives of post-industrial capitalism and that these will offer the means to deliver sustainability, provided that they are adequately policed and adjusted. They argue accordingly for solutions that retain, and in fact rely on, these basic operating principles, including a commitment to economic growth, to market competition, to progressive individualism and to capital or, more broadly, to creating financial wealth. But they insist on curbing excesses in so far as they render the operation of capitalism unsustainable in the longer term.

This view suggests that while it would be necessary to modify *how* we secure economic growth to ensure sustainable development – 'decoupling' growth from social and environmental externalities through, for example, investment in green technologies and so on (Jackson, 2011, chapter 5; Krugman 2014) – there is no case in principle for going further by calling for a fundamental revision of the growth objective and its role in our economic and political system (Hawken et al, 2005). It considers similarly that, appropriately incentivised, the operation of markets can be usefully engaged to achieve sustainable outcomes, relying on regulated forms of competition. Related to this is the assumption that individualism and rational economic engagement can work effectively as developmental narratives – that ultimately, what makes sustainability achievable is the striving of individuals to further their own ends, including by competitive means (Harrison, 2014). Nor is this perspective particularly concerned about the use of financial metrics to calculate the impact of sustainability as long as it encourages, say, social impact investment to develop sustainable economic forms. Instead, it actively embraces such metrics (Gore and Blood, 2011).

In so far as sustainability here functions as political objective, it justifies intervention, including by regulatory means, to impose boundaries on the operation of our economic systems – market liberalism and capitalism – but without fundamentally overhauling commitment to the existing operating principles that shape them. Figuratively speaking, this take on sustainability assumes that, much like we might trim a hedge or tree to make it fit its environment, so we must trim our established systems to align them with our political concern for sustainable development. In both scenarios, however, while we might trim them, we leave their organisms intact. In terms of bringing about systemic change, then, we might label this a *flat* version of sustainability: one built fundamentally on an optimistic view of our existing systems and their operating principles, and their ability to address, if appropriately engaged and policed, sustainability challenges. It aligns too with what others have labelled a 'weak' version of sustainability (Ekins et al, 2003; Neumayer, 2013), to the extent that the latter suggests we may continue to pursue our current economic course – of generating manufactured capital and economic growth – so long as we provide for adequate monetary compensation for environmental degradation, and seek out technological solutions to environmental problems that support sustainable development (Pelenc et al, 2015, p. 3). Sustainable-capitalism reflects this view but also places it in relation to other key narratives of post-industrial capitalism – competition, individualism, financial value and the commitment to a linear form of progress that leads to growth. It determines not only our approaches to environmental conservation, but the shape of our societies and how we see them operate.

Sowing: sustainable systems

A second perspective on sustainability, on the other hand, insists that the scope and urgency of its challenges today require a fundamental overhaul of central aspects in our current systems; one that replaces at least some of the traditional narratives of post-industrial capitalism, and its operating principles, with an alternative set of narratives and principles. Sustainability's role is here understood not in a reformative but, more accurately, in a *formative* sense: rather than policing the boundaries of existing systems and their operating principles – to curb their excesses so as to 'future-proof' capitalism – this view conceives of sustainability as foundational, a challenge to these very principles, and intent on replacing them with alternatives that frame and constitute fundamentally reformed systems altogether. Figuratively speaking, rather than trimming a hedge or tree – a process of curbing excess through intervention – this view on sustainability encourages that we should sow, and grow, alternative seeds (operating principles) that will yield alternative organisms (systems). These are designed, from the ground up, to align with an environment that accommodates sustainable development, including forms or post-capitalist organising (Frase, 2016; Mason, 2016).

This version draws on historical accounts of sustainability's origins through modernity and pre-modernity, essentially 'baking' the *counter*-narratives of sustainability, which have evolved through its history, into new systems as they grow and expand. Broadly speaking, where our economic system is built on the idea of development as growth, this perspective on sustainability challenges the feasibility of (unlimited) economic growth. It links up to an ecological tradition of sufficiency (Schumacher, 1973; Princen, 2005) as well as an economic counter-tradition that points out the limits of growth (Daly, 1991; Jackson, 2011). In fact, it calls into question the dominance of financial wealth as a way of measuring our prosperity and what we value (Schor, 2011), emphasising instead the importance of natural forms of value-creation for human prospering and the flourishing of life on Earth. It builds up economic models that define our choice of what we (should) value as a fundamentally political one (Mazzucato, 2018). Related, it defies an economic characterisation of humans in broad terms as fundamentally individualist and competitive and embraces additional forms of cooperative, commons- and solidarity-based economic organising (Bollier, 2014; Raworth, 2017). But it also challenges a modernist understanding of progress as a linear process that can be measured in one-dimensional or financial terms. Instead it suggests greater complexity and circularity in the way that our social and natural systems work (Meadows et al, 2004).

Where sustainable-capitalism is aligned with ideas that others have labelled 'weak' sustainability, sustainable-systems sits close to their 'strong' version of sustainability, calling on us to change our economic course in fundamental ways and acknowledging that 'certain human actions can entail irreversible consequences' (Pelenc et al, 2015: 3). Sustainable-systems highlights that to do so depends on our ability to successfully formulate a set of counter-narratives to the stories of market liberalism and post-industrial capitalism, and the institutions they have created. The aim of this perspective is not only to formulate these narratives but also to form new economic organisations – from businesses and regulators to new forms of property or consumer law – that incorporate them and put them into practice. Far from operating predominantly at the intellectual level, the challenge of sustainable systems – of 'sowing' sustainability – is very concretely to ask what these alternative organisations might look like and how they might work. A quote usually attributed to Buckminster Fuller sums up its approach – that 'you never change things by fighting against the existing reality. To change something, build a new model that makes the old model obsolete.' However, this is not to say that this perspective considers sustainability as a justification to replace capitalism with a uniform alternative model. Rather, it relies on experimentation with a set of ideas, and a set of concrete shapes that these ideas might take in the form of organisations, to identify what alternatives will bring about systemic change (Schor, 2011; Kelly, 2012; Parker et al, 2017).

Relating trimming and sowing

In conceptual terms, clearly there is contention between sustainable-capitalism and sustainable-systems – a logic of dichotomy, tension and contrast. One advocates adjustments to 'future-proof' our existing systems, the other a systemic shift, including a structural rejection or revision of trusted narratives such as growth, competition and individualism. One is closer to a 'weak' version of sustainability, the other to a 'strong' version, and, according Pelenc et al (2015), the 'fundamental debate regarding sustainable development is whether we choose to adopt a strong or a weak conception of sustainability' (Pelenc et al, 2015: 1; see also Neumayer, 2013). The two trajectories, in other words, represent two competing visions of where exactly sustainability, as political objective, should take our future. To be logically consistent, our choice must, surely, be *either* to replace prevailing narratives with counter-stories (sustainable-systems) *or* to accept what we have, provided that we can curb its excesses (sustainable-capitalism). We cannot accept *both* that the potential growth (on a finite planet) is inherently limited *and* that we must continue to pursue it (infinitely), albeit in 'smart' or 'sustainable' ways. We cannot embrace individualism and competition as central human characteristics and at the same time maintain that economic systems should be built to reject these, instead nurturing the human character as fundamentally cooperative. The functional concern here would be that, if we are trying to embrace both these perspectives at the same time, we might end up undermining either one. So, if we subscribe to sustainable-capitalism, we implicitly weaken the substantive arguments that might speak for a more radical, sustainable-systems view. Yet, by advocating the latter, we risk that our arguments talk down the very tools – markets, a dedication to (sustainable) economic growth and financial incentives and so on – that will help us in promulgating the former. In conceptually purist terms, then, these are opposite perspectives.

To leave it here, however, would be to leave two further important aspects unconsidered. The first is that there exists a great deal of uncertainty about what we can and cannot achieve by pursuing either of those perspectives in real life. Scientific evidence can be inconclusive or only just emerging, and our knowledge of risks is vague. Discussions on economic growth can illustrate this. In debating whether we should revise or continue our commitment to growth we may find, according to Jackson, that '[s]trangely, the answer is not so simple. Both positions have elements of truth in them' (Jackson, 2011: 85). From a sustainable-capitalism perspective, the key question is 'whether we can achieve enough efficiency gains in the future to continue to purpose economic growth, indefinitely, while still remaining within the "safe operating space" of a finite planet'. And while we have science to help us identify some answers, as Jackson points out, it still remains difficult to 'get a clear handle on it' (Jackson, 2011: 86). Conversely, before accepting a sustainable-systems perspective, we must be sure that we can safely give up growth and rely on a sufficiency-based alternative in the first place – that by adopting this perspective in search of systemic alternatives, we can continue to secure our own prosperity. Jackson engages this by pointing out that 'growth may not be a useful end in itself. It might still be the means to that end. Could it be that, without growth, our ability to flourish diminishes entirely?' (Jackson, 2011: 66).

The second aspect to consider is political context. Their differences notwithstanding, what unites sustainable-capitalism and sustainable-systems is the fact that they are both counter-perspectives to prevailing economic systems (and their political implementation and underlying narratives). As a result, both face formidable challenges and barriers in terms of attracting political support and finding an effective regulatory frame (nationally or internationally) that accommodates their concerns. The question is then whether, given these challenges facing proponents of either perspective, they can afford to be too purist in conceptual terms; whether to do so would instead mean to pass up opportunities to build momentum, and potentially weaken the argument for sustainability altogether. There is, in other words, a case for political pragmatism that suggests at this stage, given the urgency of sustainability concerns and, corresponding to it, of generating further political and regulatory momentum to address them, that we should run every single argument for sustainability for which we can find a sensible and effective forum. This is not to discard important distinctions between the two perspectives we set out here but, rather, to account for the reality of the dynamics of social change (Green, 2016).

Both aspects, political context and existing uncertainty, would seem to support an approach that is less purist and instead more pragmatic and experimental, encouraging both perspectives to 'run' in political discussions and regulatory environments, potentially even to *reinforce* one another, whenever possible, for supporting the wider case for sustainable development and testing out various methods to bring it about. Again, this is not to deny underlying conceptual tensions and the need for political choices, but simply to highlight that these choices are, in practice, shaped not only by concepts but also by scientific and political realities. Our later discussion will eventually return to this argument by making the point that, in developing a *sustainable framework for corporate law and governance*, there is room for a 'pincer movement' (Kelly, 2012: 13) in which sustainable-capitalism and sustainable-systems can reinforce one another to drive forward the wider case for sustainability. Before reaching this point in the argument, however, the discussion first addresses a preliminary question, namely, why (and how) the conceptual distinctions between sustainable-capitalism and sustainable-systems matter in the regulatory context of corporate governance in the first place.

Sustainable corporate governance

Corporate firms are central to our economic and political organisation. Arguably, more than any other social institution, they currently shape both our ability to address the challenge of sustainability and our attitudes towards it. They are influential not only for the institutional (corporate) power they wield and the (political) interests they represent and diffuse, but also because, as organisations in which politics is 'made durable' (Parker et al, 2017), they hold extensive *ideational* power: the manner in which they are organised and governed shapes wider ideas, expectations and systemic behaviours. So, 'greed is good' is not just a principle of corporate organisation and management, often related to the pursuit of shareholder value (as well as incentivised risk taking and short-termism) in corporate governance. The more pervasive it becomes, and the more widespread and influential corporate firms become in our societies, the more we can expect this principle to take on a taken-for-granted character that translates into social paradigms and systemic behaviours – a 'life attitude' aligning with a certain historical narrative of human character, development, organisation and progress.

Recognising these effects of business organisation on issues of sustainability opens opportunities for sustainable development: levying corporate influence to improve, say, global supply chains to secure labour standards and environmental guarantees can be a powerful route to reinforcing sustainability standards. But it also highlights real risks where the very same power is deployed without regard for sustainability, or even to undermine sustainability levels (for example, by exploiting supply chains and their workers). From a governance perspective, it raises the important question of how we might incorporate these opportunities – but at the same time respond to the risks inherent in corporate power – into the governance structure of the corporate firm itself. What, in other words, does a sustainable framework for corporate governance look like?

Linking corporate governance expressly to concern for sustainability is a relatively recent phenomenon. The earliest efforts to make this linkage explicit appear in the field of sustainability reporting (see Villiers and Tsagas, Chapter 3 in this book). In other areas of corporate law and governance, sustainability concerns appeared for some time mostly indirectly, usually in critical discussions over the public or private character of our corporations and of their wider responsibility towards stakeholders and society (for example, Parkinson, 1995). During the 1980s and 1990s, while both political and academic aspirations were focused on classic economic theory as underpinning of corporate governance, these discussions often remained marginal. However, following the turn of the millennium, we have seen this incrementally changing. Not only has an evolving body of international scholarship sprung up that discusses sustainability, company law and corporate governance as explicitly linked issues, from a variety of disciplinary perspectives (Lazonick and O'Sullivan, 2002; Lambooy, 2014; Sjåfjell and Richardson, 2015; Jones, 2017; Sjåfjell and Lynch Fannon, 2018; Goergen and Tonks, 2019), but these linkages also appear, one initiative at a time, increasingly in debates between these academics and policy makers (European Commission, 2019).

From a conceptual perspective, this raises the question of whether the same fault lines that we identified previously in general debates on sustainability – what we termed a perspective of sustainable-capitalism as distinct from one of sustainable-systems – have any noticeable or significant impact on these discussions over the future direction of business and its governance, and particularly of corporations. Do the distinctions, which we identified in the debate on sustainability generally, make a difference to what path we might suggest for a sustainable corporate governance framework? What concrete changes to these frameworks does, or might, each perspective require, including on issues such as boardroom representation, share ownership and accountability? And, finally, are they in tension as mutually exclusive approaches or complementary, even mutually reinforcing, paths? The following sections briefly address these questions by sketching the priorities of either perspective, applied to the context of corporate governance.

Trimming corporations for sustainability

From the point of view of sustainable-capitalism, reshaping corporate governance to align with sustainability concerns is centrally about reforming current regulatory and governance frameworks to ensure that they avoid and address excessive – that is, destructive and extractive (Kelly, 2012) – corporate behaviour. Reforms target the short-term and risk-intense decision making that characterises highly financialised corporate management, focused exclusively on shareholder value and a quarterly rise in share price (see, for example, Stout, 2012). But the aim is to do so without changing the fundamental principles according to which corporations currently operate, at least no more than is essential or necessary. At the very least, this view proposes, corporate managers will be incentivised to consider the long-term economic impact of their decisions; to, in other words, 'pursue shareholder value in a more "enlightened" manner and to focus on long-term rather than short-term financial returns' (Ireland, 2018: 33). A range of regulatory interventions may be necessary to put the requisite incentives in place, including, for example, a set of stewardship obligations to motivate 'active ownership' (McNulty and Nordberg, 2016) among investors, but also fine-tuning of corporate takeover rules to reverse overly financialised interference with corporate management by activist hedge-fund investors (Deakin, 2018). A regulatory discussion on executive pay, with an aim to incorporate long-term incentive structures into corporate remuneration policies, also features here (Villiers, 2016).

Some, still following the sustainable-capitalism mould, would go considerably further and argue for a wider 'culture shift' (B Lab, 2019) to align corporate governance with social and environmental sustainability concerns, especially by engaging corporate business itself to actively take on the responsibility of achieving this shift (Levitt, 2017). In this vein, B Lab, an internationally operating non-profit organisation promoting a sustainability-oriented 'benefit corporation' and 'b corp' format, for example, encourages a 'global movement of people using business as a force for good' and to 'harness the power of business to help address society's greatest challenges'. This organisation's vision is, accordingly, that 'one day all companies will compete to be not just best in the world but also best for the world' (B Lab, 2019) – a vision of promoting 'doing well by doing good' and of delivering corporate 'profit with purpose'. Through two promoted corporate formats (the 'benefit corporation' offers a statutory choice and the 'b corp' a certification process), B Lab encourages corporations to commit to these responsibilities not just as a matter of business policy but by force of their corporate charter.

Their reference to competition highlights, on the other hand, that this perspective still is fundamentally about embracing the *existing* corporate governance principles in so far as they assist in refocusing corporate activity towards concern for sustainability. At its centre, then, lies an aspiration to produce a set of adjusted, but still fundamentally capitalist, operating principles. This aspiration includes the (re)structuring of investment incentives and competitive market dynamics as well as nurturing of individual (entrepreneurial) responsibility to reorient corporations and corporate governance towards sustainability, but without changing their fundamental character. While the goals shift, the methods remain to some considerable extent intact. There is continuity, notably, in the basic allocation of decision-making competencies within the firm to shareholders and management, as responsibilities for taking decisions on sustainability-related innovation are placed squarely with investors (for delivering social or sustainable investment) and directors (for delivering purpose).

Others go further still, with suggestions to give greater decision-making powers to other stakeholders, notably labour, and to allow greater diversity into the corporate boardroom by regulating for effective worker representation (Deakin, 2018). And some propose to incorporate sustainability concerns directly into the legal duties imposed on directors in managing the corporation and suggest that corporations be governed effectively not in the interest of their shareholders, but for sustainability (Sjåfjell, 2018a, 2018b). Some of these reform proposals are a radical departure from existing frameworks in Anglo-American corporate governance, especially where they would impose on directors a duty to go beyond the 'business case' for sustainability (Johnston, 2014). Some are explicitly set up as initiatives towards *systemic* change (Sjåfjell, 2018b). But they do align themselves with a sustainable-capitalism view in so far as they impose more or less far-reaching reform on existing corporate legal and governance structures, rather than generating alternative business organisations, legal and governance structures. These interventions are reformative rather than formative – aiming to curtail any excessive and destructive tendencies of the corporation in its current legal format and to adjust its governance principles to reduce these to sustainable levels.

Sowing sustainable business

Initiatives that align with sustainable-systems thinking, on the other hand, tend to take a different path towards change. Their challenge to the current legal and governance structure of the corporation rests on the basis that its very foundations – the narratives it is designed to incorporate – are fundamentally unsuitable to our concern for sustainability. To fully meet sustainability concerns, interventions are necessary not just to avoid excessive corporate behaviour or to redirect it, but instead to identify fundamentally new, or different, operating principles and to incorporate them into the organisation of business and its governance. Importantly, this perspective goes beyond ideas of reforming the legal and governance structure of the corporation, however radical they might be. It is a more diverse movement, focused not primarily on – more, or less, radical – corporate reform but, more broadly, on developing alternative business forms. This movement considers that to impose changes by regulating the corporation's existing legal and governance frameworks does not necessarily suffice to create sustainable economic systems. In addition, the underlying paradigms of business would need to be looked at and templates developed for alternative business organisations capable of creating and supporting these systems.

From a historical perspective, rather than critiquing corporations and their excess while tracing the development of these harmful patterns through history, this view's natural starting point is to study the evolution of alternative forms of business and economic organising – including in the format of partnerships, cooperatives, social enterprises, employee-owned and mutual firms. The point is then to see if it is possible to develop and build up these templates to set up sustainable business governance in the modern economic context. This view, in other words, takes the process of 'sowing' almost literally. It is dedicated to setting up micro-organisms – business organisations – as seeds of alternative economic systems and to creating an environment (including in legal terms) in which they may thrive and grow.

This might start with a focus on sufficiency and business size. Parker, for example, has made the argument that 'a localized small business system is more resilient to economic shocks, as well as providing clear advantages in terms of environmentally friendly business practices and the reduction of inequality' (Parker, 2017: 419). As for generating sustainable value, Bentham et al (2013: 7) suggest focusing initially on the 'foundational economy' – 'that part of the economy that creates and distributes goods and services consumed by all (regardless of income and status) because they support everyday life'. The cooperative sector, according to Mayo (2017: 3), helps to identify that business *values* are equally important motivators as, say, individualism and competitive advantage to ensure sustainable business success, as they allow businesses 'to engage staff, customers and suppliers in an emotional way that touches on their own core motivations'. Abrams (2008: 3) reports that employee ownership coupled with keeping things locally focused helped him to build 'a community of enterprise that we hope will have the strength to nurture stable relationships, the flexibility to shift with changing times, and the ability to sustain itself for generations'. Similarly, the growth of social enterprises – firms that have a clear social or environmental mission set out in their governing documents and that re-invest more than half of their profits for this purpose or mission – shines a critical reflection on the assumption that sustainable success relies foremost on profit (Social Enterprise UK, 2018).

These are some examples of what Kelly (2012: 12) refers to as a movement towards 'private ownership for the common good', defying the choices between private and public ownership. From the perspective of law, this movement tends to focus on enabling sustainable business formats that entrepreneurs may choose. Law here acts primarily in a facilitating role (a private law function). Following a regulatory (or public law) perspective, on the other hand, law would be seen typically as an intervention, designed to revise aspects of corporate law and governance frameworks, to impose responsibilities in the interest of sustainability on all corporations (Sjåfjell, 2018a, 2018b).

Conclusion

Based on these sketches, the argument thus far is that in this concrete field – where the practical challenge is to develop a sustainable corporate legal and governance framework – our conceptual understanding of sustainability clearly matters as a way of determining the institutional path we choose to take, and the methods we choose to deploy, in achieving change. How we frame sustainability generally – in terms of sustainable-capitalism or sustainable-systems – will directly influence what starting points we may consider to be most sensible or effective, and what trajectories we are most inclined to follow, in attempting to shape the sustainable governance of business. Sustainable-capitalism leads us, broadly speaking, to focus on rethinking aspects of the corporation and its governance, but it does not, in this reform effort, necessarily mean that we reject existing governance principles, nor the overarching objectives of growth, the dynamics of competition and its financial incentives. Fundamentally, it is optimistic about achieving sustainability by deploying existing principles in so far as they can be adjusted to curb excessive (unsustainable) corporate behaviour. Sustainable-systems leaves us with a different developmental path; one that is inclined to look beyond mainstream corporate models and their governance principles altogether and to draw on alternative business models governed by different principles – including from within the solidarity and cooperative economy – as templates to build and expand. Calling for business to organise itself as part of a 'new' economy (Sjåfjell, 2018b), this view is prepared to engage with ideas of fundamentally revising existing economic narratives and governance structures.

The argument invites, once more, the follow-on question of where these two perspectives stand relative to one another: are they competing and contending for influence – and thus, to an extent at least, mutually exclusive – or are these, on the other hand, complementary, even mutually reinforcing, perspectives that we may pursue simultaneously, perhaps even interactively? Can they both be right? The general discussion recognised that, from the point of view of logical consistency and functionality, the perspectives of sustainable-capitalism and sustainable-systems are best seen as opposing counter-points in the sustainability debate. The point is to avoid a 'cake and eat it' approach where, by trying to pursue both simultaneously, we risk undermining their respective arguments for sustainability. However, such a purist standpoint in conceptual terms will always have to be contextualised, by way of reality check. There is a case for engaging both perspectives simultaneously – to be less purist and more pragmatic – where to do so serves to address political constraints (inertias) and opposition to sustainability, and where it is helpful to manage existing uncertainties about how we might achieve sustainable development.

In the area of corporate governance, where the political context in many jurisdictions (and internationally) is shaped by strong corporate interests and resulting struggles to implement change, these factors are highly relevant (see also Villiers and Tsagas, Chapter 3). So are, on the other hand, concerns that, by pursuing both perspectives simultaneously in this context, one might end up politically interfering with the other. For example, by talking up the corporate format of the 'b corp' – a format in the sustainable-capitalism mould – are we at risk of confusing the public about (and potentially drawing resources from) why we need businesses that choose to go further by setting themselves up as social enterprises in the sustainable-systems mould (Boeger and Hunter, 2018; Hunter, 2018)? Conversely, by polarising the debate between the 'new' and traditional economies and their preferences for certain corporate governance structures, is there a risk that we might be downplaying what sustainable-capitalism can do to reform corporations pragmatically, to build sustainable capitalist organisations, with a wider impact than, say, the cooperative movement could/might ever have?

Needless to say, there are no easy answers. What can be said is that, in Britain, against the backdrop of a corporate legal and governance framework that for some time, despite far-reaching technical reforms, has proved mostly change resistant in political terms, these questions are currently being played out at the sharp end of political and legal debate. The search for improving the governance of UK companies has been long standing, and, while its focus has been on public companies, many private companies too are in the spotlight. To date, we have seen extensive corporate law reform (Barker and Chiu, 2018), the introduction and frequent revision of corporate governance codes (Mor, 2019) and various other initiatives including international instruments (see McNulty and Nordberg, 2016; Deakin, 2018). Most of these reforms have been designed to introduce greater transparency, and checks and balances, to ensure primarily that managers will be held accountable for protecting the interests of shareholders as capital owners (and, to a lesser extent, those of other stakeholders including labour); and that shareholders in turn will act more like actual 'owners' rather than distant, absentee rentiers. However, despite these long-standing efforts, many would argue today that corporate governance reform in the UK has been slow to truly make a difference to business practice and policy in terms of sustainability. Even among traditionally doctrinal English company lawyers, there is growing concern that these reforms have failed to introduce the changes necessary to revise the corporation's critical role in financialised capitalism, to take sustainability more seriously (Talbot, 2016).

On the other hand, just to lament political inertias (Green, 2016) that have muffled attempts at further-reaching reform of these frameworks would be to neglect an important flip-side in the story of modern business law and governance in Britain that does appear to take sustainability more seriously; suggesting that the British story is about a polarisation of corporate governance more than purely about stagnation or resistance to change. This flip-side comprises various sustainable business models that tend to organise as movements (Boeger, 2018) – social enterprises, cooperatives, community businesses, b corps (Hunter, 2018) or, more generally, 'purposeful' companies (Big Innovation Centre, 2017). These alternative corporate forms have gained momentum, especially since the 2008 financial crisis and its aftermath committed the UK politically to a period of public austerity (see contributions to Boeger and Villiers, 2018). Some of these formats incorporate ideas of sustainable-capitalism while others reflect a sustainable-systems perspective. They all, however, position themselves at a distance from traditional corporate for-profit business, and attempt to employ this position as a strength, making use of legal and economic opportunities to do so.

What is of interest here is less the general issue of how these counter-models manage to develop successfully (on this, see for example, Boeger and Villiers, 2018), but more concretely how their diversity – the fact that some of these will be in pursuit of sustainable-capitalism while others are commit more fully to sustainable-systems – affects their evolution and success. What evidence is there, in other words, of a tension between these two perspectives in the practical development of these sustainable corporate governance trends, whereby one perspective might in fact undermine the other? The issue recently fell into focus in the context of a government-led review on 'mission-led business' in Britain (Boeger and Hunter, 2018). In this review the government sought concrete recommendations on the future role in Britain's economy of companies that are led by a wider social purpose beyond profit, which they enshrine in their corporate constitution (much like a 'b corp' would), and which they are therefore committed to but without fundamentally curtailing their ability to generate and distribute profits. It is an extraordinarily flexible concept, attracting some criticism for that reason (see Boeger and Hunter, 2018). The advantage in financial terms, on the other hand, is that the company becomes attractive to social impact investors who feel a responsibility to support sustainable initiatives with their capital; but it does so without curtailing its economic flexibility as much as, say, a social enterprise, which is committed to the reinvestment of its profits to further its social purpose, would (see Social Enterprise UK, 2018). This is a model for sustainable-capitalism: committed to the existing mould of corporate governance, including the concern for shareholders and profit, but ready to curb excess and an overly narrow focus by committing to a wider social purpose (and stakeholders). As such, it is attracting the attention of a growing number of entrepreneurs, academics (Big Innovation Centre, 2017) and practising company lawyers (Bourne, 2012) with an interest in sustainability.

A critical contribution to the review's call for evidence, on the other hand, came from Social Enterprise UK (SEUK), the membership organisation representing British social enterprises. It observed, first, that the review's 'mission-led business' terminology was vague and ill-defined. It seemed to water down our established understanding of existing forms of sustainable business, some of them long-standing examples of sustainable-systems, including cooperative forms. By including the ability to distribute profits as part of their definition, the review panel effectively excluded from the concept of mission-led business precisely those firms which are most committed to social purpose: social enterprises themselves. In addition, SEUK was concerned that the attention that mission-led business might draw from social impact investors would in effect divert resources away from genuine social-purpose businesses, that is, social enterprises (Social Enterprise UK, 2016).

This short episode highlights that in the specific, and challenging, context of developing more sustainable forms of corporate governance in Britain there are examples where the two perspectives of sustainable-capitalism and sustainable-systems stand in contradiction and create tension. However, the broader direction of travel currently appears to be one that embraces a diversity of approaches – which is perhaps unsurprising, given the strength of political inertia in the face of reform that is affecting the sustainability movement more widely. There is a discernible case for saying, then, that the two perspectives on sustainable business governance that we have sketched out here – moulded by sustainable-capitalism or sustainable-systems, respectively – should more usefully be treated as complementary than as mutually exclusive. They could even be seen as mutually reinforcing, in so far as both highlight what type of changes are possible to move businesses towards a more sustainable governance framework. In this vein, engaging them together can help to create what Kelly (2012: 13) describes as a useful 'pincer movement: one arm moving to rein in corporate abuse and reform corporate governance at existing corporations, the other arm moving to develop generative alternatives'. This is so, not only because engaging them together helps to address political barriers and problems of marginalisation that both perspectives encounter to some extent; it also helps to overcome technical barriers and scientific uncertainty – to work out, by way of experimentation, which of these perspectives might, ultimately, bring effective solutions that deliver sustainability.

References

Abrams, J. (2008) *Companies We Keep: Employee Ownership and the Business of Community and Place*, White River Junction: Chelsea Green Publishing.

B Lab (2019) 'About B Lab'. Available at: https://bcorporation.net/about-b-lab (accessed 23 March 2019).

Barker, R. and Chiu, I. (2018) 'Unfinished work in UK company law, reforms: a normative and European perspective to addressing the gaping holes in directors' duties', *European Company Law* 15(6): 194–4.

Bentham, J. et al (2013) *Manifesto for the Foundational Economy*, CRESC working paper 131. Available at: http://hummedia.manchester.ac.uk/institutes/cresc/workingpapers/wp131.pdf (accessed 23 March 2019).

Big Innovation Centre (2017) *Purposeful Company Report*. Available at: http://biginnovationcentre.com/media/uploads/pdf/TPC_Policy%20Report.pdf (accessed 27 March 2019).

Boeger, N. (2018) 'The new corporate movement', in N. Boeger and C. Villiers (eds), *Shaping the Corporate Landscape: Towards Corporate Reform and Enterprise Diversity*, Oxford: Hart Publishing, pp 189–212.

Boeger, N. and Hunter, D. (2018) 'Mission-led business: CSR reboot or paradigm shift?', *Bristol Law Research Paper Series* 2018(1): 1–26.

Boeger, N. and Villiers, C. (eds) (2018) *Shaping the Corporate Landscape: Towards Corporate Reform and Enterprise Diversity*, Oxford: Hart Publishing.

Bollier, D. (2014) *Think Like a Commoner: A Short Introduction to the Life of the Commons*, Gabriola Island: New Society Publishers.

Bourne, T. (2012) 'Why lawyers have a part to play in sustainable development', *The Guardian*, 16 February. Available at: www.theguardian.com/sustainable-business/blog/sustainable-business-development-law (accessed 25 March 2019).

Capra, F. and Luisi, P. (2016) *The Systems View of Life: A Unifying Vision*, Cambridge: Cambridge University Press.

Caradonna, J. (2014) *Sustainability: A History*, Oxford: Oxford University Press.

Daly, H. (1991) *Steady-State Economics* (2nd edn), Washington, DC: Island Press.

Deakin, S. (2018) 'Reversing financialization: shareholder value and the legal reform of corporate governance', in C. Driver and G. Thompson (eds), *Corporate Governance in Contention*, Oxford: Oxford University Press, pp 25–41.

de Sadeleer, N. (2002) *Environmental Principles – From Political Slogans to Legal Rules*, Oxford: Oxford University Press.

Du Pisani, J. (2006) 'Sustainable development – historical roots of the concept', *Environmental Science* 3(2): 83–96.

Ekins, P., Simon, S., Deutsch, L., Folke, C. and De Groot, R. (2003) 'A framework for the practical application of the concepts of critical natural capital and strong sustainability', *Ecological Economics* 44(2–3): 165–85.

European Commission (2019) *Programme, DG Justice and Consumers Conference on Sustainable Corporate Governance*, 24 January 2019. Available at: https://ec.europa.eu/info/events/conference-sustainable-corporate-governance-2019-jan-24_en (accessed 22 March 2019).

Frase, P. (2016) *Four Futures: Life after Capitalism*, London: Verso Books.

Goergen, M. and Tonks, I. (2019) 'Introduction to special issue on sustainable corporate governance', *British Journal of Management* 30: 3–9.

Gore, A. and Blood, D. (2011) 'A manifesto for sustainable capitalism', *Wall Street Journal*, 14 December. Available at: www.algore.com/news/a-manifesto-for-sustainable-capitalism (accessed 21 March 2019).

Green, D. (2016) *How Change Happens*, Oxford: Oxford University Press.

Harrison, N. (2014) *Sustainable Capitalism and the Pursuit of Well-being*, Abingdon: Routledge.

Hawken, P., Lovins, A. and Lovins, H. (2005) *Natural Capitalism: The Next Industrial Revolution* (2nd edn), Abingdon: Routledge.

Hunter, D. (2018) 'The advent of B Corps in Britain: another milestone towards a more nuanced economy?', in N. Boeger and C. Villiers (eds), *Shaping the Corporate Landscape: Towards Corporate Reform and Enterprise Diversity*, Oxford: Hart Publishing, pp 253–70.

Ikerd, J. (2005) *Sustainable Capitalism: A Matter of Common Sense*, Boulder, CO: Lynne Rienner Publishers.

Ireland, P. (2018) 'Corporate schizophrenia: the institutional origins of corporate social irresponsibility', in N. Boeger and C. Villiers (eds), *Shaping the Corporate Landscape: Towards Corporate Reform and Enterprise Diversity*, Oxford: Hart Publishing, pp 13–40.

Jackson, T. (2011) *Prosperity without Growth*, Abingdon: Routledge.

Johnston, A. (2014) 'Reforming English company law to promote sustainable companies', *European Company Law* 11(2): 63–6.

Jones, G. (2017) *Profits and Sustainability: A History of Green Entrepreneurship*, Oxford: Oxford University Press.

Kelly, M. (2012) *Owning Our Future: The Emerging Ownership Revolution*, Oakland: Berrett-Koehler Publishers.

Kingman, J. (2018) *Independent Review of the Financial Reporting Council: Final Report*. Available at: www.gov.uk/government/publications/financial-reporting-council-review-2018 (accessed 24 March 2019).

Korten, D. (2015) *Change the Story, Change the Future*, Oakland: Berrett-Koehler Publishers.

Krugman, P. (2014) 'Errors and emissions', *New York Times*, 18 September. Available at: www.nytimes.com/2014/09/19/opinion/paul-krugman-could-fighting-global-warming-be-cheap-and-free.html (accessed 23 March 2019).

Lambooy, T. (2014) 'Reforming company law for sustainable companies', *European Company Law* 11(2): 54–7.

Lazonick, W. and O'Sullivan, M. (eds) (2002) *Corporate Governance and Sustainable Prosperity*, London: Palgrave Macmillan.

Lent, J. (2017) *The Patterning Instinct: A Cultural History of Humanity's Search for Meaning*, Amherst, MA: Prometheus Books.

Levitt, T. (2017) *The Company Citizen: Good for Business, Planet, Nation and Community*, Abingdon: Routledge.

Mason, P. (2016) *PostCapitalism: A Guide to Our Future*, London: Penguin.

Mayo, E. (2017) *Values: How to Bring Values to Life in Your Business*, Austin: Greenleaf Publishing.

Mazzucato, M. (2018) *The Value of Everything: Making and Taking in the Global Economy*, London: Allen Lane.

McNulty, T. and Nordberg, D. (2016) 'Ownership, activism and engagement: institutional investors as active owners', *Corporate Governance* 24(3): 346–58.

Meadows, D. (2009) *Thinking in Systems: A Primer*, Abingdon: Routledge.

Meadows, D., Randers, J. and Meadows, D. (2004) *Limits to Growth: The 30-Year Update*, White River Junction: Chelsea Green Publishing Company.

Monbiot, G. (2017) *Out of the Wreckage: A New Politics for an Age of Crisis*, London: Verso Books.

Mor, F. (2019) *Corporate Governance Reform*, House of Commons Library Briefing Paper Number 8143, 4 January. Available at: https://researchbriefings.parliament.uk/ResearchBriefing/Summary/CBP-8143#fullreport (accessed 27 March 2019).

Neumayer, E. (2013) *Weak versus Strong Sustainability: Exploring the Limits of Two Opposing Paradigms* (4th edn), Cheltenham: Edward Elgar.

Parker, M. (2017) 'Alternative enterprises, local economies, and social justice: why smaller is still more beautiful', *Management (France)* (20): 418–34.

Parker, M., Cheney, G., Fournier, V. and Land, C. (2017) 'Organization is politics made durable: principles and alternatives', in G. Baars and A. Spicer (eds), *The Corporation: A Critical, Multi-Disciplinary Handbook*, Cambridge: Cambridge University Press, pp 538–45.

Parkinson, J. (1995) *Corporate Power and Responsibility: Issues in the Theory of Company Law*, Oxford: Oxford University Press.

Pelenc, J., Ballet, J. and Dedeurwaerdere, T. (2015) 'Weak sustainability versus strong sustainability', *Brief for GSDR 2015*. Available at: https://sustainabledevelopment.un.org/content/documents/6569122-Pelenc-Weak%20Sustainability%20versus%20Strong%20Sustainability.pdf (accessed 27 March 2019).

Princen, T. (2005) *The Logic of Sufficiency*, London: MIT Press.

Ratner, B. (2004) '"Sustainability" as a dialogue of values: challenges to the sociology of development', *Sociological Inquiry* 74(1): 50–69.

Raworth, K. (2017) *Doughnut Economics: Seven Ways to Think Like a 21st-Century Economist*, New York: Random House Business.

Reich, R. (2019) 'Donald Trump tells a fake American story. We must tell the real one', *The Guardian*, 4 March. Available at: www.theguardian.com/commentisfree/2019/mar/04/donald-trump-american-story-robert-reich (accessed 4 March 2019).

Schor, J. (2011) *True Wealth: How and Why Millions of Americans Are Creating a Time-Rich, Ecologically Light, Small-Scale, High-Satisfaction Economy*, London: Penguin.

Schumacher, E. (2010) *Small is Beautiful: A Study of Economics as if People Mattered*, New York: Harper Perennial (reprint of the 1973 original).

Sjåfjell, B. (2018a) 'Beyond climate risk: integrating sustainability into the duties of the corporate board', *Deakin Law Review* 23: 41–61.

Sjåfjell, B. (2018b) 'Redefining the corporation for a sustainable new economy', *Journal of Law and Society*, 45(1): 29–45.

Sjåfjell, B. and Lynch Fannon, I. (2018) *Creating Corporate Sustainability: Gender as an Agent for Change*, Cambridge: Cambridge University Press.

Sjåfjell, B. and Richardson, B. (eds) (2015) *Company Law and Sustainability: Legal Barriers and Opportunities*, Cambridge: Cambridge University Press.

Social Enterprise UK (2016) *Response to the Mission-Led Business Review: Call for Evidence*. Available at: www.socialenterprise.org.uk/consultation-responses (accessed 27 March 2019).

Social Enterprise UK (2018) *Hidden Revolution.* Available at: www.socialenterprise.org.uk/the-hidden-revolution (accessed 23 March 2019).

Stout, L. (2012) *The Shareholder Value Myth: How Putting Shareholders First Harms Investors, Corporations, and the Public*, Oakland: Berrett-Koehler Publishers.

Talbot, L. (2016) 'Trying to save the world with company law? Some problems', *Legal Studies* 36(3): 513–34.

Thwink (2019) *Definition of Sustainability.* Available at: www.thwink.org/sustain/glossary/Sustainability.htm (accessed 18 March 2019).

Villiers, C. (2016) 'Executive pay: a socially-oriented distributive justice framework', *Company Lawyer* 37(5): 139–54.

PART III

Trade

5

The International Trade Regime and SDG 2: Reforming Agricultural Markets for Food Security

Clair Gammage

Introduction

The political economy of agriculture is complex, and reforming the rules on agricultural trade has been a point of contention among states for decades. Agricultural markets have evolved significantly since the beginning of the 21st century, and as global demand for agricultural commodities has grown, international trade expanded (FAO, 2018:20). In the period 2000–15 agricultural trade volumes have tripled from $550 billion to $1.8 trillion, with a growing volume of commodities destined for emerging economies like China and India (Schleifer & Sun, 2018). Historically, the agricultural trade rules have been shaped by the protectionist normative preferences of the United States (US) and the European Union (EU) (McCalla, 1969; Clark et al, 2000), but there are now many state and non-state actors shaping and contesting the normative frameworks through which agricultural trade is liberalised (Thies, 2011; Smith, 2015; Scott, 2017).

In the World Trade Organization (WTO), and its predecessor the General Agreement on Tariffs and Trade (the GATT), agriculture has been conceptualised as an exceptional sector. There was a shared consensus among states in the GATT era (1947–94) that agriculture should be treated differently under the international trading rules, in part because of its 'multifunctionality' (Minju and Lee, 2017: 172). Multifunctionality finds its origins in forestry policies of the 1950s and it was later adopted as a concept for sustainable agricultural governance, most notably in the 1997 Luxembourg European Council (Brouwer, 2004). There is no single definition of the concept of multifunctionality but it generally characterises the trade and non-trade concerns of agricultural production and consumption (OECD, 2008: 19). In WTO terms, multifunctionality refers to the 'idea that agriculture has many functions in addition to producing food and fibre [such as] environmental protection, landscape preservation, rural employment [and] food security' (WTO Glossary, 2019).

Food security is a multidimensional concept, and for the purposes of WTO law it is classified as a 'non-trade concern'. Nevertheless, there is a close relationship between food security and the modes of production and availability of food, both of which are governed by international trade rules. Food security exists where 'all people at all times have physical, social and economic *access* to sufficient, safe and nutritious food that meets their dietary needs and food preferences for an active and healthy life' (FAO, 2003). However, food security is not simply a scientific or technological problem that can be resolved by improving crop yields to increase the quantity of food available. Rather, it has legal, political, social and cultural dimensions that require an understanding about who has access to adequate food and why (Orford, 2015; Scott, 2017; Vivero-Pol et al, 2018).

What role, then, does international trade law have in promoting sustainable agriculture and food security? This chapter posits that international trade law 'stands between food availability and food entitlement' (Sen, 1981: 166), and that rights-sensitive interpretation and transformation of the international trade rules on agriculture is needed. The significance of agricultural exceptionalism for the realisation of food security and sustainable agricultural markets will be explored and it will be argued that achieving food security requires the creation of a level playing field in international trade through the elimination of distorting trade measures in a manner that recognises the social, environmental and cultural dimensions of food security. The reframing of sustainable development through the Sustainable Development Goals (SDGs) presents an opportunity to revisit the debate on the governance of agricultural trade. SDG 2, which aims to 'end hunger, achieve food security and improved nutrition, and promote sustainable agriculture' foresees, alongside SDG 17, an important role for the WTO in reforming global agricultural markets sustainably. Target 2.b provides that trade restrictions and distortions in the world agricultural markets need to be corrected, 'including through the parallel elimination of all forms of agricultural export subsidies and all export measures with equivalent effect, in accordance with the Doha Development Agenda'.

With a focus on food security as a trade concern this chapter will argue that the WTO has a fundamental role to play in (re)shaping *sustainable* agricultural governance for food security. The purpose of the chapter is to map the limitations and possibilities of world trade law in reforming agricultural markets in a sustainable way that promotes food security. Central to this enquiry is an analysis of the ideational frameworks of meaning through which the international trading system and SDGs operate. The international trading system has been shaped through the frame of liberalism and operates on the fundamental premise that trade will be non-discriminatory, reciprocal and mutually advantageous (Lang, 2011). The liberal normative frame is embedded in the trade rules and, it is submitted, the economic rationality of the multilateral trading system fails to adequately accommodate for non-trade concerns like food security.

Conversely, the analytical frame of this chapter is informed by the capabilities approach advanced by Amartya Sen (1999) and conceives of the strategic orientation of the SDGs as inherently rights based, seeking to maximise the global redistribution of public goods to ensure that 'no one is left behind'. The liberalisation of trade promotes economic freedom and this, in turn, has a significant bearing on the ability of individuals to realise other social and political freedoms. Development is to be understood as both a discourse and a process to expand human freedoms, capabilities and agency (Sen, 1999: 3). At the heart of the capabilities approach, development is a process that achieves freedom from the deprivation of capabilities and entitlements (Sen, 1999: 87). This chapter explores the contours of these conflicting ideational frameworks and examines the extent to which they can be reconciled in the pursuit of a common goal – food security.

The chapter is organised into three sections. In the first section the ideational frameworks of meaning through which the SDGs and agricultural trade liberalisation operate will be discussed. The second section analyses the evolution and contestation of agricultural policy from the GATT era to the birth of the WTO (1947–94). The shifting paradigms of agricultural trade will be examined through the many rounds of negotiation in the WTO era (1995–present). The final section will explore the ideational divide between international trade rules on agriculture and food security. This chapter proposes that there is, in theory at least, the potential for these conflicting ideational systems of law to be reconciled through the implementation of SDG 17, which promotes inter-institutional cooperation. It will be argued that food security requires international solutions beyond international trade. Nevertheless, international trade can play an important role in enabling food security.

Agricultural trade and food security: the ideational divide

Since the end of the Second World War the international order has been underpinned by the logic of liberalism, which is characterised by economic openness, multilateral institutions operating in accordance with a loosely rules-based system, security cooperation and democratic solidarity (Ruggie, 1982). There have been considerable geopolitical shifts in this period which have threatened to undermine the logic of liberalism. Emerging economies – those countries that have experienced rapid economic growth but are not classified as developed countries – have become powerful actors in the global order and they have disrupted the logic of liberal internationalism (Ikenberry, 2018). As the hegemonic power of the US has gradually declined over the past two decades, the international order has become multipolar. A consequence of multipolarity is the increased likelihood of ideational dissonance and conflict between different actors; 'the fact that several of the new players around the table do not share the same visions of global order as those espoused by the established powers makes it even more difficult to keep the existing global institutions in functioning order' (Narlikar, 2017: 93).

The crisis of liberal internationalism is one of 'legitimacy and social purpose' (Ikenberry, 2018: 19) and it is the assertion of this chapter that the SDGs aim to reorient the social purpose of the international community around the 'supernorm' (Fukuda-Parr and Hulme, 2011) of sustainable development. However, there are two considerable challenges facing the reconciliation of the ideational divide between the SDGs, which promote sustainable development, and the rules governing trade liberalisation. First, the normative content of the SDGs is set out in ambiguous and imprecise terms (see Chapter 2 in this book). There is little guidance for institutions and other actors on how the broadly articulated goals and targets are to be realised. Second, the SDGs cannot be realised unless and until the WTO is reimagined as more than a 'political marketplace' (Lang, 2014).

From poverty eradication to sustainable development

In 2015 the international community committed to the 2030 Agenda for Sustainable Development (Agenda 2030) and rearticulated the concept of sustainable development. Agenda 2030 is normatively framed in the tradition of the human development approach (Sen, 1999; Nussbaum, 2011), which emphasises the significance of realising human rights and capabilities through a global strategy for development. The analytical framework of this chapter draws insights from Amartya Sen's capabilities approach, famously set out in *Development as Freedom* (1999).

Sen proposes a theory of development where human freedom is both the principal means and the principal end of development. He identifies two types of freedoms – constitutive and instrumental – and argues that the focus of development should be on human capabilities to achieve a life that each individual values (Sen, 1999: 44). Constitutive freedoms are those freedoms that we intrinsically value, and include the ability to be nourished, the ability to live a peaceful life, the ability to access education, the ability to participate in political processes and so on. On the other hand, instrumental freedoms are those freedoms which contribute to, or expand, the realisation of constitutive freedoms. In the context of this chapter, the ability to participate in the market and sell one's labour (an *instrumental* freedom) to generate income enables an individual to purchase food and be nourished (a *constitutive* freedom).

Through a capabilities lens, the liberal international trade rules on agricultural governance can be inverted and the 'ends' of trade can be reimagined (Gammage, 2019). Rather than focusing narrowly on the 'ends' of trade as productivity, efficiency and economic growth, the focus can shift toward the expansion of human freedoms, capabilities and entitlements. It is suggested that the point of intersection between sustainable development and international trade is to remove obstacles to human freedom, and the purpose of redistribution through the international trading system is to promote and enhance freedoms for more just and inclusive societies.

Agenda 2030 is a 'plan of action for people, planet and prosperity' that extends beyond the limited framework of the Millennium Development Goals (MDGs), wherein development was defined as 'poverty eradication'. Sakiko Fukuda-Parr and David Hulme (2011: 31) refer to the goal of eradicating poverty as a 'supernorm'; a 'carefully structured set of interrelated norms that pursue a grand prescriptive norm'. They trace the life-cycle of this supernorm, identifying the state and non-state actors involved in shaping and articulating the normative framework that came to be the MDGs (see also Chapter 2 of this book).

In doing so, they propose that the MDGs 'powerfully communicated the antipoverty agenda', in part because 'they directly referred to concrete human conditions with which people could empathise rather than the abstract term "poverty" that was open to interpretation' (Fukuda-Parr and Hulme, 2011: 23). It was the simplicity of the goal-oriented approach – with just eight goals specified – and the time-limited targets for achieving those goals that also contributed to the perceived success of the MDGs at the time of their drafting.

From a capabilities perspective, poverty is understood to be 'capability deprivation', and the process of development promoted by the MDGs was, therefore, one that achieves freedom from the deprivation of capabilities (Sen, 1999: 87). The MDGs were premised on the human development approach, and one that was normatively framed on the concept of human rights (OCHR, 2008). Human rights and the MDGs were seen as 'a natural fit, driven by the same objectives, using very similar means, facing common obstacles, and relying on closely related constituents and political dynamics in order to make progress' (Alston, 2005: 760). However, the MDGs unduly narrowed the concept of development to mean the alleviation of poverty. As a result of the narrow conception of development, coupled with the focus on the use of metrics and indicators, a narrative of development emerged that was 'strangely alien to the vision of the Millennium Declaration for a people-centred development motivated by universal values of equality, respect for nature, solidarity and freedom' (Fukuda-Parr et al, 2014: 115). In part, the failure of the MDGs stems from the lack of ideational consensus about how the global development agenda should be operationalised. The ideational divides between the various state and non-state actors who had battled to reach an intersubjective framework of meaning for the global development agenda were deeply entrenched (Fukuda-Parr and Hulme, 2011: 30).

On the other hand, the SDGs are integrative and embody a range of universalised economic, social and environmental objectives to reflect the indivisible nature of the three dimensions of sustainable development: social, economic and environmental (Agenda 2030, para 17). The SDGs marked a normative shift toward a global strategy for sustainable development and away from the aid-driven rationale of the MDGs, which primarily sought to alleviate suffering in poorer developing countries (Fukuda-Parr, 2016). In this respect, the SDGs reflect a shared intersubjective meaning of sustainable development. That is not to say that there is agreement among the international community of the conceptual boundaries of sustainable development but, rather, the SDGs are symbolic of a global normative commitment to pursuing the various rights and obligations which attach to the 'matrix' of sustainable development. It is important to note that the SDGs are not intended to be prescriptive. Each state must be able to exercise regulatory autonomy and implement its own measures, albeit in accordance with its commitments under international law, including world trade law.

SDG 2, which sets out targets in relation to agricultural governance and food security, is normatively rooted in rights discourse. International responses to food crises and famines were framed around the norm of food production, in part because the powerful grain-producing states were prominent actors in the United Nations' (UN) specialised agency, the Food and Agriculture Organisation (FAO). Sen's capabilities approach was influential in reorienting the international community toward a 'multifaceted understanding of hunger' (Margulis, 2013: 56), and this formed the basis of the concept of food security which was adopted in the 1996 World Food Summit. There are multiple causes of hunger, and Sen's theory of entitlements captured the social, political, economic and cultural dimensions of the food system. At the heart of Sen's theory of entitlements is the idea that 'ownership of food is one of the most primitive property rights, and in each society there are rules governing this right' (Sen, 1981: 434). Hunger is understood to be a deprivation of entitlements, or 'entitlement failures' (Sen, 1981: 436), relating to not just food supply and availability but also utilisation and access.

Food security is closely linked to the right to food. The right to food was first recognised as falling into the international human rights framework by the UN in Article 25 of the Universal Declaration of Human Rights, and subsequently in Article 11 of the International Covenant on Economic, Social and Cultural Rights (ICESCR), both of which relate to the right to 'an adequate standard of living'. While there were many obstacles in recognising the right to food as a human right (Alston and Tomasevski: 1984), the right to food is legally binding on any state that has ratified the ICESCR. This right was interpreted in General Comment No 12 by the Committee on Economic, Social and Cultural Rights and thereafter defined by the UN Special Rapporteur on the Right to Food as meaning:

> The right to have regular, permanent and unrestricted access, either directly or by means of financial purchases, to quantitatively and qualitatively adequate and sufficient food corresponding to the cultural traditions of the people to which the consumer belongs, and which ensure a physical

> and mental, individual and collective, fulfilling and dignified life free from fear.

The number of undernourished people in the world has risen since 2014 and it is estimated that 821 million people were experiencing food insecurity in 2017 (FAO, 2018) and suffering capabilities deprivation. Food insecurity is not evenly distributed, mainly affecting those living in developing countries where the primary source of trade is in agricultural products. In general, the agricultural sectors in developing countries are characterised by low productivity rates and a lack of competitiveness on the international market. Hunger is on the rise in most areas of sub-Saharan Africa and South America and the 2018 FAO Report states that 'without increased efforts, there is a risk of falling far short of achieving the SDG target of hunger eradication by 2030' (FAO, 2018: xiii).

The human rights-based frameworks of the UN and FAO recognise the importance of international trade for promoting food security (SDG 2), improving rural livelihoods and creating more inclusive societies (SDG 8), but their support for international trade 'is tempered by the recognition of asymmetrical power relations where powerful food-exporting countries and several transnational agri-food companies disproportionately shape market outcomes' (Marguilis, 2013: 61). Recent data indicates that the 2030 zero-hunger target (target 2.1) will not be met unless there are significant changes to agricultural governance (FAO, 2019), including through the international trade regime.

International trading system

While the world trade system views free trade as enabling for food security, there is a tension in the literature about the role of the multilateral trading system in promoting food security. For some scholars, food insecurity results from market distortions in agricultural trade and, therefore, the role of the WTO should be to remove harmful barriers to agricultural trade liberalisation and to prevent the abuse of the trade rules, for example in relation to the export of food aid (Howse, 2016) For others, this reductivist approach to food security, which frames it merely in terms of agricultural trade liberalisation, is extremely problematic because it overlooks the social, cultural and political dimensions of food production and consumption (Orford, 2015; Scott, 2017).

The strategic orientation of the international trading system, from the GATT to the WTO, is inherently economic. The economic rationality underpinning the agricultural sector has not been superseded by rationality-oriented social or environmental concerns (Orford, 2015). Andrew Lang (2011) attributes the legal transformations of the international trading system to the intersubjective frameworks of meaning through which organisational and substantive norms and preferences are shaped and contested. He argues that the 'imagined purposes of the GATT/WTO have always been multiple' (2014: 411) and he identifies three distinct paradigm shifts in trade law: embedded liberalism, neoliberalism and post-neoliberalism. The first period of the GATT (1947–70s) reflects the embedded liberalism approach of the international order (Ruggie, 1982), which sought to balance international stability with domestic stability. The idea that economic trade liberalisation in the post-war era would foster cooperation among states at the international level and stimulate economic growth, create jobs and improve welfare at the domestic level was dominant in the thinking of this era. In this way, liberal economic policies were adopted, with the need to protect domestic welfare 'embedded' within them. In this period, 'the imagined purpose of the post-war GATT was to provide the international conditions necessary for the domestic flourishing and global projection of the Western welfare state' (Lang, 2014: 414). Where international freedom and domestic stability were in conflict, the latter would prevail. This is evident in terms of agricultural policy, which fell outside the scope of the GATT.

Lang (2011) identifies a normative reorientation, the 'neoliberal turn', towards liberalisation and away from stability from the Tokyo Round (1973) through to the post-Uruguay Round of the GATT (1986–2000). With the shift toward neoliberalism came the reimagined purpose of the GATT as a 'smooth-running political marketplace for the exchange of trade concessions' (Lang, 2014: 417). It is the purpose of the GATT and WTO Agreements to regulate and set limits on state interference in the market, with some exceptions to preserve regulatory autonomy of states, such as the General Exceptions under Article XX GATT and through sanitary and phytosanitary (SPS) standards on food safety (Report of the Appellate Body, *EC – Measures Concerning Meat and Meat Products (Hormones)* WT/DS26/AB/R of 19 January 1998). However, not all WTO members are market economies and the WTO Agreements address governments in their capacity as *regulators* of economic activities but not as *participants* in economic activities through state intervention (Du, 2014: 427). This omission becomes problematic when governments intervene in the pricing of commodities through domestic support, for example. Article XVII GATT provides limited rules on state trading enterprises but there are no rules governing the behaviour of state-owned enterprises (SOEs) and all members are free to establish SOEs should they wish to do so. While this 'ownership-neutral position' (Du, 2014: 427) stems from the recognition of state sovereignty, it becomes problematic when states disagree on what constitutes unwarranted or illegitimate state intervention.

This period brought with it an increasing focus on technical expertise coupled with the judicialisation and formalisation of legal rules and norms (Lang, 2011: 253). In the context of agriculture, it was in this period that an international regime for agricultural trade emerged. Toward the end of this period, the WTO entered its first notable legitimacy crisis. In 1999 the Seattle Ministerial Conference was a focal point for anti-globalisation protestors who sought to challenge the emerging 'constitutionalism' at the multilateral level, which was ideologically rooted in neoliberal economic programmes and which privileged corporate interests over social welfare. The inescapable connection between trade and labour standards, human rights and the environment became a point of enquiry for eminent scholars as the social purpose of the WTO was explored and contested (Petersmann, 2000; Alston, 2002; Howse, 2002; Marceau, 2002. See also Chapter 6 of this book). Ernst-Ulrich Petersmann (2000), one of the first scholars to engage with the human rights and international trade debate, proposed that the rationality of both regimes is based on the same values: individual freedom and responsibility, non-discrimination, rule of law, natural justice, promotion of social welfare through peaceful cooperation and parliamentary approval of national and international rules.

He proposed that the WTO's enforcement mechanisms could provide the optimal realisation and protection of freedom and non-discrimination (Petersmann, 2000: 20), leading to accusations of 'merger and acquisition' of human rights law (Alston, 2002). The basis for Petersmann's claim lies in the assertion that trade law and human rights law share the same ideational basis. However, his understanding of the trade:rights interface is inherently Hayekan, favouring liberalism and the protection of economic freedoms. There is, for example, no real focus on assessing the merits for the WTO's dispute settlement mechanism to analyse a dispute, which draws into question social or cultural rights, like the right to food.

To assimilate the rights arising under the WTO agreements with 'human rights' is conceptually flawed. Human rights and trade rights have fundamentally different purposes and conceptual origins. Human rights are constitutive freedoms based on the 'inherent dignity of all persons', while trade-related rights and entitlements are instrumental freedoms (Alston, 2002: 826). Trade-related rights empower individuals as economic agents but they do not confer political agency in the same way as human rights or constitutive freedoms. While the WTO legal texts do not make explicit reference to human rights, it is a primary objective of the WTO 'to produce certain market conditions which would allow ... individual activity to flourish'(Report of the Panel in *US – Section 301–310* [1999] WT/DS152/R, para 7.72–7.73). If individual activity is to flourish, to expand freedoms and promote human dignity in accordance with the normative values underpinning the SDGs, the trade rules need to be reframed in line with this ideational framework of meaning. Promoting the social, economic and environmental dimensions of sustainable development *through* trade liberalisation requires a rights-sensitive approach, but perhaps one that involves delegation or deference to other appropriate UN supervisory bodies, as proposed by Alston (2002). The next two sections of this chapter offer a critique of the (neo)liberal framing of agricultural rules, with a focus on the harmful effects of domestic agricultural farm support programmes for the realisation of food security.

The final paradigmatic shift identified by Lang is one of a post-neoliberal (re)imagination of the international trading system. In part a response to the legitimacy crisis of the WTO in the late 1990s, this period 'seeks to draw new boundaries around the operation of trade law and the trade regime, so as to ensure that WTO law does not become a mechanism for the global projection and entrenchment of a single form of state-market relations, and a single vision of appropriate and legitimate regulatory intervention' (Lang, 2011: 343). This paradigm also introduced the stated objective of the WTO that international trade should be liberalised in accordance with the principle of sustainable development (Marrakesh Agreement, 1994: Recital 1).

In 2001 the WTO officially launched the Doha Development Round, which sought to place development at the centre of the multilateral trading system's agenda. The Doha Ministerial Declaration recognises that 'international trade can play a major role in the promotion of economic development and the alleviation of poverty' (Article 1) and highlights the importance of placing the needs of developing countries at the 'heart' of the WTO's programme. In the context of agriculture, Article 13 of the Doha Ministerial Declaration (WTO, 2001) reiterates the 'long-term objective' of the WTO 'to establish a fair and market-oriented trading system through a programme of fundamental reform encompassing strengthened rules and specific commitments on support and protection in order to correct and prevent restrictions and distortions in world agricultural markets'. However, this long-term objective of the WTO will be realised only if the development needs of developing countries are taken into account.

The shift from embedded liberalism to neoliberalism has provided the architecture for the WTO rules to reinforce and perpetuate structural inequalities in agricultural trade. While the US and EU have influenced the ideational framework in which agricultural trade operates for many decades, this normative space is now being contested by emerging powers, like India and China. A rights-sensitive interpretation of the agricultural trade rules for food security requires a more nuanced understanding of the interconnections between the trade and non-trade concerns of food:

> Guaranteeing food security to a population in times of crisis requires complex political choices about the obligations of states to protect their own populations versus their obligations to protect the rights of those in need in other countries, how national communities might protect particular kinds of rural livelihoods, the forms of political action that are necessary to preserve democracy in the face of rural despair and dispossession, how states can support non-industrial approaches to agriculture, and how states might enable the survival of traditional relationships to land within their territory or jurisdiction. (Orford, 2015: 9)

In the post-neoliberal era Lang (2011: 353) calls for a 'collective moral responsibility' among WTO members through which the purpose and consequences of international trade law can be restated. While there is a legal basis for promoting sustainable agriculture at the WTO, as set out in the Doha Ministerial Declaration, the political will to give meaning to this objective has been lacking. Ultimately, the conflicting agendas of WTO members in relation to agricultural trade liberalisation has led to the collapse of the Doha Development Round altogether. It is now in its 16th year and is regarded widely as an irretrievable failure (Howse, 2016; Scott, 2017).

Shifting paradigms of agricultural trade liberalisation

Agricultural trade policy has been a story of 'institutionalising inquality' (Gonzalez, 2002). As the organisation moved from the GATT to the WTO, the political economy of agricultural trade policy has undergone a number of transformative shifts. Agricultural negotiations have a long history of being protracted in nature, in part, because domestic agricultural producers blocked efforts to liberalise markets (Thies, 2001: 403). In the pre-GATT era the first notable period of agricultural protectionism occurred in the late 1870s, in response to a general depression that followed the expansion of wheat and livestock markets in the Americas and Australia (McCalla, 1969: 332). Preferential treatment for liberalisation of agricultural trade can be traced as far back as the 1920 Havana Charter establishing the International Trade Organization. Agricultural and fisheries products were excluded from the general elimination of quantitative restrictions (Article 20.2(c) Havana Charter, 1920) and, while export subsidies were eliminated for all other commodities, agricultural export subsidies were permitted (Articles 26–28 Havana Charter, 1920). The cumulative effect of this 'special' treatment was to protect domestic agricultural markets and buffer them from the gains and losses associated with the international reduction of tariffs.

Shaping agricultural trade norms

Exceptionalism was a prominent feature of the GATT era. Import quotas known as 'quantitative restrictions' are prohibited under Article XI GATT, but in 1951 a GATT Working Group found that the US had been imposing import quotas on dairy products. This was a clear violation of Article XI GATT. However, the US Congress passed a domestic law, Section 22 of the Agricultural Adjustment Act, which enabled the import quotas on agricultural goods where this was necessary to avoid interference with domestic production (Schoenbaum, 2011: 1168). Section 22 was to be applied notwithstanding existing commitments under international agreements, including the GATT, and the US sought a waiver under the GATT rules. Agriculture has enjoyed a special status in the international trading system, but it would be misleading to say that agriculture fell outside the GATT disciplines altogether (Bureau et al, 2019: 5). Article XXVI:3, which sets out the disciplines on subsidies, provided that states could subsidise 'primary products' for export, provided that the provision of such subsidy did not result in the state having 'more than an equitable share of world export trade in that product'. What constitutes 'more than an equitable share of world export trade' is not defined by the GATT, nor in the Interpretive Note to Article XVI. However, and in short, this provision constituted permission to use export subsidies for agriculture – and not other sectors – provided they were not *too* distortive.

A radical transformation to the architecture of agricultural governance emerged in the Uruguay Round negotiations (Clark et al, 2000).

The Uruguay Round (1986–94) had a broader agenda than previous rounds, as it invited negotiation on trade in services, investment and agriculture for the very first time. In relation to agriculture, Margulis attributes this normative shift to the changing ideational perspectives of the US and EU, both of which were 'fiscally exhausted in part by massive agricultural subsidy programmes from a prolonged transatlantic food trade war' (2014: 330). The shift in agricultural policy was not, therefore, a response to illiberal practices of WTO members like the EU and Japan but, rather, it was a response to exogenous shocks, including the food crisis of 1972–74.

The US and EU effectively insulated their markets from liberalisation for a long period of time, but the conflict between the two trading nations became more pronounced when the EU (then the European Community (EC)) began its enlargement process, bringing more countries under its controversial Common Agricultural Policy (CAP). With the ongoing enlargement of the bloc there have been subsequent treaties and amendments; in terms of agriculture, the most significant of these amendments in the GATT era was the Maastricht Treaty. Article 38 of the Maastricht Treaty codifies the CAP in EU law and empowered the European Commission to negotiate on behalf of the EU in the GATT trade talks. The CAP was established in 1962 as a mode of protection against global market fluctuations and support of regional farm incomes through high product prices. The US criticised the accession process in the EC because there had been no Article XXIV:6 GATT negotiations in accordance with GATT protocol. If the prescribed negotiations under Article XXIV:6 GATT had been held, it would be for the purpose of discussing compensatory measures for the losses incurred to other trading members as a result of the EC enlargement process.

The EU had been dependent on its colonial lands for raw materials, including primary agricultural commodities (Orford, 2015). In this respect, the CAP symbolised capabilities deprivation in developing countries for the enhancement of freedoms in the EU member states. Introducing the CAP, a programme of domestic support that heavily subsidises agricultural production to stabilise supply, enabled the member states to become increasingly self-sufficient. With the accession of Eastern European countries the agricultural commodities produced in the EU was vastly diversifying, and therefore the focus of the CAP shifted to rural development and supply management (Fransden and Walter-Jørgensen, 2006: 35). In the early 1990s the EU was forced to reconsider its position on agriculture and the CAP in light of the integration of agriculture into the multilateral trading negotiations of the GATT. As a result of both internal and external pressures to reform, the EU revised the CAP, using the proposals submitted during the GATT negotiations as a guideline. The revision, known as the McSharry reform, was brought into force in 1993 and was implemented in two successive reforms known as Agenda 2000 and the CAP 2003 reform, also known as the Mid-term Review. The Mid-term Review was centred on bringing the expenditure of the CAP within the budgetary confines of the EU and, in addition, it promotes the inclusion of a more accommodating policy for developing countries. Arguably, the most 'radical and innovative' initiative under the Mid-term Review was the decoupling of some direct support programmes from production (Gersfelt and Jensen, 2006: 59).

In the US, agricultural and food policy is largely determined by Congress through the 'Farm Bill' – a comprehensive omnibus legislation reviewed every five years. The first farm bill, the Agriculture Adjustment Act 1933, paved the way for Congress to set out the programmes and measures available to domestic farmers. Over the years, the US farm bills have courted controversy for their distortive market effects. Support to US farmers is provided through a range of financial and non-financial measures, and, while government expenditure on subsidies accounted to only 15% of the US Department of Agriculture spending in 2018 (Smith, 2018: 3), the use of market access tools like tariffs and quotas has enabled the US to protect its agricultural market (Sumner, 2018). When introducing the proposed revisions to US agricultural policy, representatives of Congress often depict a bleak economic outlook for domestic production. In other words, the justification for agricultural exceptionalism is the avoidance of capabilities deprivation in the domestic setting. For example, the 2002 Farm Bill, which was implemented shortly after the launch of the Doha Round, increased domestic support on the protectionist grounds of 'national security' for the purposes of 'ensuring a safe, abundant, and affordable domestic food supply' (Orden, 2006: 80). In 2017 one Congressman sought to justify domestic support programmes on the basis that 'there is a real potential here for a crisis in rural America' (Smith, 2018: 5).

Arguably, the EU and US respective positions on the provision of agricultural support may appear to enhance the freedoms, capabilities and entitlements of domestic agricultural workers and consumers. However, in reality the beneficiaries of these measures tend to be large agri-processing companies, like Coca-Cola, for whom corn-syrup is a major ingredient in its soda products (Bujalski, 2016). The US programme for domestic support favours production by corporate mega-farms, often to the detriment of small and medium-sized farms. For decades, the four largest grain traders – ADM, Bunge, Cargill and Dreyfus – have benefited from US farm policies. However, the recent crisis of liberal internationalism has brought unexpected challenges for these mega-farms. In response to the Trump administration raising tariffs on imported goods from China, the Chinese government cross-retaliated by levying higher tariffs on soybeans and corn. This raised the price of US commodities and resulted in a temporary decrease of soybeans exported to China and, although US trade has now recovered, the trade war signals a shift in global agricultural export patterns (*The Economist*, 2018).

Distorting agricultural markets

The Agreement on Agriculture (AoA) internationalised agricultural trade policy and introduced legally binding commitments in relation to tariffs and subsidies. Arguably, the Uruguay Round 'ushered in a new equilibrium in the institutional nature of the WTO' because agriculture now formed part of multilateral trade negotiations (Thies, 2001: 401). Introducing agriculture governance at the WTO level in the AoA enabled the US and EU to dictate the terms of international trade and to shape it to their vision. The AoA is structured around modalities of agricultural trade: export competition, domestic support (subsidies) and market access (tariffs and tariff-quotas). Non-trade concerns, such as special and differential treatment for developing countries and Least Developed Countries, also form part of the negotiating modalities.

The AoA sets out disciplines on market access in Article 4 and Article 5. Article 4.2 AoA requires that all agricultural customs duties be 'converted into ordinary customs duties'. This process, known as 'tariffication', requires the elimination of non-tariff barriers at the border – like quantitative restrictions – which are then converted into tariffs that can be included within a member's schedule of concessions. The purpose of tariffication was to improve transparency, with the goal that 'ordinary customs duties would, in principle, become the only form of border protection' (*Peru – Additional Duty on the Imports of Certain Agricultural Products* WT/DS457/AB/R adopted on 31 July 2015, para 5.38). Tariff-rate quotas (TRQs) are now used to enable members to protect their markets. TRQs operate by allowing a certain volume of imports in at a lower tariff, and once that quantity has been exceeded, the higher tariff is imposed.

Domestic support refers to financial aid programmes to farmers for either product-specific support or non-product-specific support.

Agricultural subsidies include both agricultural domestic support measures and export subsidies. Domestic support is a particularly contentious aspect of agricultural trade. The disciplines on domestic support are set out in Articles 3, 6 and 7 AoA and collectively they set out a classificatory system for protectionist policies, including trade-distorting measures, with members establishing a binding level of support using the Aggregate Measurement of Support (AMS). In brief, the AMS provides a system of measuring the distortion of domestic support and classifies the policies into three distinct categories or 'boxes' analogous to a traffic-light system: green box, blue box and amber box.

Green box expenditures are those that 'have no, or at most minimal trade-distorting effects or effects on production' (Annex 2 AoA), while blue box expenditures are granted to farmers to limit their production. Blue box expenditure includes direct payments with production-limiting characteristics and trade-distorting policies that fall below the *de minimus* levels set out in the AMS. The AMS refers to the annual level of financial support given to a particular agricultural product by the state and is considered to be a 'trade distorting subsidy'. As the purpose of the AoA is to eradicate trade-distorting measures, each WTO member scheduled their levels of AMS in a country-specific Schedule at the time of the Uruguay Round negotiation. The value of the support is taken for the period 1986–88. The AoA does not set a limit on green box or blue box expenditures.

Amber box expenditures, on the other hand, are defined in Article 6 AoA as support prices or subsidies related to production quantity. Amber box policies are the most trade-distorting measures and include those measures for which members have reduction commitments. WTO members have agreed to reduce the level of domestic support in the agricultural sector of trade and their reduction commitments are detailed in Part IV of the Schedule. The use of AMS is generally limited to WTO negotiations with regard to compliance with reduction commitments. However, at the time the AMS was determined, many developing countries did not schedule any trade-distorting domestic support, and, therefore, this limits the extent to which domestic support can be offered to the 10% prescribed by the AoA (Diaz-Bonilla, 2014: 6). Developed countries, on the other hand, scheduled a substantial amount of trade-distorting domestic support within the AMS at the time of the Uruguay Round negotiations and this has led to a significant power imbalance and asymmetry between agricultural exporting countries in the global North and global South (South Centre, 2015).

Export competition, the second pillar of the agricultural modalities, includes financial contributions from the state to stimulate agricultural production for export in the form of export subsidies, export credits, agricultural state trading enterprises and international food aid. Articles 9 and 10 of the AoA set out the members' commitments in relation to trade-distorting export subsidies. For the 2018 fiscal year the US spent nearly USD 7 billion, or 30% of total spending on agricultural programmes, on conservation subsidies and expenditures on research and development (Smith, 2018: 4). These are classified as green box payments, and therefore do not count toward US commitments on AMS. A similar amount was dedicated to federal crop insurance (approximately USD 7 billion) and programmes for agricultural risk coverage and price loss coverage (approximately USD 8 billion), with support primarily directed to three commodities: corn, soybeans and wheat (Smith, 2018: 4).

There is some overlap between WTO disciplines, since domestic support is also covered in the Agreement on Subsidies and Countervailing Duties (SCM Agreement). This agreement addresses specific subsidies for all non-agricultural commodities. While the SCM Agreement stipulates that export subsidies on non-agricultural products are expressly prohibited, the rules in relation to agricultural products and export subsidies are more ambiguous. The SCM Agreement prohibition on export subsidies applies on agricultural subsidies with the exception of those specified in the US Uruguay Round Agreements Act (URAA), such as bona fide food aid. In basic terms, an export subsidy is a subsidy contingent upon export performance, albeit the subsidy may be contingent *de jure* or *de facto* (Article 3 SCM Agreement). Where a subsidy is contingent *de jure* this will be evidenced either explicitly from, or 'derived from necessary implication from the words actually used in the measure' of, the relevant legal instrument or legislation (*Canada-Autos* WT/DS142/AB/R of 31 May 2000, para 100). However, *de facto* contingency must be inferred from the cumulative configuration of the facts surrounding the grant of the export subsidy. In other words, there must be a 'close connection' or nexus between the granting of the subsidy and the export performance.

It is,therefore necessary to distinguish between export subsidies applied to agricultural products listed in Section II of Part IV of a member's GATT Schedule of Concessions and export subsidies applied to agricultural products that are not listed within the Schedule. This distinction is important for three fundamental reasons. First, the export subsidies applied to agricultural products listed in the Schedule are subject to reduction commitments. Twenty-five WTO members are permitted to subsidise agricultural exports, but only within prescribed limits. The reduction commitments were negotiated by the members at a level of 36% by value and 21% by volume for developed countries and 24% by value and 14% by volume for developing countries. Second, WTO members cannot apply export subsidies that are not listed in the URAA where such action may threaten or lead to circumvention of export subsidy commitments, as this would constitute a violation of Article 9 of the AoA. Finally, members may not employ export subsidies on those agricultural products which are not listed in the relevant parts of their Schedule.

In the Uruguay Round the US refused to categorise its own export credit system as an export subsidy. This creates problems, particularly in regard to the provision of food aid, which can contribute to food security. The US export credit system guarantees financing of domestic agricultural commodities but does not fall within the discipline of Article 9.1. URAA, and therefore the US does not have reduction commitments in respect of export credits. Furthermore, in accordance with Article 10.2. URAA the US stated that export credits are not considered export subsidies within the plain language of the URAA. Article 10.2. URAA states that 'members undertake to work toward the development of internationally agreed disciplines to govern the provision of export credits, export credit guarantees or insurance programmes and, after agreement on such disciplines, to provide export credits, export credit guarantees or insurance programmes only in conformity therewith'.

Following the *US-Upland Cotton* case the Appellate Body explicitly confirmed the Panel's ruling that export credits are 'a *per se* export subsidy' (WT/DS267/AB/R of 3 March 2005, para 7.869) within the meaning of the SCM Agreement and therefore should be correctly classified as prohibited export subsidies under Article 3.1. SCM Agreement. The Appellate Body provided further clarification on when an agricultural export credit is an export subsidy. In essence, there must be an export subsidy component to the export credit in order for the measure to fall within the scope of the URAA (WT/DS267/AB/R of 3 March 2005, at para 68). Thus, not all export credits will necessarily constitute an export subsidy per se. In the particular case of *US-Upland Cotton* it was found that export credits in relation to cotton did amount to prohibited export subsidies, and as a result the US had failed to comply with its obligations under Part V of the AoA. It is somewhat of a paradox that the export credit system of the US is now openly considered an export subsidy and yet the US has failed to implement reduction commitments for export credits for decades.

Agricultural trade liberalisation for food security

Food security falls under the AoA, but not as a core discipline. Rather, it is 'subsidiary' to the overarching goals of the agreement (Margulis, 2014: 330). Preambular recital 6 notes that the legally binding commitments set out under the AoA 'should be made in an equitable way among all Members, having regard to non-trade concerns, including food security and the need to protect the environment'. Article 20 AoA provides that 'non-trade concerns, special and differential treatment to developing country Members, and the objective to establish a fair and market-oriented agricultural trading system' should form part of the reform process for agricultural trade. However, the AoA does not define what constitutes 'non-trade concerns'. Furthermore, Article X AoA, which deals with the circumvention of rules relating to export subsidies, explicitly refers to food aid which is closely connected to food security. Furthermore, public stockholding for food security purposes is an exemption to the reduction of legally binding commitments on domestic support set out in Article 3 of Annex 2 AoA. Overall, it is evident that the AoA embeds the liberal market approach that the 'removal of state support for and protection of agricultural production is the best way to achieve food security in the longer term' (Orford, 2015: 55).

The lack of a shared intersubjective meaning of what constitutes fairness in the agricultural trade rules is evidenced in the various reform proposals submitted to the Committee on Agriculture since the mid-2000s. In 2001 the Doha Round was launched with the intention of concluding the matters left unresolved in the Uruguay Round. One of the most significant actors in the Uruguay Round was the Cairns Group of Fair Trading Nations (Cairns Group), which is a coalition of 19 diverse agricultural exporting countries, founded in 1986. Although the group is not comprised of similarly situated countries in development terms, their success comes from a shared commitment to the pursuit of a single policy: agriculture. In the early stages of the negotiations for agricultural reform at the WTO, the Cairns Group proposed that export subsidies and export competition measures should be eliminated for all agricultural products (Cairns Group: 2000). This proposal noted the concerns of the Cairns Group, namely that 'export subsidies force [developing countries] to compete with the richest treasuries, contributing to increased rural poverty, the swelling of overcrowded cities, and the promotion of social unrest' (Cairns Group, 2000).

The Doha Round

Typically, a trade negotiation round should last a few years, but the Doha Round negotiations have yet to be concluded. The Doha Ministerial Declaration outlined the broad consensus of the members and set out the general objectives for the current negotiating round but the Doha *acquis* was narrowed and clarified through a number of negotiating stages between 2003 and 2005. A major stumbling block to the negotiations has been agriculture. The global food crisis of 2008, which saw the disruption to global food supplies as a result of volatile price spikes, widened the divide between small-scale farmers and multinational corporations, since small-scale producers, unlike multinational agri-businesses, were unable to profit from the higher prices (Margulis, 2014). Procurement prices for food security stocks – which would appear to fall within the scope of Article 20 AoA – have been a challenge for WTO members. While food security is not a new issue, the context in which countries are experiencing food security has changed. Historically, food security was understood in the context of low food prices, but since the 2007–08 food crisis and 2008 financial crisis, food security has been framed in the context of higher prices and price volatility (Diaz-Bonilla, 2014).

Developing countries and their negotiating coalitions, including the Africa Group and the G33, have proposed amendments to the AoA. In the Doha negotiations developing countries proposed including Footnote 5 of Annex 2 (becoming Annex B of Rev 4), which excluded the 'acquisition of stocks of foodstuffs by developing country Members with the objective of supporting low-income or resource-poor producers' from the AMS. However, this was not included. As part of the revised draft Modalities, developing countries then fought for the inclusion of a 'Food Security Box' (WTO, 2008b TN/AG/W/4/Rev 4 of 6 December 2008). The 2008 Draft Modalities, which are not legally binding on the members and cannot be the subject of dispute settlement, were not accepted by the members, but some of the proposals were raised again in the negotiations leading up to the Bali Ministerial Conference.

For the first time since the launch of the Doha Round in 2001, the WTO members concluded comprehensive multilateral agreements in the Bali Ministerial Conference. As part of the Bali package, members concluded agreements in respect of a number of issues relating to agriculture. Notably, among these issues are public stockholding for food security purposes and the decision to eliminate export subsidies. The decision to eliminate export subsidies and export measures with equivalent effect ('export competition') pursuant to Article 20 AoA gives effect to the objective set out in the 2005 Hong Kong Declaration.

Public stockholding for food security purposes

Public stockholding for food security purposes represents a site of contestation between the rights-based approach to food security and the rational strategic orientation of the international trade rules. The so-called Bali Package set out commitments to negotiate on various aspects of international trade, and this chapter will focus only on the public stockholding issue (WTO Ministerial Declaration, 'Public Stockholding for Food Security Purposes' WT/MIN(13)/W/10). Public stockholding of agricultural commodities has been a response to rising food prices as countries seek to protect their own domestic production.

Many developing countries have public stockholding programmes in place. Article 3 of Annex 2 AoA provides that public stockholding for food security purposes is exempt from the rules on domestic support. It provides that 'Expenditures (or revenue foregone) in relation to the accumulation and holding of stocks of products which form an integral part of a food security programme are identified in national legislation. This may include government aid to private storage of products as part of such a programme.' Footnote 5 to Article 3 stipulates that:

> governmental stockholding programmes for food security purposes in developing countries whose operation is transparent and conducted in accordance with officially published objective criteria or guidelines shall be considered to be in conformity with the provisions of this paragraph, including programmes under which stocks of foodstuffs for food security purposes are acquired and released at administered prices, provided that the difference between the acquisition price and the external reference price is accounted for in the AMS.

In the lead-up to the 2013 Bali Ministerial Conference, the G33 submitted a proposal that included expenditure for public stockholding for food security and food aid as green box measures – in other words, such expenditure would be exempt from the AMS methodology. Under the proposal, procurement of food for food security purchases would need to be paid at market value (that is, not a preferential rate), but the food can be sold at subsidised prices on the domestic market to confer greater availability of food to the poor and rural communities. If the agricultural product was not purchased at the market value, and instead the state procured the product at 'administered prices', then the difference between the purchase price and the external reference price will be accounted for in the AMS (Diaz-Bonilla, 2014: 7). It is important to note that the 'external reference price' referred to in the AoA relates to the prices of goods in 1986–88. Using this reference period makes 'no economic sense' (South Centre, 2015: 5) because it fails to take into account price inflation that has subsequently taken place.

India, a member of the G33 and a country that has implemented domestic legislation for public stockholding, was concerned that this proposal would push it beyond its permitted levels of support under the AMS. Food procured at 'administered' or minimum prices is considered to be trade-distorting subsidy under the WTO legal framework and, since developing countries have a zero-AMS entitlement, developing countries can grant subsidies only to a value of 10% percent of the value of an agricultural product, within the rules of the AoA. By contrast, developed countries can grant subsidies to a value stipulated in the levels of the AMS plus a further 5% (Article 6(4) of Part IV AoA). Furthermore, India argued that the differential between the administered price and the external reference price does not accurately reflect the current trading reality and would give a distorted figure. In its 2015 Analytical Note the South Centre presents a useful example of trade distortion:

> In Kenya, maize fetched USD 100 per Ton on average during 1986, 1987 and 1988. Its current administered price is around USD 400. Thus, the Agreement on Agriculture considers that the government provides a trade-distorting subsidy of USD 300 per Ton of maize. If the government does not set a clear purchasing limit well in advance of the planting season, USD 300 needs to be multiplied by total production.
>
> Kenya's annual maize production is around 3.3 million Tons. Thus, according to the Agreement on Agriculture, Kenya provides a 'trade-distorting' subsidy of 990 million, close to USD 1 billion, to its maize farmers. Kenya's maize production equals roughly USD 750 million (in 2010), i.e. Kenya has a 'de minimis' of trade-distorting domestic supports of USD 75 million. The country is therefore in violation of its WTO commitments. (South Centre, 2015: 6)

However, while the AoA assumes the administered price to be trade distortive in many developing countries, it can be low (South Centre, 2015). Instead, India wanted to adjust the reference prices for inflation and relied on Article 18.4 AoA, which provides that members give 'due consideration to the influence of excessive rates of inflation on the ability of any Member to abide by its domestic support commitments' when reviewing the implementation of their commitments. In the months leading up to the MC9 (9th Ministerial Conference), tensions were growing among WTO members. In November 2013 India stepped away from the negotiating position of the G33 in relation to food security. Ultimately, it was this decisive step that stalled the pre-Bali negotiations (Wilkinson et al, 2014).

The outcome of the Bali Ministerial Conference was to adopt the Ministerial Decision (WT/MIN(13)/W/10) on Public Stockholding for Food Security Purposes, also known as the 'Peace Clause'. This will operate as an interim measure until a permanent solution has been concluded. On 24 November 2015, in advance of the Nairobi Ministerial Conference, the G33 presented a revised proposal on agriculture which would see a new annex, Annex 6, included in the AoA (WT/MIN(15)/W/22). Under this proposal, programmes for public stockholding for food security purposes would be exempt from AMS. Australia, Paraguay and Canada put forward an alternative proposal which would see the Peace Clause used as the basis for a permanent solution. However, the US has rejected the proposals of the G33 (South Centre, 2015: 10). While the G33 proposal for reform would constitute a 'significant contribution to the improvement of international trade rules for food security' (South Centre, 2015: 11), the framing of the Peace Clause is arguably narrow.

WTO members agreed to the Peace Clause on the basis that the developing countries had concluded negotiations on the Trade Facilitation Agreement. Ideational division remains pronounced in relation to the other two pillars of agricultural trade: domestic support and market access. Arguably, 'the splits that emerged within developing country coalitions ... actually eroded their collective bargaining power' (Wilkinson et al, 2014: 1034). Furthermore, the WTO members abandoned the single undertaking in the Nairobi Ministerial Conference (2015). This means that other aspects of international trade can be negotiated without agreement on agricultural trade having been achieved. Revising the negotiating principles of the WTO will have profound implications for agriculture, as members have relied on the single undertaking as a mechanism for protecting negotiating space (Scott, 2017: 1167).

A permanent solution to the issue of public stockholding has yet to be found. It is not clear what bearing the outcome of the recent US–China grains dispute (*China – Domestic Support for Agricultural Producers* WT/DS511/R of 28 February 2019) will have on the future of agricultural trade negotiations, particularly in relation to public stockholding for food security purposes. This dispute related to China's use of domestic support in excess of its *de minimis* level for producers of wheat, Indica rice, Japonica rice and corn in the period 2012–15. The panel confirmed that the appropriate methodology for calculating the AMS is that set out in the AoA using the reference period 1986–88. On 15 March 2019, Guatemala requested consultations with India (DS581) in relation to domestic price support, which it claims exceeds the *de minimis* level of 10%, on sugar and sugar cane.

At the 10th Ministerial Conference, held in Nairobi (2015), WTO members adopted the Export Competition Decision (WT/MIN(15)/45), under which all export competition and measures with equivalent effect are to be eliminated. Members have agreed to eliminate their scheduled export subsidies commitments from the Uruguay Round, but in its 2016 submission to the WTO the Cairns Group (G/AG/W/153: para 1.10) identified gaps in the notifications to the Committee on Agriculture by WTO members. As a consequence, it is difficult to get a clear sense of how distorted agricultural markets remain. Since the close of the 10th Ministerial Conference multilateral negotiations have all but been suspended, at the cost of 'two decades of political paralysis' (Howse, 2016: 10).

Overall, this signals that the targets under SDG 2 are unlikely to be met unless meaningful reforms to the agricultural trading system are made. The absence of civil society actors who might advance the rights-sensitive approach to food security further exacerbates the notion that agriculture should be treated differently to other sectors. Unlike other sectors of trade, like intellectual property and services, corporations have been excluded from shaping the rules on agricultural trade (Margulis, 2014: 325). Furthermore, key actors like non-governmental organisations and civil society have traditionally fallen outside the negotiating remit of the WTO. That being said, there has been an increased willingness to engage civil society on trade matters, as evidenced in the submissions of *amicus curiae* briefs in the recent *Australia – Plain Packaging* dispute (WT/DS467/R of 20 June 2018). However, for the meantime, it seems that the narrative of agricultural exceptionalism, and capabilities deprivations, remains.

Conclusion

This chapter has examined the role for the WTO in promoting sustainable agricultural governance in the framework of SDG 2. It has shown that agriculture remains a site of normative contestation for WTO members. However, bridging the ideational divide between the strategic orientation of the international trading system and the SDGs requires the inter-institutional dynamic between the WTO and UN specialised agencies to be strengthened. SDG 17 provides the opportunity for developing and fostering intersubjective meanings relating to the other goals. Although the SDGs are framed around three dimensions – social, economic and environmental – an inter-institutional approach should also recognise the cultural dimension of food security. Food and its production can have a cultural significance to societies that differs from other sectors of the economy, and this is obscured by the formalistic rules of the international trading system (Scott, 2017: 1170). Uncertainty surrounds the extent to which adequate protection for the cultural dimensions of food security can be achieved through the General Exceptions under Article XX and SPS rules. While there is no real sense of how SDG 17 will be operationalised in practice to further trade liberalisation for food security, political will must be shown not only by international institutions but also by the WTO members themselves.

In recent years the WTO and its members have demonstrated a more cooperative approach to agricultural governance, and modest reforms promise to narrow the gap between the domestic support given to agri-processing in the global North and the global South. The collective outcomes of the WTO Ministerial Conferences at Bali (2013) and Nairobi (2015) have marked a small but progressive shift in the governance of agricultural trade at the multilateral level. Members have agreed to eliminate agricultural export subsidies, to permit public stockholding for food security and to discuss the implementation of a special safeguard mechanism for developing countries. The preceding analysis has shown that the rules on international trade liberalisation favour a liberal market approach to food security. This approach has not enhanced the freedoms and capabilities of individuals equitably. Rather, it has reinforced long-existing structural inequalities. This chapter has argued for the reimagination of the trading system as an institutional setting of collective responsibility that seeks to redress the harmful effects of the trade rules. To take seriously the demands of food security, and the redistribution of global public goods, we must try to prevent these harms (Christensen, 2017).

References

Alston, P. (2002) 'Resisting the merger and acquisition of human rights by trade law: a reply to Petersmann', *European Journal of International Law* 13: 815–44.

Alston, P. (2005) 'Ships passing in the night: the current state of the human rights and development debate seen through the lens of the Millennium Development Goals', *Human Rights Quarterly* 27: 755–89.

Alston, P. and Tomasevski, K. (1984) *The Right to Food*, the Hague: Martinus Nijhoff Publishers.

Bailé, J. et al (2017) 'Agriculture and food global value chains in sub-Saharan Africa: does bilateral trade policy impact on backward and forward participation?', IMT Lucca EIC Working Paper Series 03, February.

Bouët, A. et al (2005) 'Multilateral agricultural trade liberalisation : the contrasting forturnes of developing countries in the Doha Round', *World Economy* 28: 1329–54.

Brouwer, F. (ed) (2004) *Sustaining Agriculture and the Rural Environment: Governance, Policy and Multifunctionality*, Cheltenham: Edward Elgar.

Bujalski, J. (2016) 'The agricultural subsidy and how it affects you', *Fordham Political Review*, 24 October.

Bureau, J.C., Guimbard, H. and Jean, S. (2019) 'Agricultural trade liberalisation in the 21st century: has it been done before?', *Journal of Agricultural Economics* 70: 3–25.

Cairns Group (2000) 'Negotiating Proposal on Export Competition', G/AG/NG/W/11 of 16 June.

Christensen, J. (2017) *Trade Justice*, Oxford: Oxford University Press.

Clark, W.R., Duchesne, E. and Meunier, S. (2000) 'Domestic and international asymmetries in United States–European Union trade negotiations', *International Negotiation* 5: 69–95.

Deacon, B. (2016) 'SDGs, Agenda 2030 and the prospects for transformative social policy and social development', *Journal of International and Comparative Social Policy* 32: 79–82.

De Schutter, O. (2014) 'Report of the Special Rapporteur on the Right to Food', United Nations Human Rights Council Final Report, A/HRC/25/57.

Diaz-Bonilla, E. (2014) 'Agricultural Trade and Food Security: Some Thoughts about a Continuous Debate,' *E15Initiative*. Geneva: International Centre for Trade and Sustainable Development (ICTSD) and World Economic Forum.

Diaz-Bonilla, E., Frandsen, S. and Robinson, S. (eds) (2006) *WTO Negotiations and Agricultural Trade Liberalisation: The Effect of Developed Countries' Policies on Developing Countries*, Oxon: CABI International.

Du, M. (2014) 'China's state capitalism and world trade law', *International and Comparative Law Quarterly* 63: 409–48.

Economist, The (2018) 'Zero sum grain: trade war has given merchants a boost', *The Economist,* 13 December.

FAO (2018) 'The state of agricultural commodity markets 2018: agricultural trade, climate change, and food security', Rome: FAO.

FAO (2003) 'Trade Reforms and Food Security: Conceptualizing the Linkages' Rome: FAO.

FAO, IFAD, UNICEF, WFP and WHO (2018) *The State of Food Security and Nutrition in the World: Building Climate Resilience for Food Security and Nutrition*, Rome: FAO.

Frandsen, S. and Walter-Jørgensen, A. (2006) 'Review of the European Union Common Agricultural Policy', in Díaz-Bonilla, E., Frandsen, S. and Robinson, S. (eds), (2006) *WTO Negotiations and Agricultural Trade Liberalisation: The Effect of Developed Countries' Policies on Developing Countries*, Oxon: CABI International.

Fukuda-Parr, S. (2016) 'From the Millennium Development Goals to the Sustainable Development Goals: shifts in purpose, concept, and politics of global goal setting for development', *Gender & Development* 24: 43–52.

Fukuda-Parr, S. et al (2014) 'The power of numbers: a critical review of Millennium Development Goal targets for human development and human rights', *Journal of Human Development and Capabilities* 15L: 105–17.

Fukuda-Parr, S. and Hulme, D. (2011) 'International norm dynamics and "the end of poverty": understanding the millennium development goals', *Global Governance* 17(1): 17–36.

Gammage, C. (2019) '(Re)Imagining the trade-labour linkage: the capabilities approach', in Langille, B (ed), *The Capability Approach to Labour Law*, Oxford: Oxford University Press.

Gersfelt, B. and Jensen, H. (2006) 'The Common Agricultural Policy in an enlarged Europe: bright or bleak prospects for Africa', in Díaz-Bonilla, E., Frandsen, S. and Robinson, S. (eds), *WTO Negotiations and Agricultural Trade Liberalisation: The Effect of Developed Countries' Policies on Developing Countries*, Oxon: CABI International.

Ghale, Y. et al (2018) 'Gender dimensions of food security, the right to food and food sovereignty in Nepal', *Journal of International Women's Studies* 19: 15–31.

Gill, S. (2000) 'Toward a postmodern prince? The battle of Seattle as a moment in the new politics of globalisation', *Millennium: Journal of International Studies*, 29: 131–40.

Giménez, E.H. and Shattuck, A. (2011) 'Food crises, food regimes, and food movements: rumblings of reform or tides of transformation?', *Journal of Peasant Studies* 38, 109–44.

Gonzalez, C. (2002) 'Institutionalising inequality: The WTO Agreement on Agriculture, Food Security, and Developing Countries', *Columbia Journal of Environmental Law* 27: 433–90.

Horner, R. and Nadvi, K. (2018) 'Global value chains and the global South: unpacking twenty-first century polycentric trade', *Global Networks* 18: 207–37.

Howse, R. (2002) 'Human rights in the WTO: whose rights, what humanity? Comment on Petersmann', *European Journal of International Law* 13: 651–9.

Howse, R. (2016) 'The World Trade Organisation 20 years on: global governance by judiciary', *European Journal of International Law* 27: 10.

Ikenberry, C.J. (2018) 'The end of the liberal international order?' *International Affairs* 94: 7-23.

Kennedy, K.C. (2001) 'Reforming farm trade in the next round of the WTO multilateral trade negotiations', *Journal of World Trade* 35: 1061–79.

Lang, A. (2011) *World Trade Law After Neoliberalism: Re-Imagining the Global Economic Order*, Oxford: Oxford University Press.

Lang, A.T.F. (2014) 'World trade law after neoliberalism,' *Social and Legal Studies* 23: 408–26.

Lang, T. and Barling, D. (2012) 'Food security and food sustainability: reformulating the debate', *The Geographical Journal* 178: 313–26.

Marceau, G. (2002) 'WTO dispute settlement and human rights', *European Journal of International Law* 13: 753–814.

Margulis, M. (2013) 'The regime complex for food security: implications for the global hunger challenge', *Global Governance* 19: 53–67.

Margulis, M. (2014) 'Trading out of the global food crisis? The World Trade Organisation and the geopolitics of food security', *Geopolitics* 19: 322–50.

Marrakesh Agreement Establishing the World Trade Organization, 15 April 1994, 1867 U.N.T.S. 154

McCalla, A. (1969) 'Protectionism in international agricultural trade: 1850–1968', *Agricultural History* 43: 329–44.

Mechlem, K. (2004) 'Food security and the right to food in the discourse of the United Nations', *European Law Journal* 10: 631–48.

Minju, K. and Hyo-Young, L. (2017) 'Looking beyond the Doha Negotiations: a possible reform of the WTO Agricultural Subsidies Rules', *Asian Journal of WTO & International Health Law & Policy* 12: 171–200.

Montemayor, R. (2014) 'Public stockholding for food security purposes: scenarios and options for a permanent solution', ICTSD Issue Paper No 51.

Narlikar, A. (2017) 'India's role in global governance: a Modi-fication?', *International Affairs* 93: 93–111.

Nussbaum, M. (2011) *Creating Capabilities*, Cambridge, MA: Belknap Press Harvard University.

OECD (2008) *Multifunctionality in Agriculture: Evaluating the Degree of Jointness, Policy Implications*, Paris: OECD Publishing.

Orden, D. (2006) 'US agricultural trade policy: the 2002 Farm Bill and WTO Doha Round proposals', in Diaz-Bonilla, E., Frandsen, S. and Robinson, S. (eds), *WTO Negotiations and Agricultural Trade Liberalisation: The Effect of Developed Countries' Policies on Developing Countries*, Oxon: CABI International.

Orford, A. (2015) 'Food security, free trade, and the battle for the state,' *Journal of International Law and International Relations* 11: 1-67.

Petersmann, E. (2000) 'The WTO constitution and human rights', *Journal of International Economic Law* 3(1): 19–25.

Pogge, T. and Sengupta, M. (2015) 'The Sustainable Development Goals (SDGs) as drafted: nice idea, poor execution', *Washington International Law Journal* 24: 571–87.

Ruggie, J. (1982) 'International regimes, transactions and change: embedded liberalism in the postwar economic order', *International Organization* 36: 379–415.

Schleifer, P. and Sun, Y. (2018) 'Emerging markets and private governance: the political economy of sustainable palm oil in China and India', *Review of International Political Economy* 25: 190–214.

Schoenbaum, T. (2011) 'Fashioning a new regime for agricultural trade: new issues for the global food crisis', *Journal of International Economic Law* 14: 593–611.

Scott, J. (2017) 'The future of agricultural trade governance in the World Trade Organisation', *International Affairs* 93: 1167–84.

Sen, A. (1981) 'Ingredients of famine analysis: availability and entitlements', *The Quarterly Journal of Economics* 96: 433–64.

Sen, A. (1999) *Development as Freedom*, Oxford: Oxford University Press.

Sharma, S. (2018) 'WTO and Policy space for agriculture and food security: issues for China and India', *Agricultural Economics Research Review* 31: 207–19.

Smith, F. (2008) 'The limitations of a legal approach to the regulation of cultural diversity in the WTO: the problem of international agricultural trade', *Asian Journal of WTO & International Health Law & Policy* 3: 51–80.

Smith, F. (2015) 'Natural Resources and global value chains: what role for the WTO?', *International Journal of Law in Context* 11: 135–52.

Smith, V.H. (2018) 'US agricultural policy beyond 2018: implications for the World Trade Organisation', *ICTSD Issue Paper*, Geneva: International Centre for Trade and Sustainable Development.

South Centre (December 2015) 'WTO's MC10: agriculture negotiations – public stockholding', Analytical Note SC/TDP/AN/MC10/3.

Sumner, D.A. (2018) *Dairy Policy Progress: Completing the Move to Markets*, Washington, DC: American Enterprise Institute.

Swinbank, A. and Tanner C. (1996) *Farm Policy and Trade Conflict: The Uruguay Round and CAP Reform*, Ann Arbor: University of Michigan Press.

Thacker, C. (2005) 'Agricultural trade liberalisation in the Doha Round: the search for a modalities draft', *Georgia Journal of International and Comparative Law* 33: 721–55.

Thies, C. (2001) 'A historical institutionalist approach to the Uruguay Round agricultural negotiations', *Comparative Political Studies* 34: 400–28.

United Nations OHCHR (2008) *Claiming the MDGs: A Human Rights Approach*, Geneva: UN.

Vivero-Pol, J.L. et al (2018) *Routledge Handbook of Food as a Commons*, Abingdon: Routledge.

Wilkinson, R. (2016) 'The WTO, Nairobi and the 2030 Agenda', 19 February, *ICTSD BIORES* 10:1. Available at: www.ictsd.org/bridges-news/biores/news/the-wto-nairobi-and-the-2030-agenda (accessed 2 February 2018).

Wilkinson, R., Hannah, E. and Scott, J. (2014) 'The WTO in Bali: what MC9 means for the Doha development agenda and why it matters', *Third World Quarterly* 35: 1032–50.

Wolfe, R. (2009) 'The WTO single undertaking as negotiating technique and constitutive metaphor', *Journal of International Economic Law* 12: 835.

WTO (World Trade Organization) (2001) 'Ministerial Declaration', Ministerial Conference, 4th Session, Doha 9–14 November 2001 WT/MIN(01)/DEC/1 adopted on 20 November 2001.

WTO (2013) 'Bali Ministerial Declaration', 9th Session, Bali 3–6 December 2013, WT/MIN(13)/DEC adopted on 7 December 2013.

WTO (2015) 'Ministerial Decision of 19 December 2015: Export Competition', WT/MIN(15)/45 dated 21 December.

WTO (2019) 'Glossary.' Available at: www.wto.org/english/thewto_e/glossary_e/glossary_e.htm

Zanella, M. et al (2018) 'Deliberation in multi-stakeholder participation: a heuristic framework applied to the Committee on World Food Security', *Sustainability* 10: 428.

Zhou, W. (2018) 'Appellate Body Report on *EU-Biodiesel*: the future of China's State capitalism under the WTO Anti-Dumping Agreement', *World Trade Review* 17: 609–33.

6

Social Sustainability, Labour and Trade: Forging Connections

Tonia Novitz

Introduction

The idea of labour standards as constitutive of 'sustainability' has begun to emerge in the sphere of the academic literature on labour law (Galgoczi, 2014; Frey and McNaughton, 2016; Polomarkakis, 2019). Previously, analysis tended to be confined largely to the ways in which regulation of labour markets and trade union action could promote (or obstruct) inter-generational environmental sustainable development (Lund, 2004; Räthzel and Uzzell, 2013). The notion that labour law might be itself a key facet of the 'social' and 'economic' pillars aimed at intra- and inter-generational sustainability is only slowly taking hold. In this sense, connections are still being forged.

The notion that labour standards and sustainability are profoundly connected has been carried forward, to a limited extent, in the 2015 United Nations (UN) Sustainable Development Goals (SDGs) (Agenda 2030 Resolution A/RES/70/1). Examples include SDG 8, which aims to '[p]romote sustained, inclusive and sustainable economic growth, full and productive employment and decent work for all', alongside SDGs 5, 10 and 16. The extent to which the targets in the SDGs cohere with the International Labour Organization (ILO) treatment of 'decent work' and the norms which the EU promotes in its trade policy will be considered.

Curiously, it is the European Union (EU) that has taken the lead on labour conditionality as a feature of sustainable development in the context of trade. Examples include the 'Sustainability and Good

Governance' incentive provisions in the EU Generalised System of Preferences (Regulation (EU) No 978/2012) and design of 'labour chapters' as part of 'sustainable development' objectives in free trade agreements (FTAs).[1]

The difficulty seems to be that the global consensus around labour as a facet of social and economic sustainability reflected in the SDGs is not a neat fit with ILO standards; nor does Agenda 2030 necessarily endorse the ways in which the EU pursues sustainability through its external relations policies. This chapter considers how these tensions may be resolved.

The chapter begins by investigating links between sustainability and labour. It does so from a historical vantage point, considering the widely accepted position relating to 'social sustainability' and the relevance of collective worker representation prior to the adoption of Agenda 2030 and the SDGs. It goes on to consider the shift in perspective from 2015 onwards.

The chapter then examines the ILO approach to the intersection between sustainability and labour objectives, noting a long-standing reluctance to engage with trade-related issues and recent resistance from the employers' group to concrete protections of freedom of association. What may seem more promising are a number of developments which have taken place in 2019, the centenary of the ILO; in particular: the report of the ILO Global Commission on the Future of Work (ILO, 2019a), the International Labour Office Report submitted to the High-Level Political Forum (HLPF) titled *Time to Act for SDG 8* (ILO, 2019b) and the Centenary Declaration adopted at the International Labour Conference.

Up until now, it has been the EU, the focus of the subsequent section of this chapter, which has appeared to lead on social justice (including international labour standards) as a basis for sustainability, making these a condition of various kinds of trade concessions. As De Schutter (2015: xv) has observed, 'Europe has potentially a special role to play in this context'. In so doing, the EU has drawn explicitly on 'core' or 'fundamental' ILO Conventions reflecting the focus on four key principles set out in Article 2 of the ILO Declaration on Fundamental Principles and Rights at Work. These are freedom of association and the effective recognition of the right to collective bargaining (linked to the 'fundamental' ILO Conventions Nos 87 and 98), elimination of all forms of forced and compulsory labour (ILO Conventions Nos 29 and 105), effective abolition of child labour (ILO Conventions Nos 138 and 182) and elimination of discrimination in respect of employment and occupation (ILO Conventions Nos 100 and 111). In this way the

ILO also has a significant (if indirect) effect on the construction of sustainability norms in the context of trade. Nevertheless, the ways in which the EU has implemented trade conditionality with reference to sustainability remain uneven and have been the subject of criticism. Moreover, the EU has been reluctant to impose the ILO's broader 'Decent Work Agenda', which entails not only implementation of these four fundamental principles and rights at work but also '(i) promoting employment; (ii) developing and enhancing measures of social protection – social security and labour protection – which are sustainable and adapted to national circumstances; and (iii) promoting social dialogue and tripartism' (recognised in the ILO Declaration on Social Justice for a Fair Globalization 2008).

What is interesting, however, is that in the EU's more recent reflections on international policy coherence there is a desire to find legitimacy externally and to ensure that EU trade policy is in compliance with the 2015 SDGs. The chapter concludes by considering how the trade and policy coherence objectives set out in SDG 17 can be achieved and how the common and divergent approaches of the ILO and EU may yet evolve. It is suggested that SDG 16 could guide the processes for dialogue that are necessary to forge connections and solutions.

Links between sustainability and labour

In the first chapter in this book it became evident that the sustainability discourse has conventionally given prominence to environmental protection and ecological issues, from the 1987 World Commission on Environment and Development 'Brundtland' Report onwards. In practice, economic development (the alleviation of poverty through full integration in international trade and global capitalism) has been the *de facto* focus of sustainable development. The recent emphasis on building a 'green economy' is arguably the latest manifestation of this long-standing trend (Jacobs, 2012; Spangenberg, 2016). It has been less clear what should be the place of the so-called 'third' social pillar alongside environmental and economic concerns. Much of the literature concerns the specific technical mechanics via which trade mechanisms can promote certain social aspects of sustainable development, but an exploration of the normative dimension regarding the place of labour standards in a sustainability context is arguably under-developed (De Schutter, 2015; Perulli and Treu, 2018).

Littig and Grießler (2005) were among the first to interrogate seriously how social sustainability might be conceptualised, suggesting that this could be more than 'a catchword'. They rejected an overarching pillar model of sustainability, whereby economic and social policies would be relevant only to the extent that they affected environmental protections. They also expressed scepticism regarding a three-pillar conception in which environmental and/or economic concerns dominate. Rather, they considered the scope for a more multi-dimensional model.

Building on the notion of 'needs' of present and future generations used in the commonly referenced Brundtland definition (World Commission on Environment and Development, 1987) of sustainable development, Littig and Grießler (2005: 71) argued that needs can include 'the necessity to have food, housing, clothing, sexuality, health care, a healthy environment, access to safe drinking water and sanitary facilities, freedom from bodily harm, and protection in case of illness, old age, and social hardship'. Moreover, since some needs can be fulfilled by 'work', labour and labour standards become relevant 'not just with regard to securing people's incomes, but also with regard to the psycho-social functions of gainful employment (time structure, identity, etc.), citizens' integration (due to the high social status of paid work), and the significance of paid labour for social cohesion' (Littig and Grießler, 2005: 73). Their suggestion, then, is that how workers are protected and enabled is vital to an understanding of social sustainability. (For contemporary application of their theoretical framework, see Polomarkakis, 2019: 3–4, although he adopts a peculiarly EU definition of the norms to be applied.)

The scope of Littig and Grießler's recommendations (2005: 74) regarding labour was limited to:

- 'the ecologisation of existing employment and the creation of new, environmentally sound jobs ...';
- 'the gender-sensible re-distribution of all ... work';
- and 'the freedom to choose at any stage in life between different forms of work ... while being at all times entitled to individual social security'.

However, their analysis of social indicators did also take them into the realms of capability theory (Littig and Grießler, 2005: 75, citing Nussbaum and Sen, 2002), considering potential also for social solidarity and action. (See in this respect also our discussion in Chapter 3). Since their contribution to the debate, most of the social sustainability literature has focused less on labour and more on other aspects of social deliberation and planning (Vallance et al, 2011; Boström, 2012: 6), but displaying a continuing concern with both the substantive and procedural dimensions of a much-disputed dynamic concept.

There is little doubt that environmental and social sustainability can be interrelated. For example, a lack of worker voice to challenge employer practices (such as through whistleblowing) can mean that those who sell their labour, who are also often residents in the locality in which they work, lack the ability to challenge poor environmental practices that then may go on unabated with profound consequences to them in their homes and nearby (Schipani, Milliken and Dworkin, 2016; Chacartegui, 2018). When labour is paid an insufficient amount to meet the basic costs of living, the economic harms from a sustainability perspective are also obvious. There are not only devastating personal effects on the persons concerned (which impact on human rights to food, water, housing, health and so on), but a lack of spending in the economy, leading ultimately to the destruction of business and banks (and, with these, individual and collective savings). The labourer is personally affected by poverty, but so too are markets, namely, the economic pillar of sustainability (Stiglitz, 2016).

Yet, labour standards also have profound consequences for intra- and inter-generational justice which are also worthy of independent concern. This is perhaps best illustrated by the ways in which poor working conditions (such as long hours or other impacts on health) can have detrimental effects on reproductive labour. Where there is insufficient care for children and the elderly, this has broader effects on the underlying cohesion of society: its cultural traditions and long-term capacity to enhance the capabilities of its citizens (Fuchs, 2017; Roberts, 2016). Social unrest and crime have long been linked to systemic poverty and material deprivation (Short, 2018). Notably, poor working conditions are often imposed by multinational corporate employers on workers in developing countries in the global South, which is how terms of trade become relevant (Blackett, 2001; Gammage and Novitz, 2019). These negative sustainability effects can, in turn, lead to societal break-down and, as we shall see in the context of cross-border trading, a lack of trust between states, already evident in rising forms of nationalism, which present a threat to the 'universal peace' on which our current international legal system is predicated and which Agenda 2030 in its preamble seeks to promote (UN, 2015; Novitz, 2019).

Labour standards can, then, raise profound issues of inter- and intra-generational justice which relate to sustainability in terms of environmental, economic and social systems. Durable solutions to social problems will always have to be determined with attention to environmental constraints and planetary boundaries, as has been argued in Chapters 2 and 3. In many concrete situations, environmental and labour issues will arise in tandem and there will need to be a holistic solution, which requires careful analysis and balancing, but my suggestion is that this will not always be the case. The idea of sustainability can be relevant to matters not directly concerned with the environment. However, as we shall see from the following brief history, this notion is relatively new and its implications are not yet fully explored.

Before the SDGs 2015

Before the adoption of the SDGs it was common to view sustainability solely as a matter of environmental protection (with economic implications) which had to be navigated in a way that preserved jobs as well as terms and conditions for workers. There was self-evidently conflict between the short-term interests of trade union members, for example over retention of jobs in a particular industry, and the longer-term interests of a wider range of society in environmental protection from pollutants and other problematic ecological effects emanating from a particular industry (Lund, 2004: 45–8; Galgoczi, 2014: 63). However, it was not so very difficult to explain that there were clear health and safety benefits for workers (and their communities) if certain industries – for example, forms of mining – were shut down. Accordingly, the aim was not necessarily to prevent movement to a greener economy, but to ensure that, in the interests of not only business but also workers and their communities, there were not stark economic shocks but, rather, 'just transitions' (Doorey, 2017; Seck, 2018: 139–40). This became the dominant approach – for example, at the ILO in the building of 'green jobs', discussed later. Similarly, the European Trade Union Confederation (ETUC) has sought not only 'green jobs' but also, in the context of transitions driven by environmental objectives, 'green skills by active government training strategies; a respect for human and labour rights; and strong and effective social protection systems' (ETUC, 2010, drawing on ILO, 2010). Indeed, workers' organisations have been active generally across the globe in the facilitation of ecological policy change (see Lund, 2004: 61–6; Räthzel and Uzzell, 2013; Chacartegui, 2018).

A problem in Europe is that many national legal frameworks do not support trade union engagement with environmental issues. In the UK, for example, there is no 'legal obligation on employers to consult unions on the issue' and the Trades Union Congress (TUC) has been (unsuccessfully) arguing for years now for legal recognition of 'union environmental reps' (TUC 2014, 7 and 46).[2] Nor is there any entitlement to engage in meaningful collective bargaining, or to strike, over issues which affect the environment but not the immediate welfare of the workers taking the action.

This is due to the narrow scope of a legitimate 'trade dispute' under UK legislation (the Trade Union and Labour Relations (Consolidation) Act 1992 (TULRCA), sections 219 and 244) and further restrictions on the scope of legitimate collective bargaining imposed by the Court of Justice of the European Union and the European Court of Human Rights (Novitz, 2015, discussing Case C-176/12 *Association de mediation sociale v CGT*, Judgment of 15 January 2014; Case C-413/13 *FNV Kunsten Informatie en Media v Staat der Nederlanden*, Judgment of 4 December 2014; *UNISON v UK* Application No. 53574/99, Decision of 10 February 2002 [2002] IRLR 497; Case C-438/05 *International Transport Workers' Federation (ITF) and Finnish Seamen's Union (FSU) v Viking Line* [2006] IRLR 58; and Case C-426/11 *Alemo-Herron and others v Parkwood Leisure Ltd* [2013] IRLR 744, Judgment of 18 July 2013).The combined effects of this case law prevent engagement with the likely future consequences of events, such as the long-term implications of the sale of a business (as in *Alemo-Herron*), the privatisation of a hospital (as in *UNISON*) or the reflagging of ships (as in the *Viking* case). All of these judgments apparently remain good law in the sense that they have yet to be explicitly overturned by the Luxembourg or Strasbourg Courts.

In the UK, ecological concerns which extend beyond the immediate interests of workplace governance and require engagement in lobbying or funding of a political party (like the Green Party or Labour Party) can be pursued by trade unions only within the limitations placed on the use of political funds (see TULRCA, Part I, Chapter VI). These expansive legal limitations have implications for intra-generational distributive justice, and also for protection of the interests of future generations.

These restrictions are particularly problematic if we regard sustainability as something other than a static end-point ascertained through expert advice. In the first two chapters of this book we have shown how sustainable development has come to be regarded as a more dynamic process which entails social engagement with the previously silenced and collaborative initiatives engaging those who are vulnerable and affected by the economic, social and environmental actions of states and private actors (see also Novitz and Mangan, 2011). In order to achieve workers' access to voice, their organisations need to be able to engage with longer-term economic, social and environmental problems. Collective bargaining and industrial action should not therefore be limited to what are perceived to be current workers' immediate needs, but should include those of younger colleagues, future colleagues and even those who are currently children and those not yet born. In this respect, the recent initiative of climate change 'strikes' by school children is telling (Rose, 2019). Children may be able to take a day off school; but it is much more difficult for their working parents to join them.

After the SDGs 2015

On the one hand, the SDGs do not make the kind of provision for labour standards which many labour lawyers might expect. For example, while SDG 1 is concerned with the aspiration to 'end poverty in all its forms everywhere', there is no mention in the subsidiary targets of the ability to do so via work (cf Littig and Grießler, 2005). This is despite the achievement of inclusion of 'decent work' as a target connected to Millennium Development Goal (MDG) 1 in 2007 (Frey and MacNaughton, 2016: 5–6). Poverty and 'decent work' seem artificially separated in the Agenda 2030 Resolution itself (see para 3, where poverty is mentioned, and then later in the paragraph 'also' – suggesting apparently additionally – the question of decent work). Nor is work mentioned in any of the SDG 1 indicators, which focus instead on access to public services, land tenure and government spending.

Another disappointment is that, as has been identified by the UN Special Rapporteur on the rights to freedom of peaceful assembly and of association (UN, 2018: para. 87), while SDG 8 makes specific reference to what has become a familiar ILO prescription of 'decent work', there is no mention of either collective bargaining, trade unions or the right to strike in the targets for that SDG.

Perhaps this is not surprising, given recent employer opposition from 2012 onwards in the ILO to protection of the right to strike as a facet of freedom of association (discussed later in this chapter). Moreover, in the main text of Agenda 2030 the idea of 'decent work' is situated very much in the context of economic growth. An example is paragraph 27, where the emphasis is on building 'strong economic foundations for all our countries', which is equated with 'sustained, inclusive and sustainable economic growth'. This is to involve promoting youth employment and women's 'economic empowerment', although it seems accepted that the latter need not entail access to formal employment.

Three out of the four ILO core labour standards receive explicit attention in the main body of SDG 8 targets. As regards discrimination, target 8.5 mentions 'full and productive employment and decent work for all women and men, including for young people and persons with disabilities, and equal pay for work of equal value'. Non-discrimination is also addressed in SDG 5 on gender equality and women's empowerment (although this mentions explicitly only unpaid and domestic work) and SDG 10 on reduction of inequality within and among countries (which refers to social and economic inclusion and outcomes, including wages in target 10.4 and labour share of Gross Domestic Product in the attached indicator). There is a further commitment to 'eradicate forced labour and human trafficking and end child labour in all its forms' (Agenda 2030, 2015: para 27), elaborated on in SDG targets 8.7 and 16.2. However, it does seem strange that while considerable emphasis is placed on 'knowledge and skills' and a healthy workforce, workers' voice seems disregarded.

Arguably, SDG 16 can be understood as promoting collective representation of workers and their action, especially SDG 16.7, which aims to '[e]nsure responsive, inclusive, participatory and representative decision-making at all levels'. That would be consistent with the inclusion of freedom of association and collective bargaining in indicator 8.8.2 as a tool for protection of workers' rights and promotion of safe and secure working environments for all workers, especially for the most vulnerable. Yet we might have expected more explicit mention of trade unions in SDG 16, which does refer in SDG target 16.10 to 'fundamental freedoms' and in indicator 16.10.1 to the extent of mistreatment of trade unionists.

Nevertheless, after the 2015 SDGs it is arguably much easier to make the case for a self-standing sustainability social pillar. This is because many of the objectives set out in the SDGs relate to specific social and labour objectives which are conceptually separate from ecological needs or economic growth. From a very broad social perspective, an example is the commitment in target 16.2 to '[e]nd abuse, exploitation, trafficking and all forms of violence against and torture of children'. This has everything to do with inter-generational sustainability, protecting literally our future generations, and even with intra-generational equality, for those who have been so exploited are likely to remain impoverished and disadvantaged. However, this is an objective that can have little connection directly to environmental concerns. That said, the enhancement of children's capabilities can be connected to future economic growth for any country, as is arguably indicated by inclusion of the determination to eliminate not only child trafficking but child labour in SDG 8 (under target 8.7); and its application as a target will need to be sensitive to environmental concerns.

SDG 17, with its reference to a Global Partnership for Development, and more explicitly in SDG 17.10 to 'an equitable multilateral trading system', may be thought to raise implicitly issues regarding human rights and labour standards conditionality in trade agreements. Whether SDG 17 could be seen as a tacit endorsement of extant EU external relations policies regarding the inclusion of sustainable development chapters in EU trade agreements with third countries remains debatable. Whether conditionality is permissible might be viewed in terms of whether EU requirements are (also in the terms of target 17.10) 'universal, rules-based, open, non-discriminatory'. In terms of target 17.11 (and SDG 10), it would also be expected that such conditions would assist rather than obstruct developing-country participation in global markets. This could also align with the idea of 'policy coherence' raised in target 17.14. We might also anticipate the ILO and the EU to be part of the 'Global Partnership' and facilitate the 'multi-stakeholder partnerships that mobilize and share knowledge, expertise, technology and financial resources, to support the achievement of the sustainable development goals in all countries, in particular developing countries' under SDG 17.

ILO approaches to sustainable development: regulation and governance

The ILO has a tripartite structure which depends on ongoing cooperation between government, employer and worker delegates who attend the annual International Labour Conference (ILC) and sit on the Governing Body. In both instances, for each employer and worker representative there are two government representatives, so that state interests can (marginally) predominate. Yet the adoption of international labour standards in the form of Conventions and Recommendations in the ILC (such as the 'core' ILO Conventions listed earlier) requires a two-thirds majority, which necessitates more than merely governmental preferences but also inclusion of the social partners (ILO Constitution, Article 19, which dates from the Treaty of Versailles in 1919).

This tripartite structure has been regarded as a strength of the organisation, but requires a coalition to achieve any standard-setting. In the past, developing countries and the employers' group have allied to block ILO engagement with trade-related issues (Salazar-Xirinachs,

2000). The employers' group has also been extremely hostile to protection of the right to strike as a facet of freedom of association, staging a walk-out of one of the key supervisory mechanisms (the Conference Committee on the Application of Standards – commonly known as the CAS) and seeking ongoing reforms of ILO standards and supervisory capabilities (La Hovary, 2013; Vogt, 2017). In this context, the first part of this section considers the ILO's ambivalent view of the connections between sustainability, labour standards and trade. The second part considers the extent to which this may change following developments in the ILO in 2019.

The ILO's ambivalent treatment of sustainability, labour standards and trade

The World Trade Organisation (WTO), in the 1996 Singapore Ministerial Declaration, recognised the core ILO Conventions, but also expressed a determination that their promotion was the remit of the ILO and not WTO rules. This reassured certain developing states that feared trade conditionality (Leary, 1997). The 1998 Declaration on Fundamental Principles and Rights at Work, which identified the constitutional significance of core labour standards independently of their inclusion in Conventions, was viewed by many in the workers' group in the ILO as offering a route to identify certain standards as possible conditions for trade. However, this possibility was pre-empted by a proviso in the 1998 Declaration (Article 5) that stressed that 'labour standards should not be used for protectionist trade purposes, and that nothing in this Declaration and its follow-up shall be invoked or otherwise used for such purposes; in addition, the comparative advantage of any country should in no way be called into question by this Declaration and its follow-up'. It is therefore not surprising that a trade–core labour standards link is not endorsed by employers or many developing states (Bellace, 2015).

The ILO International Institute for Labour Standards has since commissioned research on the inclusion of ILO labour standards conditionality in FTAs (ILO, 2016a). The report sees the ILO as offering assistance to its members but not as insisting on this or engaging in standard-setting on this issue. Notably, the ILO is not currently engaging on SDG 17, but is restricting its institutional expertise to SDG 8 (as is evident from the International Labour Office submission to the HLPF (ILO, 2019b)). The Office's concern lies with supplying the methodology and statistical resources for following up on the SDG indicators (ILO, 2018).

The ILO has long been concerned with the expansion of 'green jobs', which became part of its portfolio on 'decent work' under the last ILO Director-General, Juan Somavia.[3] The current Director-General, Guy Ryder, has regarded this environmental dimension of ILO activities as part of the new ILO Future of Work programme and as a separate centenary initiative as the ILO celebrates 100 years of existence since its foundation in the Treaty of Versailles in 1919.[4] Further, the ILO has supported the idea of 'just transitions' from one form of manufacture to another, responding to ecological objectives but simultaneously managing redundancies and transfers of undertakings in responsible ways. This area of ILO activity has grown exponentially with the adoption of new Guidelines on Just Transitions (ILO, 2015a), which are linked explicitly to Agenda 2030.

There is arguably scope for the ILO to say more about social sustainability. For example, the ILO Declaration of Philadelphia of 1944 stated that economic and financial policies must be evaluated according to whether they promote social justice (Article II(c)). Furthermore, if trade and investment rules obstruct social justice, then they also have the capacity to undermine the peace emphasised by the founders of the ILO in 1919 when drafting Part XIII of the Treaty of Versailles. ILO concerns with supply chains and migrant labour suggest that the organisation cannot continue to evade policy making in the trade field indefinitely (ILO, 2016b, 2016c), but for the time being the orientation is one of defence and diplomacy.

A new conception of the 'future of work' in a sustainability context

The current ILO Director-General, Guy Ryder, has also been engaged in preparing a centenary 'future of work' initiative for 2019, which explicitly responds to environmental and broader sustainability concerns (ILO, 2015b: 11, para 47). In this respect, the developments that have taken place in the ILO in 2019 may give a flavour of the future direction of travel for ILO treatment of the SDGs. These developments have encompassed: the report published at the start of the year by the ILO-appointed Global Commission on the Future of Work; the report prepared by the International Labour Office (the ILO's secretariat) on the current state of global compliance with SDG 8 for submission to the HLPF; and the ILO Centenary Declaration adopted on 21 June 2019 at the ILC (again making specific reference to the 'future of work' alongside 'sustainable development').

The future of work and social dialogue

The Global Commission Report painted a picture of future labour markets as volatile, in part due to a need to respond to ecological and sustainability issues: 'The greening of our economies will create millions of jobs as we adopt sustainable practices and clean technologies but other jobs will disappear as countries scale back their carbon- and resource-intensive industries' (ILO, 2019a: 10). The Commission's policy prescription was a new social contract and a 'human-centred agenda', including social dialogue (ILO, 2019a: 11). The Office Report made similar observations regarding the challenges ahead, suggesting a strategy which will involve the interplay of national employment policies, instantiation of labour standards and labour market institutions, as well as social dialogue, on which again considerable emphasis was placed (ILO, 2019b: 69–71, 74–5). Much was made by the Office also of collective bargaining as 'one of the four fundamental principles and rights at work', as well as its role as 'an indicator under target 8.8' (ILO, 2019b: 34). In this way the Global Commission and the Office highlight the significance of inclusive debate promoted by SDG 16. Indeed, the Office was keen to point to the 'dynamic interlinkages' between SDG 8 and the other SDGs, including also SDGs 5 and 10 (see, for example, the tables at ILO, 2019b: 29, 32).

Notably, social dialogue was stressed in the preamble to the Centenary Declaration, but also in Article II(A), which directed ILO efforts (inter alia) towards 'promoting workers' rights as a key element for the attainment of inclusive and sustainable growth, with a focus on freedom of association and the effective recognition of the right to strike as enabling rights', and in Article II(B), which regarded 'social dialogue, including collective bargaining and tripartite cooperation' as 'an essential foundation of all ILO action'. Further, Article IV(C) emphasised the importance of promoting social partner capabilities and engagement, alongside 'the strong, influential and inclusive mechanisms of social dialogue'.

ILO and trade regulation

The Global Commission further made a proposal for the ILO to work more closely with the WTO (ILO, 2019a: 14, 56). The message given by the Commission (ILO, 2019a: 56) was that:

> There are strong, complex and crucial links between trade, financial, economic and social policies. The success of

> the human-centred growth and development agenda we propose depends heavily on coherence across these policy areas. Trade and financial policies are important means to the material welfare and spiritual development of the person through decent work.

But no specific proposals were made by the Commission report from a trade perspective.

The Office report was also very hesitant in this regard, naming SDG 8.A, on 'aid for trade', as significant for the achievement of other aspects of SDG 8, but not mentioning the specific targets and indicators in SDG 17 regarding trade. This is unfortunate, for arguably what is an 'equitable multilateral trading system' under SDG target 17.10 could come within the legitimate sphere of ILO concern. The issue of 'fair migration governance' was given specific attention (ILO, 2019b: 70–1), including the access of migrants to collective representation and worker voice through trade unions; but the relationship of migration to trade in services was not mentioned (cf Novitz, 2014).

The Centenary Declaration did, however, engage more with trade issues than had been anticipated previously. For example, Article III(C) referred to 'promoting sustained, inclusive and sustainable economic work' (which chimed with SDG 8) through, inter alia, 'trade, industrial and sectoral policies that promote decent work, and enhance productivity'. This might be a reference to merely domestic trade, but that is not immediately apparent from the wording of the provision. Article IV(D) mentioned the 'services that the ILO offers to its member states and partners', which, as we have seen earlier, might entail advice on inclusion of a social clause in an FTA (ILO, 2016a), and stated that these 'must be consistent with its mandate and based on a thorough understanding of, and attention to, their diverse circumstances, needs, priorities and levels of development, including through expanded South–South and triangular cooperation'. This is a cautious statement, and one which is obscure in its intent, arguably intentionally so. However, there is appreciation in Article IV(F), the final provision of the Declaration, that 'on the basis of its constitutional mandate, the ILO must take an important role in the multilateral system'. This suggests some appreciation of the requirements of Article II(c) of the Declaration of Philadelphia. There was also explicit reference in Article IV(D) to the objective of 'policy coherence' stated in SDG 17. Moreover, the Centenary Declaration (using language evidently borrowed from the Commission report) closed by 'recognizing the strong, complex and crucial links between social, trade, financial, economic and environmental policies', which indicates contemplation that the ILO may potentially engage more in trade policy, albeit at some unspecified future date and in unspecified ways.

A new overarching 'Universal Labour Guarantee' and 'sustainable work'

Instead, the 2019 Commission Report offered some new policy prescriptions which may indirectly have implications for the terms of trade which the EU generates (as it seeks to apply ILO standards). Much was made of assisting people through labour market transitions by offering 'lifelong learning' (ILO, 2019a: 30–3) and 'universal social protection' (ILO, 2019a: 35–6). In work (or even for independent contractors), there is to be gender equality (ILO, 2019: 34–5; cf SDG 5), and there is to be a new 'Universal Labour Guarantee' 'including fundamental workers' rights, an "adequate living wage", limits on hours of work and ensuring safe and healthy workplaces' (ILO, 2019: 38–43). This is interesting, as this recommendation reiterates the significance of the ILO 'core labour standards' on which the EU and other countries draw in their trade agreements, while giving additional force to the notion that fair wages, working time and health and safety are also being vital for everyone. This guarantee would apply regardless of employment status, with considerable implications for those engaged in ever more precarious work (McCann and Fudge, 2017). The Centenary Declaration has now given effect to this Universal Labour Guarantee in Article III(B) stating that:

> All workers should enjoy adequate protection in accordance with the Decent Work Agenda, taking into account:
> (i) Respect for their fundamental rights;
> (ii) An adequate minimum wage, statutory or negotiated;
> (iii) Maximum limits on working time; and
> (iv) Safety and health at work.

Finally, the Global Commission report made express mention of 'sustainable' work, viewed in terms of both human development and environmental needs (ILO, 2019: 45ff). It was in some ways a curious addendum to the main business of the report, in that it offered little that was new, but did at least seek to 'prioritize long-term, sustainable investments that favour human development and protect the planet' (ILO, 2019: 46). It seems that this part of the report was really directed not so much to international investment law as towards corporate social responsibility, which is why no demands are made regarding legal reform. The Commission argued for investment in sectors in which workers are currently vulnerable (the care sector, the agricultural sector and the digital economy), suggesting that ethical standards be maintained in their development. There was also attention here to the informal economy and the phenomenon of women's unpaid work (ILO, 2019: 50). While eminently worthy, and in line with the recognition of women's work including entrepreneurship under targets 5.4, 5.A and 8.3, 'sustainable work' seems the hardest part of the Global Commission's vision to be actualised, given a refusal on the part of the ILO to engage with terms of trade and investment.

The role of the EU in connecting social and labour sustainability to trade

In Chapter 1 we examined how the EU can be seen to have taken a leading role in the promotion of 'sustainable development'. The principle is deeply embedded in the EU treaties. Article 3(3) of the Treaty on European Union (TEU) sets out the ambition to 'work for the sustainable development of Europe', which includes 'social progress'. Indeed, Perulli (2018: 19) considers that sustainable development places particular emphasis on the use of 'fundamental social rights' and sees the EU as dominating in this field. Yet, as we have observed, there is little mention of the social pillar, or indeed labour standards, in EU Commission policy documentation on sustainability, except in relation to enhancement of access to employment and modernisation of labour markets, both of which arguably have a more economic than social flavour (see European Commission, (2010): 6, 17, 18, 32). However, this may change with the adoption of a Pillar of Social Rights for the Eurozone, which has the potential to offer greater protection of social sustainability norms (Polomarkakis, 2019).

Art. 3(5) of the TEU goes even further, requiring that the EU contribute to 'the sustainable development of the Earth', and 'social progress'. It is in this external relations context of labour and trade that arguably the EU has played a role as a game changer. However, its efforts have been largely derived from internationally governed understandings of 'core labour standards' as advocated by the ILO and, more recently, the content of the SDGs. We can see their influence in two key facets of EU external relations policy: the evolution of the EU's Generalised System of Preferences GSP and the inclusion of 'sustainable development' chapters in EU trade agreements. The EU is determined to provide policy coherence in the sphere of sustainable development, and the scope of those attempts is considered at the close of this section.

EU GSP

As early as 1994, the EU (then EC (European Community)) GSP enabled tariff preferences to be temporarily withdrawn (whether in whole or in part) where there was use of 'forced labour' as defined by ILO Conventions Nos 29 and 105 (see Article 9 of Council Regulation 3281 /94 and Article 9 of Council Regulation 1256/96). This was indicative of a desire to base the legitimacy of EU external relations policy regarding labour standards on ILO norms, as in the case of withdrawal of trade preferences from Burma/Myanmar (Council Regulation 552/97). In 2001 a particular 'special incentive arrangements for the protection of labour rights' was introduced (Council Regulation 2501/2001, Art.2(b)), which was kept separate from GSP systems relating to the environment, development and drugs. Once again, it was notable that 'fundamental' ILO Conventions provided a key reference point potentially determinative of withdrawal of tariff preferences (Council Regulation 2501/2001, Art. 14(2) and Art. 26). When India successfully challenged EC use of preferential tariffs in relation to drug arrangements, establishing standards of transparency and proportionality (the *EC Tariff Preferences* case of 2004, discussed in De Schutter, 2015: 105–10), the EU created a new GSP system, including a 'special incentive arrangement for sustainable development and good governance chapter'. This is now known colloquially as 'GSP+', which was initially set out in Council Regulation 732/2008 and maintained in the current incarnation of the GSP under Council Regulation 978/2012.

One point of interest here is the entry of 'sustainable development' as a justification for EU tariff conditionality alongside the continued listing of core (or fundamental) ILO Conventions as indicative of the content of that norm. What has been more problematic is the doubtful transparency of the selection process or the benefits for developing countries under the Enabling Clause (Bartels, 2007; Wardhaugh, 2013). Withdrawal of preferences has tended to be reliant on employer condemnation of state conduct in the ILO CAS, namely the very supervisory body that the employers' group exited in 2012 in order to demonstrate their disapproval of the findings of the more legally credible Committee of Experts on the Application of Conventions and Recommendations (see Vogt, 2015). The European Parliament is now proposing further modification and scrutiny of the implementation of GSP+ to lend greater credibility to its operations (EU European Parliament, 2018).

EU FTAs

The emergence of 'sustainable development' chapters in EU FTAs dates from at least 2008, when previously the EU utilised human rights clauses, which included labour standards (Bartels, 2012; Van den Putte and Orbie, 2015). These chapters reference and thereby reinforce ILO core labour standards and the ILO fundamental Conventions, but also can make reference to other labour standards.

An example is the EU–Canada Comprehensive Economic Trade Agreement (CETA), provisionally applied from 2016 (regarding which see COM(2016) 443 final and 444 final and COM(2016)470 final). The starting point for protection of labour standards is Chapter 22 ('Trade and Sustainable Development'), which mentions (and arguably encompasses) Chapters 23 (Trade and Labour) and 24 (Trade and Environment). Under Chapter 23 (Article 23.3), each Party is to ensure that its labour laws and practices embody the four core labour standards from the 1998 ILO Declaration, but the Chapter goes beyond these to refer to health and safety at work, establishment of minimum employment standards for wage earners, including those not covered by collective agreements, and non-discrimination in respect of working conditions, including for migrant workers. Article 23.4 requires that the parties also abide by the terms of the ILO Conventions they have already ratified. It will be interesting to see, given the openness to potential inclusion of labour standards beyond the ILO 'core', whether the kinds of concerns raised as part of the ILO Commission on the Future of Work's proposals for a 'Universal Labour Guarantee' (crucial matters concerning wages, working time and health and safety) will become a feature of EU FTAs.

Sustainable development chapters offer less readily enforceable means for the protection of labour standards, focusing more on discursive mechanisms. One example is the creation of 'Domestic Advisory Groups' (or DAGs) representing civil society, reflecting broadly environmental, labour and business interests, which advise on domestic concerns relating to the impact of the FTA on sustainable development (see, for example, the EU–Korea FTA). Another is a transnational 'Civil Society Dialogue' (CSD) which enables EU civil society representatives to meet with their counterparts in the other state parties so as to discuss implementation of the sustainable development chapter (see, for example, CETA, Chapter 22). These offer potential for coalitions between labour and other representatives within a broader frame of sustainable development, offering consolidation of voice. However, concerns have been raised that, even with enhancement of 'capability' for a wide group of social actors, the voice of labour can get lost in the throng of voices and recommendations which are ultimately unenforceable (Ulmer, 2015: 320–1; Ebert, 2016; Gammage, 2019).

EU 'Policy Coherence for Development'

The story of 'Policy Coherence for Development' (PCD) has evolved over more than a decade. Firstly, the EU has never sought to adopt its own distinctive critical perspective on what constitutes 'development'. Instead, PCD is born of an awareness of the need to integrate EU policies not only around a common objective but also with 'development' as defined by the international community. This has, however, not led to overt engagement with much more than the broad rhetoric of 'decent work' and, even then, at particular stages this has been absent.

The first *European Consensus for Development* (OJ C 46/1 24.2.2006) was adopted in 2006, stressing the EU's political commitment to PCD. Already, a Commission Communication (COM(2005)134 final: 3) had confirmed the determination of the EU to consider the extent to which PCD was achieved in certain key policy 'priority' areas: trade, the environment, climate change, security, agriculture, fisheries, the social dimension of globalisation, employment and decent work, migration, research and innovation, the information society, transport and energy. At this stage it was thought that 'the effective improvement in the coherence of developed countries' policies would put developing countries in a much better position' to achieve the MDGs by 2015. Development policy was no longer to be kept discretely in its own separate 'box'.

By 2009 a decision had been taken to cluster these policy areas around five 'PCD challenges'. These were to be: trade and finance, climate change, global food security, making migration work for development and strengthening links between security and development (COM(2009) 458 final 15.9.2009). Decent work was gone (despite the recent ILO Declaration of 2008), with only limited work-related issues potentially arising in the sphere of migration. Yet, following the 2011 EU Communication on the Agenda for Change (COM(2011) 637 final, 13.10.2011), the Directorate-General (DG) responsible for development cooperation (DEVCO) and the other directorates of the Commission started to take more stringent steps to measure the impacts of trade and investment on developing countries (in relation to the five PCD challenges) through:

- Impact Assessment Guidelines and the Better Regulation framework and
- a 'toolbox' for consideration by other DGs when externalising their policies.

The new Consensus on Development was signed in June 2017[5] and replaced the previous, decade-old version. It noted (at para 10) that PCD is 'a fundamental contribution to achieving the SDGs' and will be operationalised through a rights-based approach to development (para 16). The new Consensus stresses the existing priority areas, but sets these in a wider sphere of the 17 SDGs, which arguably entails a broader environmental agenda beyond climate change. SDG 8, which requires decent work and economic growth, gets a brief mention (at paras 22 and 33). What may be most significant is what is achieved by the further consultative process, initiated by the Commission in 2016 to set up a new *modus operandi* for PCD.[6] In this way the Commission is slowly approaching the idea of participatory institutions emphasised in SDG 16.

While matters concerning social policy internally within the EU were the subject of discussion between the 'social partners', that is, representatives of management and labour, and culminated in the adoption of a new European Social Pillar in 2018, there is less scope for representation of a worker voice in EU external relations. There are, then, dangers that the political modalities that have driven tariff preferences[7] and aid funding to date may yet be repeated, even when protection of labour standards is said to be at issue. It is interesting that in this 'sustainability' context of 'development' there is much less reference to the ILO, its standards and supervisory mechanisms than there is in trade. Genuine PCD may require further links to be made than are currently contemplated between development and trade policies, with worker voice included in the participatory processes envisaged.

Reconciling the global and regional: SDG 16 and the case for change at the ILO and in the EU

In the context of labour, there remains considerable scope for contestation over the content of sustainability standards. For example, do they include all four core ILO standards, or should 'freedom of association and the right to effective organisation' be regarded as secondary, given its treatment in SDG 8? If we can find room for this principle in the wide-ranging protections in SDG 16, then should we also be looking beyond the established 'core' to encompass employment standards such as wages, hours and health and safety? As noted earlier, the Global Commission on the Future of Work (ILO, 2019: 38ff) has proposed a 'Universal Labour Guarantee' covering not only the existing core labour standards but also 'an "adequate living wage", limits on hours of work and ensuring safe and healthy workplaces', since endorsed in Article III(B) of the ILO Centenary Declaration, which we might then expect to see included in EU future trade prescriptions. Indeed, there are already nascent forms of recognition of the benefits of such normative provision in recent sustainability chapters in EU FTAs, as noted earlier. However, we should not expect such changes to go unchallenged. In this respect, it may be telling that the whole of the ILO 'Decent Work Agenda' has yet to be incorporated into EU external relations. Further, Janice Bellace has argued convincingly that employers' perception of interdependence between EU trade conditionality, notions of corporate social responsibility and ILO standards has led to revolt. This culminated in the employers' walk-out from the ILO CAS and is currently manifested in ongoing review (and likely reform) of ILO supervisory mechanisms (Bellace, 2015). An interesting question is how, in future, these difficult questions will be resolved. My suggestions are two-fold.

Firstly, the ILO can no longer pretend that it does not influence the terms of trade; realistically, this issue needs to be brought openly within the ambit of the tripartite debate that the organisation offers. The ILO should therefore be offering submissions not just on SDG 8 (as it has in ILO, 2019b) but also on SDG 17. In so doing, the ILO would be working towards compliance with target 16.5, namely to develop effective, accountable and transparent institutions at all levels. Allowing that debate to take place openly, rather than being led by the normative power of the EU, would also enable developing countries more of a say in the modes by which ILO standards are respected in the context of trade in accordance with target 16.8.

Secondly, although the EU has played a leading role in placing social sustainability in a global frame through its trade policies, more still needs to be done. Sustainability, and indeed longer-term durability of any future labour laws and labour markets, needs to be based on inclusive participatory structures. Promoting labour standards as part of sustainable trade is unlikely to be achieved without a voice for workers both in the EU and in developing countries. We have seen that this is already partially recognised in sustainable development chapters within EU FTAs, which foster civil society participation. However, given the power dynamics at play, current measures seem inadequate for the realisation of genuine 'access to justice for all' under target 16.3 and 'responsive, inclusive, participatory and representative decision-making at all levels' under target 16.7. Worker voice in the creation, promotion and implementation of labour standards is unlikely to be effective in the absence of strong trade unions within legal structures which enable legitimate collective bargaining and action in relation to green issues and the future implications of current policies and measures. Without legal reform in Europe as a starting point, we are unlikely to achieve SDG 16 and the multifaceted regulatory solutions to sustainability problems that could be realised by its operation.

Conclusion

To conclude, connections are now being forged in ways that are both significant and defensible between labour standards, social sustainability and trade. However, they are still in a nascent form, requiring further attention, preferably in debate within the ILO in accordance with the norms set out in SDG 16. What may also be required is bolder ILO engagement in the global partnership under SDG 17, including that related to trade. There are hints in the ILO Centenary Declaration that this may be forthcoming, and that would be appropriate. These are not matters which should simply be delegated to the WTO (which refuses to address labour standards), or even to the EU, which possesses the normative force of a powerful trading bloc but (as the European Commission is well aware) should not be making unilateral decisions regarding sustainability for the rest of the world.

The SDGs offer connections to core ILO labour rights and other standards incorporated in the new Universal Labour Guarantee, enabling more far-reaching international recognition of their significance for the needs of present and future generations. This is possible not only by virtue of SDG 8, which makes direct reference to what would seem to be the ILO notion of 'decent work', but also SDGs 1, 5, 10 and 16 all of which, as explained earlier, have relevance to working lives and the regulation of the labour market. The ways in which established ILO norms affect interpretations and applications of the SDGs remain uncertain, as are the ways in which they could be made manifest through HLPF discussions and national implementation plans. What the SDGs do, however, is give weight to the EU's long-held view that labour standards are an important facet of social sustainability, to be given normative weight both in conjunction with other environmental and economic concerns and also independently.

There are also issues here which cannot only be resolved at the international level. Domestic and European legal frameworks within which trade unions operate will determine the extent to which they can be engaged in sustainability debates nationally, transnationally and within the ILO. The legal entitlement of unions to bargain collectively and take action on sustainability issues, regarding present and future generations, will make a difference, as will their ability to use their membership subscriptions for such 'political' purposes. Without that entitlement, their capacity for engagement in 'responsive, inclusive, participatory and representative decision-making' envisaged in SDG 16.7 will be unduly limited. There is a case for Europe to achieve such change. This could be done both within the Council of Europe human rights regime and in the EU through removal of the restrictions placed on trade union activity in the context of the exercise by employers of their market freedoms. In these ways, workers' voice could contribute to the access to justice and inclusive debates at all levels that SDG 16 envisages.

Notes

1. Labour standards are included in the Sustainable Development Chapters of the following EU-FTAs: Korea; the Comprehensive Economic Trade Agreement with Canada (CETA); Colombia/Peru (with Ecuador); Central America (Costa Rica, El Salvador, Guatemala, Honduras, Nicaragua and Panama); Moldova; Georgia; Ukraine; Singapore; Vietnam; and the SADC Economic Partnership Agreement (South Africa, Botswana, Lesotho, Swaziland, Mozambique, Namibia). See for further comment Gammage (2019).
2. Instead, UK trade unions have been setting up their own systems for 'green reps'. See https://www.unison.org.uk/content/uploads/2013/06/On-line-Catalogue189353.pdf; and https://www.pcs.org.uk/resources/green-workplaces/green-reps.
3. See https://www.ilo.org/global/topics/green-jobs/lang--en/index.htm.
4. See https://www.ilo.org/global/about-the-ilo/history/centenary/lang--en/index.htm.
5. See https://ec.europa.eu/europeaid/sites/devco/files/european-consensus-on-development-final-20170626_en.pdf.
6. See https://ec.europa.eu/info/consultations/public-consultation-evaluation-european-unions-policy-coherence-development-2009-2016_en.
7. Cf the EC Tariff Preferences case discussed earlier in the chapter, which was concerned with exclusion of India (and inclusion of Pakistan) in certain tariff preferences.

References

Bartels, L. (2007) 'The WTO legality of the EU's GSP+ Arrangement', *Journal of International Economic Law* 10: 869–86.

Bartels, L. (2012) 'Human rights and sustainable development obligations in EU Free Trade Agreements' in Legal Studies Research Paper Series, University of Cambridge Faculty of Law, Paper No 24/ 2012. Available at: www.academia.edu/1902855/Human_rights_and_sustainable_development_obligations_in_EU_free_trade_agreements

Bellace, J. (2015) 'Pushback on the right to strike', in A. Blackett and A. Trebilcock, (eds) *Research Handbook on Transnational Labour Law*, Cheltenham: Edward Elgar, pp 93–107.

Blackett, A. (2001) 'Global governance, legal pluralism and the decentered state: a labor law critique of codes of corporate conduct', *Indiana Journal of Global Legal Studies* 8(2): 401–47.

Boström, M. (2012) 'A missing pillar? Challenges in theorizing and practicing social sustainability: introduction to the special issue', *Sustainability: Science, Practice and Policy* 8(1): 3–14.

Chacartegui, C. (2018) 'Workers' participation and green governance', *Comparative Labor Law and Policy Journal* 40(1): 89–108.

De Schutter, O. (2015) *Trade in the Service of Sustainable Development: Linking Trade to Labour Rights and Environmental Standards*, Oxford: Hart/Bloomsbury, Oxford.

Doorey, D. (2017) 'Just transitions law: putting labour law to work on climate change', *Journal of Environmental Law & Practice* 30(2): 201–20.

Ebert, F. (2016) 'Labour provisions in EU trade agreements: what potential for channelling labour standards-related capacity building?', *International Labour Review* 155(3): 407–33.

ETUC (European Trade Union Confederation) (2010) *Resolution on a Sustainable New Deal for Europe and Towards Cancun*, Brussels: ETUC. Available at: www.etuc.org/en/publication/resolution-sustainable-new-deal-europe-and-towards-cancun

European Commission (2010) *Commission Communication, 'EUROPE 2020: A strategy for smart, sustainable and inclusive growth'* Brussels, 3.3.2010 COM (2010) 2020 final.

European Parliament (2018) *The Generalised Scheme of Preferences Regulation (No 978/2012): European Implementation Assessment Study*, Brussels: European Parliament. Available at: www.europarl.europa.eu/RegData/etudes/STUD/2018/627134/EPRS_STU(2018)627134_EN.pdf

Frey, D.F. and MacNaughton, G. (2016) 'A human rights lens on full employment and decent work in the 2030 Sustainable Development Agenda', *Journal of Workplace Rights* 6(2): 1–13. Available at: https://journals.sagepub.com/doi/pdf/10.1177/2158244016649580

Fuchs, C. (2017) 'Critical social theory and sustainable development: the role of class, capitalism and domination in a dialectical analysis of un/sustainability', *Sustainable Development* 25(5): 443–58.

Galgoczi, B. (2014) 'The changing role of trade unions in the sustainable development agenda', *International Review of Sociology*, 24(1): 59–68.

Gammage, C. (2019) 'Social norms in EU-free trade agreements: justiciable or not?', in C. Gammage and T. Novitz (eds), *Sustainable Trade, Investment, and Finance: Toward Responsible and Coherent Regulatory Frameworks*, Cheltenham: Edward Elgar, forthcoming.

Gammage, C. and Novitz, T. (2019) 'Trade, investment and corporate sustainability', in B. Sjåfjell and C. Bruner (eds), *Cambridge Handbook on Corporate Sustainability*, Cambridge: Cambridge University Press, forthcoming.

ILO (International Labour Organisation) (2004) Report of the World Commission on the Social Dimension of Globalization, *A fair Globalization, Creating Opportunities for All*, Geneva: ILO. Available at: www.ilo.org/global/publications/ilo-bookstore/order-online/books/WCMS_PUBL_9221154262_EN/lang--en/index.htm

ILO (2010) *Cancun Agreement: ILO Highlights Call for a 'Just Transition' with Green Jobs and Decent Work*, Geneva: ILO.

ILO (2015a) *Guidelines for a Just Transition Towards Environmentally Sustainable Economies and Societies*, Geneva: ILO. Available at: www.ilo.org/global/topics/green-jobs/publications/WCMS_432859/lang--en/index.htm

ILO (2015b) *Report of the Director General: ILO Future of Work Centenary Initiative*, ILC 104th Session, Geneva: ILO. Available at: www.ilo.org/wcmsp5/groups/public/---ed_norm/---relconf/documents/meetingdocument/wcms_369026.pdf

ILO (2016a) *Assessment of Labour Provisions in Trade and Investment Agreements*, Geneva: ILO. Available at: www.ilo.org/global/publications/books/WCMS_498944/lang--en/index.htm

ILO (2016b) *Decent Work in Global Supply Chains*, Geneva: ILO. Available at: www.ilo.org/ilc/ILCSessions/105/reports/reports-to-the-conference/WCMS_468097/lang--en/index.htm

ILO (Committee of Experts on the Application of Conventions and Recommendations) (2016c) *Promoting Fair Migration – General Survey Concerning the Migrant Workers Instruments*, Geneva: ILO. Available at: www.ilo.org/global/standards/WCMS_453917/lang--en/index.htm

ILO (2018) *Decent Work and the Sustainable Development Goals: A Guidebook on SDG Labour Market Indicators*, Geneva: ILO. Available at: www.ilo.org/wcmsp5/groups/public/---dgreports/---stat/documents/publication/wcms_647109.pdf

ILO (Global Commission on the Future of Work) (2019a) *Work for a Brighter Future*, Geneva: ILO. Available at: www.ilo.org/global/publications/books/WCMS_662410/lang--en/index.htm

ILO (2019b) *Time to Act for SDG 8: Integrating Decent Work, Sustained Growth and Environmental Integrity*, Geneva, ILO. Available at: www.ilo.org/global/publications/books/WCMS_712685/lang--en/index.htm (accessed 2 August 2019).

Jacobs, M. (2012) *Green Growth: Economic Theory and Political Discourse*. No 92, Grantham Research Institute on Climate Change and the Environment.

La Hovary, C. (2013) 'Showdown at the ILO? A historical perspective on the Employers' Group's 2012 challenge to the right to strike', *Industrial Law Journal* 42(4): 338–68.

Leary, V. (1997) 'The WTO and the social clause: post-Singapore', *European Journal of International Law* 8: 118–22.

Littig, B. and Grießler, E. (2005) 'Social sustainability: a catchword between political pragmatism and social theory', *International Journal of Sustainable Development*, 8(1–2): 65–79.

Lund, H.L. (2004) 'Strategies for sustainable business and the handling of workers' interests: integrated management systems and worker participation', *Economic and Industrial Democracy* 25(1): 41–68.

McCann, D. and Fudge, J. (2017) 'Unacceptable forms of work: a multidimensional model', *International Labour Review* 156(2): 147–84.

Novitz, T. (2014) 'Evolutionary trajectories for transnational labour law: trade in goods to trade in services?', *Current Legal Problems* 67(1): 239–71.

Novitz, T. (2015) 'The paradigm of sustainability in a European social context: collective participation in protection of future interests?', *The International Journal of Comparative Labour Law and Industrial Relations* 31(3): 243–62.

Novitz, T. (2019) 'Freedom of association: its emergence and the case for prevention of its decline', in J. Bellace and B. Ter Haar (eds), *Business, Labour and Human Rights*, Cheltenham: Edward Elgar.

Novitz, T. and Mangan, D. (eds) (2011) *The Role of Labour Standards in Development: From Theory to sustainable Practice?* Oxford: British Academy/Oxford University Press.

Perulli, A. (2018) 'Sustainable development, global trade and social rights: an evolutionary perspective', in A. Perulli and T. Trey (eds), *Sustainable Development, Global Trade and Social Rights*, Alphen aan den Rijn: Kluwer.

Polomarkakis, K. (2019) 'The European Pillar of Social Rights and the quest for EU social sustainability', *Social and Legal Studies*. Available at: https://journals.sagepub.com/doi/pdf/10.1177/0964663919829199

Räthzel, N. and Uzzell, D. (eds) (2013) *Trade Unions in the Green Economy*, London: Routledge.

Roberts, A. (2016) 'Household debt and the financialization of social reproduction: theorizing the UK housing and hunger crises', in S. Soederberg (ed), *Risking Capitalism*, Bradford: Emerald, pp 135–64.

Rose, A. (2019) 'The climate change strike: From a student who was there' *Chain Reaction* 135: 12.

Salazar-Xirinachs, J.M. (2000) 'The trade-labor nexus: developing countries' perspectives', *Journal of International Economic Law* 3(2): 377–85.

Schipani, C., Milliken, F. and Dworkin, T.M. (2016) 'The impact of employment law and practices on business and society: the significance of worker voice' *University of Pennsylvania Journal of Business Law* 19: 979.

Seck, S. (2018) 'Transnational labour law and the environment: beyond the bounded autonomous worker', *Canadian Journal of Law and Society* 33(2): 137–57.

Short Jr, J.F. (2018) *Poverty, Ethnicity, and Violent Crime*, London: Routledge.

Spangenberg, J. (2016) 'The world we see shapes the world we create: how the underlying worldviews lead to different recommendations from environmental and ecological economics – the green economy example', *International Journal of Sustainable Development* 19(2): 127–46.

Stiglitz, J. (2016) 'The measurement of wealth: recessions, sustainability and inequality', *Contemporary Issues in Macroeconomics*, London: Palgrave Macmillan, pp 63–76.

TUC (Trades Union Congress) (2014) *The Union Effect: Greening the Workplace*, London: TUC.

Ulmer, K. (2015) 'Trade embedded development models', *International Journal of Comparative Labour Law and Industrial Relations* 31(3): 305–29.

UN (United Nations) (2015) GA Resolution, *Transforming Our World: The 2030 Agenda for Sustainable Development*, 25 September 2015 A/Res/70/1. Available at: https://sustainabledevelopment.un.org/post2015/transformingourworld/publication

Vallance, S., Perkins, H.C. and Dixon, J.E. (2011) 'What is social sustainability? A clarification of concepts', *Geoforum* 42(3): 342–8.

Van den Putte, L. and Orbie, J. (2015) 'EU bilateral trade agreements and the surprising rise of labour provisions', *International Journal of Comparative Labour Law and Industrial Relations*, 31(3): 263–83.

Vogt, J. (2015) 'A little less conversation: the EU and the (non) application of labour conditionality in the generalized system of preferences (GSP)', *International Journal of Comparative Labour Law and Industrial Relations* 31(3): 285–304.

Vogt, J. (2017) 'Comments for "on the justification of the right to strike in the ILO system of standards"', *Comparative Labor Law and Policy Journal* 39: 537–42.

Wardhaugh, B. (2013) 'GSP+ and human rights: is the EU's approach the right one?', *Journal of International Economic Law*, 16:827–46.

World Commission on Environment and Development (1987) *Our Common Future*, Oxford: Oxford University Press.

Xiao, Y. et al (2017) 'How social footprints of nations can assist in achieving the sustainable development goals', *Ecological Economics* 135: 55–65.

PART IV

Places

7

Land Ownership, Use and Sustainability in a Pluriverse

Chris Willmore

Introduction

Land use is not itself a Sustainable Development Goal (SDG), but the attainment of almost every goal is affected by choices about how land is used – either directly in the case of SDG 15, about life on land, or indirectly, such as through choices about food production or as the subject matter of war. But the power of land stretches beyond the physical uses made of land. Studies have identified the centrality of landowners as wider social and economic gatekeepers (Marsden, 1993) influencing how a community lives and its priorities. This means that land use and those exercising property rights have a critical role to play in the delivery of sustainability.

Yet the law governing land ownership and use is not structured to prioritise sustainability. There is a vast body of literature about what has been described as the environmentally myopic nature of property rights (Marguerat, 2019). But this myopia is not limited to the physical environment aspects of sustainability. Graham has argued that property law's categories and structures 'have exceeded their utility' (Graham, 2010) in terms of delivering a sustainable future.

While concepts of 'ownership' of land vary across jurisdictions, all forms, except some forms of native title (Craig, 2000; Oxhorn and Dodsworth, 2013), give a degree of exclusivity of control, including the right to use or not use the land; or even to change its use to the point of destroying it, with regulation intervening to assert elite priorities about the exercise of those rights. There are limitations upon what can be owned in the current conceptual framework, such as global commons, but the majority of the landmass is covered by property systems in which specific private or public bodies have exploitation rights in relation to areas of land, conceptually unfettered by concerns for the future well-being of people or planet or, indeed, of the past – but equally potentially able to create a pluriverse of meanings and worlds.

This chapter explores the mismatch between the structures of land law and the demands of the SDGs. Whether the question is seen as a disconnect from physical (Graham, 2010) or social realities (Gray, 1998, 2003), there is widespread recognition of a problem with property law, extending beyond its relationship to sustainability. Some well-developed approaches focus upon improving property law so it can be better used to contribute to specific SDGs. Wildlaw, for example, is focused upon SDG15/16. Wildlaw rejects the anthropocentric prism of law and instead asks 'what if nature had rights?' (Cullinan, 2011). Similarly, redistributional approaches to property focus on SDG 1 and 10 (poverty and inequality) (Honore, 1977; Prosterman, 2012). These give rise to the problems of the binary and risks of substituting elite priorities – issues explored in Pieraccini and Novitz in Chapter 2 of this book.

In Chapter 2, Pieraccini and Novitz explore the significance of diverse human engagement with the sustainability objectives, and caution against seeking an elite-driven single prioritisation. Sustainability is positioned as a movement, not a unified single goal. Individuals have diverse experiences, agendas and priorities. The fact that different people will see sustainability through different prisms and inhabit different versions of reality is both a practical strength of the movement and a conceptual necessity. The people's assembly approach in the Extinction Rebellion movement exemplifies this approach. Movements are diverse, stress the journey, not a single destination, and value that diffused power, as opposed to organisations that are inherently structured and hierarchic. Sustainability is fundamentally focused on future thinking: identifying a plurality of futures, which coexist as goals, and an equally diverse set of responses to the steps needed to bring about those worlds.

One useful way of articulating this diverse approach is the concept of the pluriverse (see Chapter 1 for a fuller discussion). Its essence is that there are many ways of being and many ways of knowing: multiple ontologies and multiple worlds. Understanding that these are all valid, and together contribute to a richer, stronger movement for change, is vital. But to adopt that approach we have to be able to set aside the notion that there is *a* solution that fits the SDGs together neatly and is owned or managed centrally. It requires lawyers to think differently, to identify how law can be used to facilitate this plurality of being. Law is repositioned not as a tool to move us on a linear path to an elite-defined better future but, rather, as a tool to recognise and empower a multiplicity of paths and meaning. This is unusual ground for law and is more commonly the domain of free market thinkers.

This chapter explores ways in which property law can be used to help contribute to the attainment of a more sustainable future in a pluriversal model in which complexity is welcomed and multiple responses and priorities are valued as a positive attribute, not merely an inevitable practicality, without connotations of 'free market' economic values and individualism. In it I argue that a pluriversal understanding of sustainability requires the use of a relational approach to thinking about property, emphasising connections to land as opposed to state regulation, and in particular that (Radin, 1982) offers a rich way of thinking about land law/land-use rights that reflects this relational approach.

The chapter examines regulatory approaches, looking at the extent to which they are perceived as reflecting external elite-derived imperatives and the significance of empowerment as a core feature of delivering pluriversal approaches to sustainability. It notes a dissonance between the increasing levels of state regulatory structuring of private land use in relation to sustainability and the absence of leadership in relation to land owned by public bodies. It argues for a rethink of the role of regulation, to place the empowerment of pluriversal approaches at the core of state action and concludes that Radin's thinking offers a route to this.

The chapter is structured as follows: relational approaches to property thinking will be explored in the context of pluriversal understandings of property law. The nature of regulation in the land use context will be considered against pluriversal approaches, and then a brief exploration of the challenge of state-owned land will highlight the extent to which the state is externalising elite priorities through regulation of others rather than internal action.

Concepts of property: pluriversality and relationality

Some argue that the fundamental problem of property law is the disconnection of property rights from the physical entity of the land itself (Graham, 2010). This is at its most acute in relation to those who regard land as a fungible. Perceptions of land as a fungible underpin much of the discourse around title registration and the World Bank initiatives (Pashukanis, 1924; Hanstad, 1997; Anderson, 1998; de Soto, 2000). In these perceptions, land rights become a particular way of holding capital, in which the relationship of a particular physical parcel of land to the asset value is irrelevant, concepts of place and space are excluded and the asset is seen in the abstract. Sustainability here is commodified as part of the asset value. This chapter, however, focuses upon land itself and the articulations of property law as a relationship to that physical entity.

Whether land rights are perceived as part of the problem or a as tool that can be harnessed as part of the solution depends upon differing assessments of the capacity of property law to change, or for re-articulations of property law to make a difference. There are many discourses through which the challenge of reframing property rights within a pluriverse approach can be explored, from dissensus (Rancière, 2001) to relational thinking (Debaise, 2012). But core to the family of approaches is the emphasis upon the positive benefits of multiple paths and meaning and the centrality of relationality and interactions. These approaches can be distinguished both from responses that create a binary between public and private interests, and from responses that interpose a frame of elite determined responsibilities. The strength of property rights is the spaces that it can create within which multiple paths can be explored by those who have property rights. The owner of an estate in land has freedom to do as she wishes – up to and including destroying the land. But that freedom also creates space for landowners to use the land to contribute to their own perception of a more sustainable future – a pluriversal space.

If we start from a single view of what must be done to attain sustainability, the multiple loci of power vested in dispersed property ownership are problematic. But if we start from a pluriversal conceptualisation of the journey towards sustainability, then those multiple loci of power become a positive attribute, a means through which multiple experiments can take place, without the need for a central directing conceptualisation. This complexity of communities, obligations and sustainability priorities is recognised in the work of property theorists (Davies, 2007; Arnold, 2011; Nedelsky, 2011; Davies, 2012) who each, in different ways, draw out ways to refocus property thinking on its relational and connective aspects.

Arnold approaches the challenge from a model of a 'web of interests', which weaves together 'public' and 'private' interests into a web, rather than seeing each set of rights as discrete bundles. Within the web he sees private rights as more powerful, but problematises this. Writers such as Graham go on to argue that a key is reconnecting rights to responsibilities (Graham, 2010). This moves from the language of externality in regulation to positioning limits as an internal facet of relationships. This has the strength of seeking to overcome the externality challenge but leaves open the question of who determines the responsibilities that are to be inherent in the definition of property. Whatever the mechanisms through which these responsibilities are ascribed, they connote a degree of elite determination, not pluriversality – at best a socially constructed set of responsibilities, but potentially a government-derived structure repackaged as a set of inherent responsibilities.

Conceptualisations of property containing an internal/external paradigm have at their core a binary of things over which a person exercises property rights/obligations and things economists would consider externalities. Regulatory control is justified by reference to those externalities, and while the precise framing of which externalities will be recognised as such and which should be regulated will vary, the concept remains unchanged. The property in the form of an estate in land, or indeed the land itself, is seen in a vacuum. Some respond to this by seeking to establish a theory of environmental property, using resource allocation models (Rodgers, 2009), or by arguing that conventional models have failed to recognise the social obligation norms which are at play in the experiences of geographically situated landowners (Gray and Gray, 1998, 2003; Pascoe, 2012). This can lead to an emphasis on calls for regulatory change. In these approaches the problem is not with governance per se but with the particular concept of current regulatory controls (Marguerat, 2019). Here the focus is on the physical existence of land as a limited natural resource to be managed by the state or international community for public good, often juxtaposing this physical resource management to fungibility ideas (Singer, 1988, 2000, 2006; Davies, 2007; MacLeod, 2015). These models can embrace sustainability, but through a socially constructed, elite ontology. Pluriversal thinking requires a different approach to property regulation, as empowerment not as management.

A more productive approach, in terms of pluriversal thinking, is to start from seeing property as socially situated (Singer, 2006), a product of place and space. Here, the physical space itself becomes a place through the social ascribing of meaning and significance and requires a framing of property that recognises that social meaning (Radin, 1982; Blomley, 1994; Trachtenberg, 1997; Anderson, 1998; Blomley et al, 2001). When we look at the question of externalities not from the angle of what the state should regulate (my castle vs the domain of state intervention) but from the angle of what we consider as our home or place of belonging it becomes more complex. Our sense of belonging to a place engages not just the space over which we may have some sort of property law right, but also a wider domain, with which we interact and which forms part of our place. At a slightly wider level again there is a sense of community of belonging to a wider whole. All of these point away from a binary analysis, mine vs 'not something I have any right to comment upon', to a continuum of spheres of influence and legitimacy. This gives articulation to interpretations which are not elite derived.

Moore (1978) argues: 'Many lawyers and law professors view law as an instrument for controlling society and directing social change, but most anthropologists are concerned with law as a reflection of a particular social order.' Socio-legal approaches, particularly those informed by anthropology, move the focus towards the conduct and discourses in diverse communities: what people do, not the structures of the law (Popisil, 1971). This is inherently pluriversal.

Some argue that the common law approach already includes elements of social or normative obligations in relation to how land is used (Alexander, 2009; Pascoe, 2012), although this can be seen as more a question of mutual benefit reciprocity rather than normative social obligations (Dagan and Heller, 2001; Dagan, 2006). But, in its more normative approach it most often manifests in the language of stewardship (Lucy and Mitchell, 1996), primarily through physical environmental-focused approaches (Worrell and Appleby, 2000). The source of the obligation of care posited by stewardship varies – it can be religious, social, or even consumer-centred resource management. While this sort of approach can contribute to a pluriversal sustainability, particular uses of the concept of stewardship need interrogation to identify the source of the obligation. If used in the sense of a personal, internalised obligation, then it can facilitate a pluriversal approach, resonating with the 'ethical' approach adopted in the French hunting cases considered later. Page (2016) develops this notion of stewardship as a language through which multiple values can be reflected.

A particularly useful approach can be found in Radin (1982). Her work starts from consideration not of the physical land, as Graham's does (2010), but of the concept of place. 'Space' is used to refer to the physical entity, 'place' to connote the meaning of that physical space, derived from our multiple relationships to it. Those concepts of place are not uniform or even consistent, vary with time and are contingent. The problem is that law is firmly embedded in a universalist model of land (Page, 2016), lacking the diversity, contingency and adaptability that is a feature of practical relationships to land (Blomley et al, 2001) and which offer pluriversal approaches to sustainability. Even doctrinal property law analysts recognise the organic nature of property relationships – 'because how people use land is complex and not static' (Dixon, 2017).

This complexity and construction of place goes beyond the traditional property law categories, in which easements, covenants, trusts, leases and freeholds can coexist in relation to a parcel of land. While these defined relationships are the ones currently recognised in property law, conferring rights that bind the world, the reality of relationships to space, and the construction of place, is much more complex, contingent and varied.

Radin argues that in order to be a person an individual 'needs some control over resources in the external environment' (Radin, 1982). She distinguishes fungibles from those resources that she calls 'personal property'. This latter category is property that is not replaceable by money or other property but 'is part of the way [people] constitute [them]selves as continuing personal entities in the world' (Radin, 1982). Personal property in this sense is not equated to concepts of ownership or tenure – we may have personal property in this sense in things well beyond the limits of our freehold estate. Around a core of property that is mine to control there is an ever-weakening penumbra of property over which I have influence to which I feel an affinity. This sense goes beyond Graham's call to reconnect property law to the physical entity, as it encompasses personal responses to that physical entity and personal constructions of what constitutes the entity (Graham, 2010). It is pluriversal in its recognition of multiple worlds.

Individual mappings overlap with countless other personal mappings: what Singer describes as 'imbricated' (Singer, 2000). Boundaries of title in property law terms are seen not as absolute demarcators of boundaries of control but, rather, as points of transition in the analysis of influence. There is a tension between perceptions of property 'rights' in relation to an individual parcel of land in a vacuum and property conceived as part of a wider place or space, with mutual dependencies. The land-use planning process, for example, often encounters a tension between an applicant's desire to use his land in a particular way and the impact of that on other people's sense of place. This is often articulated as opposition to unwanted changes in the character of the community or locality, as a violation of people's 'place' (Davoudi et al, 2008). Evidence for this approach comes from responses to planning applications by third parties, where the language the respondents select maps onto this notion. Objectors do make economic arguments, for example about the impact on property values, but a very common theme in planning objections and the language chosen to articulate them is the extent to which the proposed development impacts on third-party perceptions of 'personal property' in Radin's sense of what constitutes me and my place. Regulation, when it is designed to be responsive, is seen not as regulating externalities but as charting a path through a complex weave of connections to place and space which are not fungible and are by definition connected to our sense of self and place.

Lametti (2003) described property as:

> a social institution that comprise[s] a variety of contextual relationships among individuals through objects of social wealth and is meant to serve a variety of individual and collective purposes. It is characterized by allocating to individuals a measure of control over the use and alienation of, some degree of exclusivity in the enjoyment of, and some measure of obligation to and responsibilities for scarce and separable social wealth.

This graduated statement brings us in a different way to a similar place, that private property is part of a weave, and that this weave is located in a place and space.

Which of these overlaps or 'harms' will be afforded normative relevance and therefore be subject to legal management is the question posed by discussions about the legitimate scope of regulation. Radin uses the concept of 'human flourishing' to guide which personal property claims should be given normative relevance. Her argument is that property connected to who we are should be protected differently from fungible property, as the latter can be replaced, but the personal connection cannot. As an example, she argues that the tenant of a property, living in it as their home, has a stronger connection to that place than the landowner who is renting it out for an income. Originally, she saw this as having an objective basis, but latterly located it in a philosophical pragmatism, grounded firmly in the meaning afforded to connections to land in the real world (Radin, 1993). In planning law, as an example of complex regulation, we see an approach to normative relevance that is elite determined, varying with time according to changes in elite prioritisation rather than accommodating the pluriverse of people's sense of place (Willmore, 2017).

This approach is not without criticism (for example, Schnably, 1993), but offers a language through which to explore the anthropological reality of people's connection to land and their construction of their ontology and world.

Regulation or empowerment?

A core characteristic of land law systems, which has been the subject of criticism by many writers seeking to reframe land law systems in relation to sustainability, is its emphasis upon 'neutrality' as between individuals – a 'Blue Peter' approach setting out a system of defined rights that enables people to create and transfer rights which bind the world – without expressing any purposes for which such rights might be created or transferred. A pluriversal analysis raises different questions about this feature of land law systems. Most jurisdictions place an emphasis on regulation to interpose the elite's interpretation of one or more directing principles as limits to the exercise of those powers, but it is difficult in the context of property law to see the operation of de Sadeleer's notion of sustainability as a directing principle (de Sadeleer, 2002).

Regulation can offer a vehicle through which priorities about property use can be articulated, but views differ about whether regulation can, ultimately, provide a sufficient redirection of the use of property rights. Sax has argued that the property law promotes conduct that militates against sustainability (Sax, 2008). McDonald has argued that 'institutions that are resistant to change or that change in small increments', including property rights, are barriers to adaptation (McDonald, 2010). However, others, such as Shoard, have argued that a characteristic of English property rights has been the capacity of the approach to bend and adapt just enough to head off arguments for fundamental change (Shoard, 1987; Graham, 2010).

The options for more regulation are well documented, with writers considering how particular regulatory regimes could be modified, or indeed whole new regulatory regimes established. But, more significantly to the concept of sustainability, regulation is too often positioned as control based within an elite-determined ontology. It is about the identification and regulation of problems as defined by centres of power, not the construction of a pluriverse.

However, the form of the regulatory regime profoundly affects whether it is an externalised voice, disconnected from both the property rights owner and those who have a sense of connection to that place. Planning law, for example, is still, at least structurally, based upon local decision making in which there is a potential for place and the voices of place to play a role. But most regulatory regimes, particularly those which impact on markets, offer no recognition of the importance of constructs of place or of wider community views – any more than they do the views of the landowner – because they are elite-priority expert systems.

Planning law has the potential to put pluriversal perceptions of place at the core of community engagements with development control: a sense of it being legitimate to oppose land use changes because of their community impacts. Residents opposing unwanted development believe they have a legitimacy in their objection. They do not articulate their activity as about interference with a developer's rights to use their own land but, rather, as an attempt to vindicate their own rights as individuals and communities. If we believe that law needs to reflect the realities of people's perceptions of their rights, then there is a need to consider how these strongly articulated claims of rights of place are to be factored in – not because they fit elite priorities but because they reflect pluriversal views. By doing that, we undermine the bipolar notion of private/public and start to create a space for exploring shared understandings. Radin's approach explains why and how pluriversal approaches to the SDGs are crucial.

Few systems make any attempt to articulate the purpose of land and land rights in society, let alone its connection to sustainability or pluriversal approaches. The silence as to the goals of land law has the potential to create pluriversal spaces. From a pluriversal perspective, articulation of a single-elite ontology as the directing principle of land law could itself be problematic unless framed in pluriversal terms. A rare and interesting exception can be found in the Land Reform (Scotland) Act 2016, which required the Scottish Government to issue a statement of principles in keeping with the human rights and sustainability approach to land rights and responsibilities. The resulting statement says:

> The overall framework of land rights, responsibilities and public policies should promote, fulfil and respect relevant human rights in relation to land, contribute to public interest and wellbeing, and balance public and private interests. The framework should support sustainable economic development, protect and enhance the environment, help achieve social justice and build a fairer society. (Scottish Government, 2017)

This is a wide statement that, while not framed explicitly in terms of the SDGs, provides scope for pluriversal approaches. It moves the focus of the question from how we redirect the use of property rights to achieve particular goals, to one of looking at the opportunities for a range of different meanings and priorities to flourish. So far it is unclear whether this sort of formulation has an impact on the contribution of land and land rights to sustainability. As the Scottish Government review (2015) concludes, while there is 'widespread anecdotal evidence, systematic assessments of the social, economic or environmental impacts of land and asset ownership by communities … are somewhat limited in Scotland'.

This is perhaps the closest we get to a pluriversal approach to land ownership legislation. The Welsh Wellbeing of Future Generations Act 2015 places duties upon public bodies: when exercising regulatory or dominium powers, those are converted into the primary purpose of action, but it does not facilitate pluriversal approaches explicitly.

In most cases, state responses to sustainability create regulations focused on specific aspects, leading to complex webs of regulatory structures with inherent contradictions and unresolved tensions. The failures of regulation tend to lead to more calls for better regulation, redefined regulation, more regulation (Bromley, 2007; Fisher, 2007; Prosser, 2010; Scotford and Oliver, 2013). So, sustainable land use has increasingly become a public law sphere of influence. This externalises sustainability, rather than normalisingit. Sustainability, in the particular manifestation of multiple regulatory controls, is posited as an external barrier, not an internal system driver. While some have sought to argue that regulation is internal to our concept of property law, rather than an external limiting factor (Scotford and Walsh, 2013), Sax argued that the property regime itself creates a 'deep structure of incentives and disincentives … about how people are actually going to behave' (Sax, 2008, 10–11), whereas regulation is seen as an externalised counter force, seeking to control or limit the 'normal'.

It is easy to see regulation, in all its forms, as imposing an elite ontology. But that is not necessarily the case: regulation can be used differently to create space for pluralist responses, to empower landowners/users to act sustainably or to prohibit conduct which serves as a barrier to them doing so. However, such approaches require us to de-problematise landowners.

Writers such as Farrier (2011) bemoan the problems of getting landowners to use land for sustainable goals. Legal efforts to address the role of land in creating a sustainable future have tended to focus upon modernist tools, in particular, direct regulation by states, coupled with a complex array of incentives. Even responsive or reflective regulation can be seen as focused on getting people to do things they don't want to do.

Perceptions of landowners as requiring elite intervention to deliver an externally determined good points towards such command-and-control tools. A common feature of these approaches is a perception that there is a 'right' way forward, embedded in elite capture of policy making and the use of regulation to deliver elite-imposed priorities. The result is calls from populist movements for reductions in regulation, particularly where they are perceived to transfer the cost of elite prioritisation to poorer landowners. In such analyses the state is positioned as a necessary regulator of what would otherwise be bad choices by landowners (Shoard, 1987; Marsden, 1993). Such approaches tend to concentrate on regulating particular aspects of sustainably, thereby producing a fragmentation of thinking in which landowners are subject to an array of regulation, not necessarily entirely consistent or integrated. Not only do they not really engage in more transformative action, but such regulation does not do so through sustainable processes, notably partnership and the shared ownership of goals. The ultimate focus is compliance, not transformation or empowerment.

Owners of property rights are not all bad. Many want to use their land to contribute to a more sustainable future (Reinhardt, 2008) – see for example, Gill, Klepis and Chisholm's case study of amenity migration (Gill et al, 2010). Many are the victims of societal failures; for example, many of the world's climate change refugees are landowners no longer able to use their land sustainably. That is the stark starting point of this section of the chapter. In focusing on problematic users of land, law may be failing to support, or even hindering, positive users; and while the worst conduct will continue to need regulatory prohibitions, there is scope to think more positively about how law could facilitate those who want to use land sustainably. While there is an array of agri- and development incentives to landowners, the models within which they operate position landowners as people who will not want to act more sustainably needing to be incentivised to do so.

The problematising of landowners occurs despite a lack of evidence to suggest that landowners are any less committed than others to delivering their perception of a sustainable future; indeed, there is some evidence that long-term security of tenure can affect future planning – a key feature of sustainability thinking (Scottish Government, 2015). Working within the property law system and providing tools to assist those seeking to act sustainably has had impact (Rodgers, 2009). It might not reflect elite preoccupations about sustainability, but it is nonetheless a response to the challenge of creating a more sustainable future. So, we need to disentangle whether the concerns are about landowners not embracing sustainability or about their not embracing a specific elite version of sustainability. In a pluriversal model there is a need to reflect a far wider range of approaches. This is not to suggest all landowners will be committed in this way – they are no more immune from short-termism than governments, multinationals or individuals. But, where landowners have a desire to pursue their perspective of a more sustainable future, are there elite imposed barriers to doing so? Some of these barriers, such as the complexity of grant incentives, can distort choice and act as a disincentive to holistic thinking about the role of particular areas of land in a more sustainable future. They may even go further and externalise the whole sustainability question.

The question for those wanting to contribute to a more sustainable future becomes what is needed to remove barriers and to positively facilitate that pluriverse of understandings and uses. That is not to say that there is no need for limitations on the acceptable range of answers or to facilitate opportunities for those who do not have the opportunities to develop their own sense of meaning that property rights entail, but that there is a need to focus more attention on how the law can enable, empower or at the very least stop getting in the way of a pluriverse of sustainability responses in the context of land.

Ultimately, regulation of land use to deliver the positive outcomes sought by the SDGs requires a different type of regulatory approach: empowerment, signposting and recognition of a plurality of positive conduct. Jurisdictions have shown a marked reluctance to adopt these sorts of positive approaches, even where specific manifestations of problems are highly geographically specific. A classic example of this is in relation to habitat conservation, where it is an offence to damage Sites of Special Scientific Interest as protected locations, but there is not a commensurate process for ensuring that the sites are positively cared for, let alone restored under the UK Wildlife and Countryside Act 1981. Regulation here stops bad conduct but is silent about helping positive conduct. Instead, positive conduct tends to be promoted through fiscal or other financial incentives, focusing on short-term financial gains, not long-term sustainability choices by the landowner. This can, in extreme cases, actually undermine a landowner's long-term sustainability choices by creating short-term economic incentives.

More commonly, rather than barriers, there is a deficiency, a lack of suitable provision, in current property thinking. Conservation covenants (Reid, 2011; Hodge, 2013) offer a good example of the opportunities to rethink land law within current models so as to address that deficiency. These operate as geographically specific agreements between landowners about what they will or will not do on their land for conservation purposes. They operate within current property law systems, empowering landowners to determine their contribution to conservation, but then using property law to ensure that those decisions bind successors in title. They enable a landowner who wishes to protect land long term to put in place obligations that will bind their successors. As such, they offer a good example of a pluriversal adaptation of property law.

While there are relatively few restrictions upon a private landowner who wants to pursue a more sustainable use of the land, as they see it (and in a pluriversal model their perception may not accord entirely with elite priorities), there are opportunities to review regulation from this prism of empowerment. The primacy of private property rights results in a space in which landowners can do much to contribute to the SDGs without state restriction. That is not to say that landowner freedom is entirely unlimited.

The ways in which particular elite formulations of a hierarchy between facets of sustainability can constrain landowners seeking to use their land more sustainably can be tracked through the jurisprudence of property rights provisions in human rights instruments (for example, Trachtenberg, 1997; Willmore, 2001). Purely private bodies are entitled to peaceful enjoyment of their property and, as part of that, the pursuit of sustainability (or not, as they wish). The absolute nature of the right to exclude the world, and to sue for trespass, makes these rights potentially very powerful.

A challenge for the empowerment of property ownership to pursue pluriversal approaches is the inequalities which underpin current property allocations. There is a real risk that using property-rights claims can reinforce inequalities, resulting in 'to him that hath', but in many cases those at the sharp end of poverty, ill health or forced migration do have property rights – even if not well recognised or documented – to the lands they have lived on for generations, and are being placed in that position because of climate change and a failure of governments to recognise and protect their right to continue to own and use that land sustainably. Climate change refugees, displaced from their land are victims of a collective social denial of their property rights, prioritising particular forms of consumption over land ownership or use rights. Users of land too often find states denying them title to the lands they have used for long periods. Writers have reflected on the legal empowerment of the poor through property rights reforms (Gray, 1991; Lucy and Mitchell, 1996; Grear, 2003), but articulating property rights as empowerment is not necessarily beneficial to those land users; for example, the project for title registration, derived from de Soto's work (de Soto, 2000), which has had a very mixed impact on the vast tracts of land invisible to global capital as a result of customary or neocustomary land tenure, and the impact upon wealth in new urban environments (McAuslan, 2003; Boone, 2014; Zartaloudis. 2016).

One approach is to seek to use property rights, however limited, as the basis for challenging state inaction or harmful action. As Lord has argued, in the context of climate change, relatively little consideration has been given to how private landowners could use property rights provisions to challenge state inaction as a restriction of their property rights (Lord et al, 2011; Thornton and Goodman, 2017). The argument here is that climate change, by limiting the ability of owners to use their land, is a denial of property rights under Article 1 of the First Protocol to the European Convention on Human Rights (ECHR) or a rights valuation under other jurisdictional rights provisions. How far human rights language is useful depends on the wording of the provisions and, in particular, on how far they create space for pluriversal approaches. A body of French cases under the ECHR illustrate the limitations of the property rights protections and offer a possible future for regulation. French legislative attempts to regulate hunting, in a manner that prevented a landowner from going further, and banning hunting on his land, was held to be a breach of the landowner's right to peaceful enjoyment of his possessions under Article 1 of the First Protocol to the ECHR (*Chassagnou and others v France* [1999]). This illustrates an elite prioritisation, which had the consequence of preventing a landowner whose own sustainability response was to go beyond the collective state-based solution from doing so. The French solution was to retain the elite prioritisation – which drove out the least sustainable solutions – but to enable landowners to set higher standards on ethical grounds (*Chabauty v France* [2012]). This exactly mirrors the way, in relation to consumer products, that law prohibits the worst conduct but, through labelling, creates space for better conduct. It articulates a societal 'bottom line' while using the 'ethics' concept to create the space for pluriversal approaches. This exceptionalism approach enables a state to require a particular position – unless the landowner is doing something better – but, crucially, gives the landowner some freedom to determine what 'better' means to them.

However, there is no general basis in law for an 'ethics'-based departure from elite-determined provisions. In the case of purely private landowners, their motive is utterly irrelevant, and in the case of public bodies as landowners, ethical or social values are not a proper reason for the exercise of powers, unless explicitly provided for in the legislation conferring the power. In *R v Somerset County Council ex parte Fewings* [1995], for example, the County Council had concluded that stag hunting was cruel and wanted to prohibit stag hunting on land it owned in Devon. The prohibition was quashed in the Court of Appeal on the basis that this was a moral decision, rather than a decision within their specific statutory powers to manage land. While individuals can interpose their personal moral choices in land use and management, statutory bodies can act only within their remit.

In terms of using regulation not to impose uniform standards but to create the space for pluralistic perceptions while regulating the worst, *Chabauty* offers a generalisable way forward: through the explicit recognition of personal grounds for landowner decision making either in individual regulatory systems or as a systemic legal basis. This sort of approach does not require a fundamental rethinking of the nature of property or property rights, but instead requires recognition of the right to make decisions that further sustainability as a defence to regulatory control. Initially that sounds scary, as it transfers the judgement about what is an appropriate stance from the elite power in the state taking a universal decision to a pluriverse model in which multiple ethical priorities coexist. The test is not one of whether the state or court agrees with the priorities of the landowner, but whether the landowner can satisfy the court that the priorities are genuinely held. For individual landowners, committed to a more sustainable future, considering regulation through the prism of 'how does this affect those who want to do more?' as well as 'how does this bring the reluctant or disinterested to a higher standard?' offers new opportunities to think about regulation and the pluriverse.

Public body landowners

This far, the private landowner has been the focus of attention. One final aspect of thinking about land and sustainability conceptually is the role of the state as landowner. States are the single biggest landowner in most jurisdictions. Even in the UK, a country perceived to have low levels of state ownership of land, 20–25% of the land mass of the is owned by an emanation of the state in one form or another. We do not know the precise figure, as the state does not even record the scale of state ownership, let alone seem to use that collective strength to deliver sustainability goals (Home, 2009). Figures have to be treated with caution, comparatively, as the definition of state-owned land varies by jurisdiction according to land ownership regimes, but, however inconsistently defined, state-owned land is substantial in all jurisdictions.

Whatever the scale and spatial characteristics of state-owned land, there is scope for action across the SDGs to use that land to contribute to the SDGs in an integrated manner. Inevitably, the emphasis here will be on elite-determined priorities, although those priorities could include empowerment of diverse local responses developed in partnership with communities rather than centrally determined ones. As a key landowner, the state has a strong gatekeeper/influencer/empowerment role, extending well beyond ownership. In one sense, emanations of the state as landowners have less freedom than other landowners, because each piece of land is held for specific statutory purposes. In the absence of any overriding constitutional principle upon government to use resources sustainably, in the UK this depends on a patchwork of particular property obligations (Willmore, 2003). Some jurisdictions do have more general constitutional provisions obliging public bodies to deliver or prioritise particular outcomes, but the provisions are not framed in the holistic language of the SDGs, but rather fragment the SDGs, offering partial commitments, often through complex hierarchies of obligation. The Wellbeing of Future Generations (Wales) Act 2015 is the most radical of the UK models and sits alongside leading global initiatives, but it, too, fragments the SDGs and does not make them an overriding purpose.

There are, of course, specific statutory obligations upon some parts of the state landowning structure to deliver aspects of sustainability; for example, the UK National Health Service (NHS) holds land for the purpose of delivering a health service under the National Health Service Act 2006. We would expect a health service to view sustainability primarily through SDG 3, but this obligation operates not only to require the NHS to deliver on SDG 3 but provides barriers to their taking into account other SDGs at all, and not only when the other SDGs might conflict with SDG 3. Rather than being a lens, the health obligation becomes a telescope where things beyond the direction of focus are institutionally excluded from view. In the UK, and commonly elsewhere, efforts to widen the line of sight have focused on specific statutory provision, which goes no further than requiring state bodies to have regard to the need for sustainable development in taking decisions, including land use/resource decisions as one of a nested set of objectives – for example, s3A of the Electricity Act 1989. Where stronger duties have been imposed – for example, s44 Climate Change (Scotland) Act 2009, which requires public bodies to exercise their functions in the way 'best calculated to achieve climate change targets' and 'in a way that it considers most sustainable' – these appear to strengthen the obligation, but that always has to be read in the context of the primary purpose for which the land is held (Willmore, 2005). These are chaotic, partial attempts to add in specific other SDGs to the decision making of a public body.

Subject to that, there is little discernible coherence in the way public bodies approach sustainable development. Within the Dicean legacy, Britain treats public bodies the same way as private landowners, subject to a statutory overlay. The result can be a complex layering of obligations, in which the public body is required to have regard to multiple factors, derived from multiple sources, without guidance as to their relative priority; or, in some cases, a single but complex statutory layering of obligations. But, crucially, if sustainability features, it tends not to be framed in relation the SDGs or pluriverse understandings and does not go as far as to treat sustainability as a holistic issue.

This leaves the contradiction of states pursuing efforts to get landowners to exercise their property rights in particular modes in pursuit of elite-determined sustainability goals, rather than in support of a pluriverse of futures – while at the same time largely failing to articulate or structure its own activity as a landowner to secure its articulated sustainability goals. Where the state does interpose an obligation on public bodies in relation to some or all sustainability objectives, the emphasis on using land for its primary statutory purpose can serve to hinder the nuanced, complex approach that the SDGs require. In the absence of generic legislation authorising such a complex nuanced approach, public bodies are less able to use their land for complex and integrated sustainability activity than are private landowners. We started by considering the extent to which all the SDGS involve how land is used, yet the biggest landowner in any state is not equipped to address that in its own land use, because of failures not with land law but with the structure and powers of public bodies.

Conclusion

While there is widespread recognition of the weaknesses of current land law paradigms for addressing the SDGs, there is a risk that some concepts, such as wildlaw, embed a prioritisation of some SDGs rather than facilitating a pluriverse of responses. In this chapter I have argued that Radin's thinking about place and space resonates with public perceptions in relation to property rights, and offers a route towards interpretations of property law that support pluriversal responses to sustainability. Anthropologically grounded in popular constructs of place and our multiple connections to particular places, it is capable of working with the realities of our located relationship to land.

Without a rethinking of the human relationship to land we are left to posit fiscal and other incentives, coupled with regulation to prohibit the worst conduct. The urgency of the SDGs does not suggest that a model of fiscal and other incentives is sufficient. In a situation where the state is not even able to ensure that its own land use is orientated consistently towards sustainability, a different approach is needed.

Current concepts of property and our relationship to land at once offer almost unlimited opportunities to the willing to make progress towards sustainability, and at the same time provide major obstacles to comprehensive progress.

More regulation is not the answer, positioned as it is in an elite ontology rather than a pluriversal model. A rethink of the role of regulation as being to create spaces for nuanced, complex, diverse action at a local level and by individuals could offer a way ahead – but one that would require elite decision making to be replaced by diverse, multi-source empowerment.

References

Alexander, G. (2009) 'The social obligation norm in American Property law', 94 *Cornell Law Review*, 745.

Anderson, S. (1998) 'The 1925 property legislation: setting contexts', in S. Bright and J. Dewar (eds), *Land Law: Themes and Perspectives*, Oxford: Oxford University Press.

Arnold, C. (2011) 'Sustainable webs of interests: property in an interconnected environment', in D. Grinlinton and P. Taylor (eds), *Property Rights and Sustainability: the Evolution of Property Rights to Meet Ecological Challenges*, Dordrecht: Martinus Nijhoff.

Blomley, N. (1994), *Law, Spaces and the Geographies of Power*, New York: Guilford Publications.

Blomley, N., Delaney, D. and Ford, R.T. (eds) (2001) *The Legal Geographies Reader: Law, Power and Space*, Oxford: Blackwell Publishing.

Boone, C. (2014) *Property and Political Order in Africa, Land Rights and the Structure of Politics*, New York: Cambridge University Press.

Bromley, D. (2007) 'Environmental regulations and the problem of sustainability: moving beyond "market failure"', *Ecological Economics* 63: 676.

Chabauty v France [2012] ECHR 1784, EHRR 38.

Chassagnou and others v France [1999] ECHR 22.

Craig, D. (2000) 'Native title and environmental planning: indigenous land use agreements', *Environmental and Planning Law Journal* 17(5): 440.

Cullinan, C. (2011) *Wild Law: A Manifesto for Earth Justice* (2nd edn), Vermont: Chelsea Green.

Dagan, H. (2006) 'The Social Responsibility of Ownership', 92 *Cornell Law Review*, 1255.

Dagan, H. and Heller, M.A. (2001) 'The Liberal Commons', 110 *Yale Law Journal*, 549.

Davies, M. (2007) *Property, Meanings, Histories, Theories*, Oxford: Cavendish.

Davies, M. (2012) 'Persons, property, and community', *2 feminists@law* 37. Available at: http://journals.kent.ac.uk/index.php/feministsatlaw/article/view/37

Davoudi, S. and Strange, I. (eds) (2008) *Conceptions of Space and Place in Strategic Spatial Planning*, London: Routledge.

Debaise, D. (2012) 'What is relational thinking?', *INFLeXions No 5 – Gilbert Simondon*, 1–11.

de Sadeleer, N. (2002) *Environmental Principles: From Political Slogans to Legal Rules*, Oxford: Oxford University Press.

de Soto, H. (2000) *The Mystery of Capital*, London: Bantam Press.

Dixon, M. (2017) 'The organic nature of the law of real property: reforming modern land law', in H. Conway and M. Hickey (eds), *Modern Studies in Property Law*, Oxford: Hart.

Farrier, D. (2011) 'The structure and scope of environmental law', in D. Farrier and P. Stein (eds), *The Environmental Law Handbook* (5th edn), New South Wales: Thomson Reuters (Professional) Australia Limited.

Fisher, E. (2007) *Risk Regulation and Administrative Constitutionalism*, Oxford: Hart Publishing.

Gill, N., Klepis, P. and Chisholm, L. (2010) 'Stewardship among lifestyle oriented rural landowners', *Journal of Environmental Planning and Management* 53(3): 317.

Graham, N. (2010) *Lawscape: Property, Environment, Law*, Oxford: Routledge.

Gray, K. (1991) 'Property in thin air', *Cambridge Law Journal* 50(2): 252.

Gray, K. and Gray, S.F.(1998) 'The idea of property in land', in S. Bright and J. Dewar (eds), *Land Law Themes and Perspectives*, Oxford: Oxford University Press.

Gray, K. and Gray, S.F. (1999) 'Private property and public propriety', in J. Maclean (ed), *Property and the Constitution*, Oxford: Oxford University Press.

Gray, K. and Gray, S.F. (2003) 'The rhetoric of reality', in J. Getzler (ed), *Rationalising Property, Equity and Trusts, Essays in Honour of Edward Burn*, Oxford: Oxford University Press.

Grear, A. (2003) 'A tale of the land, the insider, the outsider and human rights (an exploration of some problems and possibilities in the relationship between the English common law property concept, human rights law, and discourses of exclusion and inclusion)', *Legal Studies* 23: 40.

Hanstad, T. (1997) 'Designing land registration systems for developing countries', *American University International Law Review* 13: 647.

Hodge, I. (2013) 'Conservation covenants: a policy perspective', *Conveyancer and Property Lawyer* 6: 490.

Home, R. (2009) 'Land ownership in the United Kingdom: trends, preferences and future challenges', *Land Use Policy* 26: S103–8.

Honoré, A.M. (1977) 'Property title and redistribution', in C. Wellman (ed), *Equality and Freedom: Past, Present and Future*, Wiesbaden: Franz Steiner Verlag GMBH.

Lametti, D. (2003) 'The concept of property: relations through objects of social wealth', *University of Toronto Law Journal* 53: 35.

Lord, R., Goldberg, S., Rajamani, L. and Brunnée, J. (2011) *Climate Change Liability: Transnational Law and Practice*, Cambridge: Cambridge University Press.

Lucy, W.N.R. and Mitchell, C. (1996) 'Replacing private property: the case for stewardship', *Cambridge Law Journal* 68(3): 566.

McAuslan, P. (2003) *Bringing the Law Back In: Essays in Land, Law and Development*, Oxford: Ashgate Publishing.

McDonald, J. (2010) 'Mapping the legal landscape of climate change adaptation', in T. Bonyhady, A. Macintosh and J. McDonald (eds), *Adaptation to Climate Change: Law and Policy*, New South Wales: Federation Press.

MacLeod, A. (2015) *Property and Practical Reason*, Cambridge: Cambridge University Press.

Marguerat, S.H. (2019) *Private Property Rights and the Environment*, Switzerland: Palgrave Macmillan.

Marsden, T., Murdoch, J., Lowe, P. and Munton, R.C. (1993) *Constructuring the Countryside: An Approach to Rural Development (Restructuring Rural Areas)*, London: UCL Press.

Moore, S.F. (1978) *Law as Process: An Anthropological Approach*, London: Routledge & Kegan Paul Ltd.

Nedelsky, J. (2011) *Law's Relations: A Relational Theory of Self, Autonomy, and Law*, Oxford: Oxford University Press.

Oxhorn, P. and Dodsworth, S. (2013) *The Challenge of Sustainable Resource Development in Indigenous Communities*, Montreal: Institute for the Study of International Development, McGill University.

Page, J. (2016) *Property Diversity and its Implications*, Abingdon: Routledge.

Pascoe, S. (2012) 'Social obligation norm and the erosion of land ownership?', *Conveyancer and Property Lawyer* 76(6): 484.

Pashukanis, E. (1924) *The General Theory of Law and Marxism* (current edition 1989), London: Pluto Press.

Popisil, L. (1971) *Anthropology of Law: A Comparative Theory*, New York: Harper & Row.

Prosser, T. (2010) *The Regulatory Enterprise: Government, Regulation and Legitimacy*, Oxford: Oxford University Press.

Prosterman, R. (2012) 'Land rights and the rule of law', in J.C. Botero et al (eds), *Innovations in Rule of Law: A Compilation of Concise Essays*, the Hague: Hague Institute for the Internationalisation of Law and the World Justice Project, 43. http://worldjusticeproject.org/sites/default/files/wjp_hiil_compilation.pdf

R v Somerset County Council ex parte Fewings [1995] EWCA 24.

Radin, M. (1982) 'Property and personhood', *Stanford Law Review* 34: 957.

Radin, M. (1993) 'Lacking a transformative social theory: a response', *Stanford Law Review* 45: 409.

Rancière, J., Panagia, D. and Bowlby, R. (2001) 'Ten theses on politics', *Theory and Event* 5(3), Baltimore, MD: Johns Hopkins University Press.

Reid, C. (2011) 'The privatisation of biodiversity? Possible new approaches to nature in conservation law in the UK', *Journal of Environmental Law* 23: 203.

Reinhardt, F. (1999) 'Market failure and the environmental policies of firms: economic rationales for "beyond compliance" behavior', *Journal of Industrial Ecology* 3(1): 9.

Rodgers, C. (2009) 'Nature's place? Property rights, property rules and environmental stewardship', 68 *Cambridge Law Journal*, 550.

Sax, J. (2008) 'Environmental law forty years later: looking back and looking ahead', in M. Jeffery, J. Firestone and K. Bubna-Litic (eds), *Biodiversity Conservation, Law and Livelihoods*, Cambridge: Cambridge University Press

Schanbly, S.J. (1993) 'Property and pragmatism: a critique of Radin's theory of property and personhood', 45 *Stanford Law Review*, 347.

Scotford, E. and Oliver, R. (2013) 'The state of UK environmental legislation: opportunities for reform', 15 *Environmental Law Review*, 225.

Scotford, E. and Walsh, R. (2013) 'The Symbiosis of Property and English Environmental Law – Property Rights in a Public Law Context', 76 *Modern Law Review*, 1010.

Scottish Government (2015) *Impact Evaluation of the Community Right to Buy*, Edinburgh: Scottish Government.

Scottish Government (2017) *Scottish Land Rights and Responsibilities*, Edinburgh: Scottish Government.

Shoard, M. (1987) *This Land Is Our Land: Struggle for Britain's Countryside*, London: Grafton Books.

Singer, J.W. (1988) 'The reliance interest in property', 40 *Stanford Law Review*, 611.

Singer, J.W. (2000) *Entitlement, the Paradoxes of Property*, New Haven, CT: Yale University Press.

Singer, J.W. (2006) 'The ownership society and taking of property: castles, investments, and just obligations', 30 *Harvard Environmental Law Review*, 309.

Thornton, J. and Goodman, M. (2017) *Client Earth*, London: Scribe.

Trachtenberg, Z. (1997) 'The takings clause and the meanings of land', in A. Light and J. Smith (eds), *Space, Place, and Environmental Ethics*, London: Rowman & Littlefield.

Willmore, C. (2001) 'Of missiles and mice: property rights in the USA', in E. Cooke (ed), *Modern Studies in Property Law, Volume 1: Property 2000*, Oxford: Hart Publishing.

Willmore, C. (2003) 'The use of land owned by public bodies to deliver National Park objectives', *Journal of Planning and Environmental Law* 2003: 148.

Willmore, C. (2005) 'Constructing "public land"', *Stellenbosch Law Review* 16(3): 378.

Willmore, C. (2017) 'Planning law reform and reconceptualising the regulation of land use', in H. Conway and R. Hickey (eds) *Modern Studies in Property Law, Volume 6*, Oxford: Hart Publishing.

Worrell, R. and Appleby, M. (2000) 'Stewardship of natural resources: definition, ethical and practical aspects', *Journal of Agricultural and Environmental Ethics* 12: 263.

Zartaloudis, T. (ed) (2016) *Land Law and Urban Policy in Context, Essays on the Contributions of Patrick McAusland*, Oxford: Blackwell.

8

Sustainability and Marine Conservation Law

Margherita Pieraccini

Introduction

Oceans, seas and coastal areas provide countless ecosystem services,[1] from provisioning services such as harvestable biological resources to regulating services such as carbon storage to recreation services (Peterson and Lubchenco, 2003). At the same time, oceans are perhaps the quintessential 'common pool resource', that is, a resource system where 'the exclusion of potential appropriators is costly or limiting appropriation rights of existing users is nontrivial (but also not necessarily impossible) and the yield of the resource system is subtractable' (Ostrom, Walker and Gardner, 1994: 4). Indeed, oceans' physical characteristics are such that they lack clear boundaries and fixed owners/occupiers, making it more difficult to exclude users. At the same time, oceans host a vast array of attractive resources and biodiversity that are subtractable and are often subject to over-exploitation. It is not by chance that Hardin included the oceans as one example of commons destined to tragedy (Hardin, 1968). Thus, it is not surprising that calls for the conservation of oceans abound in international and national policy and law.

Indeed, Sustainable Development Goal (SDG) 14 of Agenda 2030 (life below water) is fully centred on the conservation and sustainable use of the oceans, seas and marine resources. SDG 14 reiterates and gathers together previous international policy commitments related to the conservation of the marine environment, found in Chapter 17 of Agenda 21 (UN, 1992), in the Plan of Implementation of the World

Summit on Sustainable Development (UN, 2002) and in *The Future We Want* (UN, 2012, ss 158–77), as well as in Conferences of the Parties' decisions on the Convention on Biological Diversity (for example, UNEP, 2004; UNEP, 2011) and in Aichi target 11 (Secretariat of the Convention on Biological Diversity, 2010). Indeed, SDG 14 sits within a wider policy and legal context that for decades has pushed for the conservation of the marine environment, listing programmes of measures and tools for its achievement.

Thus, the novelty of SDG 14 cannot be found in its targets. Commentators correctly argue that some of the targets of SDG 14 are narrower than what was expressed under previous international commitments. More specifically, the qualitative aspects of Aichi target 11 are diluted in SDG 14.5 (Rees et al, 2018). This point links to the cautious observations made in Chapter 2 of this book regarding the potential lowering of standards once sustainability discourses trespass on previously regulated areas of international law and policy. Other commentators also argue that SDG 14 is too narrow, but for a different set of reasons. Some argue that the social and economic dimensions of SDG 14 are less prominent than the environmental dimensions (Ntona and Morgera, 2018). Differently, others criticise SDG 14 for not being ecocentric enough (Kotze and French, 2018). Despite these readings being different and contradictory, they all condemn SDG 14 for being too narrow.

I argue that the narrowness of SDG 14 can perhaps be overcome if we read SDG 14 purposively, that is to say, within the context of Agenda 2030. As discussed in Chapter 2, Agenda 2030 is underpinned by a holistic vision of interdependent policies and goals. Such holistic vision can be interpreted fruitfully as an opportunity to overcome the more fragmented three-pillar approach to sustainability, which has directed the discourse on sustainability at least since the World Summit on Sustainable Development (2002). Drawing on the theoretical insights developed in Chapters 1 and 2 of this book, it will be argued that holism should be understood not as an attempt to integrate separate pre-existing pillars and unify all voices and perspectives, but in terms of inter- and intra-pillars' relational ontology and the ability to bring in plural perspectives on conservation to decision-making fora, to foster procedural inclusivity.

The chapter is structured as follow: SDG 14.5 will be introduced, drawing on existing scholarship and interpreting it in the wider context of Agenda 2030. Three main sustainability criteria will be identified in line with a purposive reading of SDG 14.5 and drawing on theoretical insights developed in Chapter 1 of this book. Such sustainability criteria are: (1) substantive socio-ecological inter-pillars relationality, (2) intra-pillar relationality, unpacking the 'environmental' pillar, (3) procedural inclusion through participatory decision making. They will inform the assessment of selected European Union (EU) marine conservation law, namely the Habitats Directive. The Habitats Directive is chosen because it is the cornerstone of conservation law in the EU and it is among the instruments listed by the European Commission for the implementation of Agenda 2030 and SDG 14.5 (see European Commission, nd).

SDG 14.5 and its context

Target 14.5 of SDG 14 calls for the conservation of at least 10% of coastal and marine areas by 2020, recalling previous international commitments. SDG 14.5 is quantitative in orientation and only focuses on environmental protection, thereby being quite narrow, especially when compared to Aichi target 11. Aichi target 11 also specifies that by 2020, 10% of coastal and marine areas are to be conserved 'through effectively and equitably managed, ecologically representative and well-connected systems of protected areas and other effective area-based conservation measures, and integrated into the wider landscapes and seascapes'.

Thus, the Aichi target, in comparison to SDG 14.5, brings to the fore also the qualitative dimensions of conservation such as equitable management, the concept of environmental integration and a systemic/networked view of conservation (Rees et al, 2018). As argued in Chapter 2, when sustainability discourse appropriates and trespasses on pre-existing international law and policy standards, there is a risk that those standards become diluted and reduced. However, if we read SDG 14.5 in its context, that is, Agenda 2030, then it becomes evident that we are concerned with much more than just an exercise in marine conservation quantification. This is because Agenda 2030 mainstreams the sustainability discourse in every sector of life, unpacks and expands on the traditional three pillars of sustainability and emphasises the importance of inclusion, most evidently through SDG 16. Therefore, marine conservation with Agenda 2030's holistic and inclusive approach to sustainability in mind involves an acknowledgement of fundamental entanglements between people(s) and nature(s) and the building of institutions facilitating the inclusion of multiple views and perspectives.

Commentators have begun to look at SDG 14 in its context, articulating links between SDG 14 and other SDGs. For example, Le Blanc et al (2017) show how SDG 14 links with many other SDGs and how SDG 14.5 in particular links with SDG 1 on poverty alleviation, SDG 2 on food security, SDG 4 on education, SDG 8 on decent work and economic development, SDG 10 on reducing inequality, SDG 13 on climate action, SDG 15 on life on land and SDG 16 on peaceful and just societies. Therefore, the list of SDGs explicitly related to SDG 14.5 includes substantive goals of a social and economic nature, such as SDG 1, SDG 2, SDG 8 and SDG 10, and substantive goals of an environmental nature such as SDG 13 and SDG 15. It also includes procedurally oriented social goals such as SDG 16 and SDG 4. Another way in which links have been discussed is presented by Ntona and Morgera (2018), who have attempted to connect SDG 14 with other SDGs using the conceptual tool of Marine Spatial Planning (MSP). They argue that MSP is a participatory tool for integrated ocean management and therefore a useful tool for 'mainstreaming considerations regarding equity and the synergistic pursuit of the SDGs into relevant decision-making processes and strategic frameworks for action' (2018: 216).

This chapter also looks at SDG 14.5 in context but, rather than considering specific goals that can be connected to SDG 14.5, as Le Blanc et al (2017) do, or a specific legal and/or policy tool that could provide the connections between SDG 14. 5 and other goals, as Morgera and Ntona do (2018), it takes a broader view by focusing on the salient traits of Agenda 2030, validated by the theoretical observations and arguments made in Chapters 1 and 2 of this book.

Agenda 2030 aims to elaborate a holistic approach to sustainable development, presenting the list of SDGs as an 'integrated and indivisible whole'. If we interpret this holistic ambition following the theoretical insights developed in Chapter 1, it means that SDGs and their targets should not be read as isolated attempts to foster a particular social, environmental or economic goal but should be put in mutually constitutive dialogue with each other. The current United Nations (UN) discourse on sustainability seems to characterise the goals not as atomistic and sectoral preoccupations but as integrated, with sustainability no longer the product of a trade-off between three distinct pre-existing pillars. Agenda 2030 also forces us to think about each 'traditional' pillar in a more nuanced way. For example, rather than proposing a monolithic and unproblematised view of the environment like Millennium Development Goal n. 7, Agenda 2030 presents a much more expansive representation of the environment, with various goals on different environmental sectors, such as climate, land, energy, fresh and marine water. Besides, with SDG 16 the emphasis is put also on procedural dimensions of sustainability and on processes of inclusion.

It follows that once we situate SDG 14.5 within the wider context of Agenda 2030, it becomes evident that we should be concerned with much more than just narrow, quantitative marine conservation goals. Conservation cannot happen in isolation, as it is integrated in wider social-ecological settings and its meaning(s) should be subject to discussions in inclusive decision-making fora.

This holistic, integrated and inclusive view is validated by the Resolution of the UN conference on the implementation of SDG 14 (UN, 2017), which reiterates the need for an integrated, interdisciplinary and cross-sectoral approach (para 8) and underlies the integrated and indivisible character of all the SDGs, as well as the interlinkages and synergies between them (para 13(a)). The Resolution indeed recognises that 'the well-being of present and future generations is inextricably linked to the health and productivity of our oceans' (para 5) and calls for actions aimed at increasing the knowledge pool related to the oceans, the strengthening of multi-stakeholder partnerships in ocean-governance decision making, ocean-related education initiatives and increasing access to marine resources for small-scale and artisanal fisheries in developing countries, inter alia.

Although such complex framing of sustainability under Agenda 2030 can be difficult to navigate, complexity is a step towards a view of sustainability, or better sustainabilities, underpinned by relational ontology. Indeed, as argued in Chapter 1, in order to move forward in the sustainability discourse, sustainability should be understood not as an integration of distinct pillars but as a move towards relationality, overcoming Western dualisms, residual of a Cartesian logic. Besides, as argued by critical legal scholars (Grear, 2015; De Lucia, 2017), both *eco* and *anthropos* need unpacking, as monolithic views mask more than they reveal and may contribute to distributive injustice. Finally, it should be recalled that the ontological overcoming of dualisms should be interpreted not as an annulment of difference but as a move towards pluriversality and the acknowledgement of different visions of sustainability, achievable through procedural openness. Taking these insights seriously and linking them with a wide purposive reading of SDG 14.5 in the context of Agenda 2030 means that reaching a target of 10% conservation of coastal and marine areas entails at least three key steps:

1. An ontological acknowledgement of substantive social-ecological inter-pillar relations in line with a relational view, moving beyond a view of sustainability as a trade-off between pillars.
2. An ontological unpacking of the 'environment' to overcome monolithic understandings of nature and society and therefore to

consider the interactions between marine conservation and other environmental sectors, such as climate.

3. A call for procedural inclusion through participatory decision making in line with the epistemic pluralisation of sustainability.

These three steps are used in the next section as sustainability criteria to assess measures on marine protected areas (MPAs) under the Habitats Directive.

MPAs under EU law

The indicator linked to SDG 14.5 is the coverage of protected areas in the marine context (14.5.1). The choice of indicator reflects the overwhelming use of MPAs as a key regulatory tool in marine conservation law. However, there is no agreed definition of what MPAs are, and MPA is more an umbrella term than a term to signify a specific entity. The International Union for the Conservation of Nature (IUCN), which has championed the establishment of MPAs for decades, provides one of the most comprehensive and well-known classifications of protected areas according to their management objectives (Dudley, 2008). Protected areas indeed range from strict nature reserves (category Ia), that is, no-take no-entry areas, to protected areas with sustainable use of natural resources (category VI). Clearly, then, the way in which different MPAs relate to sustainability varies greatly, given that category I has only environmental objectives at its core while category VI also aims at the protection of cultural, social and economic ecosystem services. This is also complicated by the fact that these categories are not necessarily mutually exclusive, as one MPA can host different levels of protection. As there is no single definition of MPAs, there is no universally applicable legal regime for the establishment and management of MPAs. Hence, the relationship between MPAs law and sustainability will inevitably vary depending on the jurisdictional scale that is chosen. This chapter focuses on the EU scale.

Under EU law a key instrument for establishing MPAs is the Habitats Directive. The aim of the Habitats Directive is to contribute towards the protection of biodiversity through the designation of protected areas for habitats and species of community interest (Art 2). Those habitats and species are listed in Annex I and II of the Directive. To achieve such aim, the Habitats Directive requires member states to contribute to the establishment of an ecologically coherent network of protected areas, known as Natura 2000 (Art 3). The Natura 2000 network comprises Special Protection Areas (SPAs) established under Directive 2009/147/EC of the European Parliament and of the Council on the Conservation of Wild Birds, OJ L 20/7 (hereafter the 'Birds Directive') and Special Areas of Conservation (SACs) under the Habitats Directive.

It is important to stress from the outset that the Habitats Directive explicitly engages with the term 'sustainable development'. Under the Habitats Directive, the conservation of biodiversity shall happen with a view to promoting sustainable development. The preamble of the Directive states that although 'the main aim of this Directive [is] to promote the maintenance of biodiversity, taking account of economic, social, cultural and regional requirements, this Directive makes a contribution to the general objective of sustainable development'. Moreover, Article 2(3) requires that 'measures taken pursuant to the Directive shall take account of economic, social and cultural requirements and regional and local characteristics'. Besides, when contextualising the Habitats Directive within the *aquis communautaire*, it becomes evident that sustainable development needs to be considered in interpreting the Directive. Indeed, primary EU legislation makes explicit the need to consider sustainable development (Art 3(3) Treaty on the European Union and the integration principle under Art 11 of the Treaty on the Functioning on the European Union). Given the legal hierarchy between the Treaties and the Directives, it follows that the Habitats Directive cannot disregard such general objectives of the EU. However, the Treaties do not define what sustainable development is. Hence, they offer little guidance on what sustainability should mean in the Habitats Directive. To understand how sustainability is approached in the Habitats Directive it is essential to have a closer look at the key provisions of the Directive, also as interpreted by the jurisprudence of the Court of Justice of the European Union (CJEU) and the European Commission Guidance on Article 6 (European Commission, 2018). Although the European Commission Guidance is not legally binding, it provides important insights in interpreting the Habitats Directive and, consequently, references to it will be made. The key provisions of the Habitats Directive can be divided broadly into three groups: those related to the designation of sites, those related to the management of sites and those related to the establishment of the Natura 2000 network.

As will be shown, analysing these groups of provisions of the Habitats Directive against the three sustainability criteria identified earlier generates negative results. The Habitats Directive presents an approach to sustainability based on a trade-off between current socio-economic and environmental interests, hence very far from a substantive relational approach. The Directive does not score high even in relation to sustainability criterion 2, looking at the environment in a narrow, not integrated way. Finally, there is little in the Directive on procedural justice in the sense of inclusive and informed decision making, thereby not meeting sustainability criterion 3. However, a closer reading of the Habitats Directive supported both by the CJEU case law and the European Commission Guidance (2018) shows that the Directive can accommodate a more complex and integrated view of conservation through the concept of the Natura 2000 network, offering fruitful links with terrestrial and climate-change mitigation and adaptation, hence unpacking 'nature' and moving towards sustainability criterion 2. However, both judicial and policy interpretations continue to portray the relationship between socio-economic and environmental issues as an antagonistic one, and processes for inclusion of different viewpoints and perspectives are limited. Therefore, overall, the Habitats Directive and its interpretations present a weaker version of sustainability than that produced by a purposive reading of SDG 14.5 within the context of Agenda 2030 and underpinned by relational ontology.

Designation provisions and sustainability

SACs under the Habitats Directive are chosen in an iterative process involving the member states and the Commission and based on relevant scientific evidence and criteria contained in Annex III (Art 4). For SPAs under the Birds Directive the process is somewhat different and simpler as compared to the Habitats Directive, in that it is member states only that have the task of selecting sites. Like the Habitats Directive, though, site selection is based exclusively on scientific criteria, in this case ornithological criteria, including species listed in Annex I of the Birds Directive and migratory species not listed in Annex I (see Art 4(1) and 4(2)).

Article 2(3) of the Habitats Directive, which states that measures taken pursuant to the Directive shall take account of economic, social and cultural requirements, does not dilute the scientific requirements at the basis of designation of Natura 2000 sites. Indeed, the CJEU has interpreted this provision not in a way to halt the designation of sites on socio-economic reasons. Social and economic factors cannot be considered as a reason for avoiding to designate sites, as designation needs to be based purely on environmental criteria (see, for example, *The Queen v Secretary of State for the Environment, Transport and the Regions, ex parte First Corporate Shipping Ltd, interveners: World Wide Fund for Nature UK (WWF) and Avon Wildlife Trust* [2000]). Recent case law, though, shows that a balance between social, economic and environmental considerations may play a small role at least in the de-designation of sites. In *Cascina Tre Pini Ss v Ministero dell'Ambiente e della Tutela del Territorio e del Mare and Others* [2014], the Court held that the obligation of a member state to propose a declassification to the Commission is even 'greater when that site includes land belonging to an owner whose exercise of his right to property is restricted as a result of that listing' (para 80). Failure to propose a declassification when the ecological interest of the site is no longer there can amount to a violation of the right to property. Although this case shows that the obligation to declassify is greater if there are socio-economic issues at stake, the key requirement is still that the site has lost its ecological interest. Hence, after all, the environmental criteria are the only ones that count in designation.

As far as designation provisions go, it can be concluded that the designation provisions of the Habitats Directive do not account for participatory decision making and procedural inclusion in line with the epistemic pluralisation of sustainability (sustainability criterion 3), as the choice of designation is one that does not require inclusive decision making but it is a choice made by member states alone or by a iterative dialogue between member states and the Commission. Besides, the choice of what to protect is based on strict predetermined ecological criteria based on the individuation of a selected and arguably narrow number of marine species and habitats of community importance. Thus, designation of sites does not encompass a relational view of social-ecological systems, as social and economic factors cannot be taken into account in selecting the sites for designation (sustainability criterion 1). As for the most modest endeavour of considering conservation in its wider environmental context (sustainability criterion 2), the designation is site specific and only a small number of pre-selected habitats and species count as nature worthy of marine conservation. Although wider network considerations are to be taken into account in selecting the sites, *taking into account* is not a very strong legal terminology, leaving much room for discretion. Hence, also sustainability criterion 2 is not met.

Management of sites and sustainability

As regards the management of sites, the key provisions are contained in Article 6. Article 6(1) applies only to SACs but there are similar provisions in Article 4 of the Birds Directive applying to SPAs. Article 6(2)–6(4) applies to both SACs and SPAs. Article 6 can be subdivided into provisions related to conservation, prevention and remediation. Measures related to conservation are to be found in Article 6(1), which requires member states to establish the necessary conservation measures for the sites and, if need be, management plans for the sites. Management plans could be important instruments in developing proactive conservation measures and in bringing in adaptive management provisions, which have been recognised by the EU Commission Guidance on Natura 2000 and climate change as being key for conservation in the context of climate change (European Commission, 2013). The European Commission has stressed the importance of adaptive management for the implementation of the Birds and Habitats Directives, especially in estuaries and coastal zones, advising a joint consideration of socio-economic development and nature conservation following an ecosystem-based approach that takes into account system dynamics and, in cases of uncertainty, adopts adaptive monitoring to be fed back to the management plans (European Commission, 2011). However, management plans are not mandatory, nor there is any guidance related to what they should contain. Article 6(1) is also silent in relation to inclusive decision making in relation to the conservation measures and in relation to the way in which it should consider social-ecological relationships. Thus, it does not meet any of the three sustainability criteria identified in this chapter (see also Garcia-Ureta and Lazkano, 2015).

As for Article 6(2), it concerns preventative measures requiring member states to take appropriate steps to avoid the deterioration of sites and disturbance of species, in so far as such disturbance could be significant in relation to the objectives of the Directive. As the Commission Guidance on Article 6 states, Article 6(2) 'takes as the starting point the prevention principle … the words "*avoid*" and "*could be significant*" stress the anticipatory nature of the measure to be taken. It is not acceptable to wait until deterioration or disturbances occur before taking measures' (European Commission, 2018: 26). This reading is to be found in recent case law too. In *European Commission v Republic of Bulgaria* [2017] (para 70), an infringement of Article 6(2) was deemed to exist where the Commission establishes that there is a probability or risk that a project will cause deterioration to the habitats of protected species of birds or cause significant disturbance to those species. A similar reasoning was present in *European Commission v Kingdom of Spain* [2016].

The preventative and environmentally focused character of the Article leaves little space for other-than-environmental considerations, and again the decision regarding which steps to take is left to member states, with little participation of others in decision making, hence sustainability criteria 1 and 3 are not met. As this is a site-specific measure (not a network measure) and does not provide for precise protective measures, it seems of no relevance for sustainability criterion 2 either. However, the Commission Guidance does state that Article 6(2) is not limited to human activities and 'in the case of natural succession or of climate change effects, measures would need to be taken to halt or counter this process if it is deemed to be negatively impacting on the species and habitat types for which the site has been designated' (European Commission, 2018: 27).

Similarly, Article 6(3), which establishes limits regarding the carrying out of plans or projects on Natura 2000 sites, focuses on prevention, though it does not put a complete ban on development. Indeed, in *Azienda Agro-Zootecnica Franchini sarl and Eolica di Altamura Srl v Regione Puglia* [2011], the CJEU considered Italian law's ban on construction of wind farms not for self-consumption in Natura 2000 sites to be more stringent that the provisions under the Habitats Directive. Article 6(3) has been interpreted by the CJEU drawing on a strong version of the precautionary principle. This was first established in the landmark *Landelijke Vereniging tot Behoud van de Waddenzee and Nederlandse Vereniging tot Bescherming van Vogels v Staatssecretaris van Landbouw, Natuurbeheer en Visserii* (*Waddenzee*) [2004], which restricted the margin of discretion of competent authorities to authorise projects following a strong precautionary logic. Article 6(3) can be divided into two stages and a strong precautionary logic has been applied to both stages.

The first stage of Article 6(3) states that a plan or project not directly connected with the management of the site but likely to have a significant effect thereon, individually or in combination with other plans or projects, shall be subject to appropriate assessment of its implications for the site in view of the site's conservation objectives. The second stage states that the plan or project in question cannot be authorised unless the appropriate assessment has ascertained that it will not adversely affect the integrity of the site concerned and, if appropriate, after having obtained the opinion of the general public. Regarding stage 1, the likelihood of a plan or project having significant effect is established when the plan or project in question may undermine the conservation objectives of the site and mitigation measures cannot be considered when carrying out screening for appropriate assessment (*People Over Wind, Peter Sweetman v Coillte Teoranta* [2018]). An appropriate assessment cannot be side-stepped by anticipating the beneficial consequences of a habitat creation that mitigates the negative effects of a plan or project (*Hilde Orleans and Others v Vlaams Gewest* (*Orleans*) [2016]).

The appropriate assessment requires that all aspects of the plan or project must be identified in light of the best scientific knowledge available (see, inter alia, *Orleans* para 51, and *European Commission v Federal Republic of Germany* [2017], para 57). The assessment cannot have lacunae and must contain complete, precise and definitive findings and conclusions capable of removing all reasonable scientific doubt as to the effects of the proposed works on the protected site concerned (see, inter alia, judgments of *Peter Sweetman and Others v An Bord Pleanála* [2013], para 44, and *Orleans*, para 50). Protective measures aimed at compensating the negative effects of the project on a Natura 2000 site cannot be considered as part of the appropriate assessment (*T.C. Briels and Others v Minister van Infrastructuur en Milieu* [2014], para 29). Finally, competent authorities are to authorise the project only if they have made certain that it will not affect the integrity of the site (*Waddenzee*).

As for the second stage, in considering whether the integrity of a Natura 2000 site will be affected, member states must have regard to the site's conservation objectives to achieve Favourable Conservation Status (FCS). No reasonable scientific doubt should remain, and the precautionary principle should apply (*Peter Sweetman and Others v An Bord Pleanála* [2013]). Notably, the opinion of the public may be obtained if deemed appropriate.

As the CJEU states, 'Article 6(3) of the Habitats Directive thus integrates the precautionary principle and makes it possible to prevent in an effective manner adverse effects on the integrity of protected sites as a result of the plans or projects envisaged' (*Peter Sweetman and Others v An Bord Pleanála* [2013], para 118). Clearly, then, Article 6(3) emphasises the role of scientific knowledge in deciding whether or not a plan or project can adversely affect the integrity of a site. The focus is strictly on the conservation of selected species and habitats, assessed purely using scientific lenses, and other factors play no role in deciding whether to grant authorisation. Although the second stage of Article 6(3) contemplates the possibility for obtaining the opinion of the public, hence striving towards more inclusive decision making (sustainability criterion 3), it is up to the national authorities to decide whether to include the public in decision making ('if appropriate').

In relation to defining the integrity of the site on the basis of conservation objectives, the CJEU has held that the site's overall conservation objectives extend beyond an isolated consideration of the habitats and species contained within the site and take account of the wider ecological context of the site as a whole in terms of its effects on the designated features (*Peter Sweetman and Others v An Bord Pleanála* [2013]). This is important in striving towards sustainability criterion 2 because the reasoning is underpinned by network considerations, thereby useful in thinking about integration of marine conservation with terrestrial ecosystems and also for contextualising conservation within global environmental change. However, Article 6(3) fails to meet sustainability criterion 1, given that social and economic factors play no role in determining whether to grant authorisation of a plan or project and given that mitigatory measures cannot be taken into account at any stage of Article 6(3). Taking account of mitigatory measures during the making of the plan or project could facilitate the integration of ecological concerns (for example, habitats creation and restoration) with social and economic considerations. This more liberal approach to mitigation could therefore be positive from a sustainability perspective, supporting plan and project proponents to have a more systemic, social-ecological view, rather than divorcing the environmental from the socio-economic. However, the CJEU's reliance on a strong precautionary approach means that this cannot happen and, as will be explained later, social and economic factors play a role only in the derogation clause of Article 6(4). The CJEU reasoning, as expressed in *T.C. Briels and Others v Minister van Infrastructuur en Milieu* [2014], indeed rests on the argument that positive mitigatory effects aimed at compensating the loss of that same habitat type on a protected site are 'highly difficult to forecast with a degree of certainty', hence mitigation efforts cannot be relied upon outside the context of the derogation clause.

Article 6(4) derogation states that, despite the negative results of an appropriate assessment, a project or plan can be carried out for imperative reasons of overriding public interest and if there are no alternatives. The imperative reasons can be of a social and economic reason, unless the site hosts priority species/habitats. In the latter case, only human health or other environmental reasons can give the green light to the plan or project in question or other imperative reasons of overriding interests further to an opinion issued by the Commission. Socio-economic issues are therefore present, but in opposition to ecological ones. Besides, the Directive offers no guidance in relation to how the socio-economic and environmental aspects are weighted against each other and therefore it is silent in relation to distributive justice. Equal access to resources plays no direct role in determining which socio-economic reasons are to be considered as imperative. Article 6(4) is thus consistent with a weak version of sustainable development, allowing a trade-off between natural, economic and social capital, instead of integration, holism and inclusivity.

However, both the European Commission Guidance (2018) and recent case law have been helpful in shedding light on the meaning of imperative reasons of overriding public interest. The Commission guidance states that only plans or projects having long-term positive consequences on society and environment can outweigh the ecological damage and the long term-conservation interests. The guidance text indeed reads as such:

> it seems also reasonable to assume that the public interest can only be overriding if it is a long-term interest; short-term economic interests or other interests yielding only short-term benefits for the society would not appear to be sufficient to outweigh the long-term conservation interests protected by the Directive

and imperative reasons of overriding public interest

> refer to situations where plans or projects envisaged prove to be indispensable: – within the framework of actions or policies aiming to protect fundamental values for the citizens' life (health, safety, environment); – within the framework of fundamental policies for the State and the Society;– within the framework of carrying out activities of economic or social nature, fulfilling specific obligations of public service. (European Commission, 2018: 59)

This purposive reading of the Directive was confirmed in *Marie-Noëlle Solvay and Others v Région Wallonne* [2012]. The CJEU held that an interest justifying the implementation of a plan or project must be both public and overriding, 'which means that it must be of such an importance that it can be weighed up against that Directive's objective of the conservation of natural habitats and wild fauna and flora' (para 75). In that case the creation of infrastructure intended to accommodate a management centre was not regarded as an imperative reason of overriding public interest. This is important in stressing the need for long-term considerations, hence contributing to inter-generational justice. However, given that socio-economic considerations and environmental ones are still put in opposition to one another and there is no article that does it more explicitly than Article 6(4), the view presented is one of trade-off rather than integration, hence sustainability criterion 1 is not met.

Besides, in the case in which imperative reasons of overriding public interest are found, the coherence of the network cannot be undermined, so that mitigatory measures are to be provided and communicated to the Commission. Mitigatory measures are independent of the project or plan. They are effectively biodiversity offset measures, to annul negative effects on the coherence of the Natura 2000 network. They may include, for example, the restoration of a degraded habitats or the creation of a new habitat in a new location, either within the same site or elsewhere. Therefore, Article 6(4), as interpreted by the CJEU and Commission Guidance, more closely align to sustainability criterion 2. However, procedural justice issues are not taken into account, hence sustainability criterion 3 is not met. Indeed, it is the Commission only that needs to be informed of the mitigatory measures adopted by the member state (see also McGillivray, 2012).

Network provisions and sustainability

The Habitats Directive provisions related to the Natura 2000 network are mostly relevant in relation to sustainability criterion 2, as unpacking 'nature' requires a consideration of conservation within the wider 'environment' and connected environmental issues, be these climate change or terrestrial protection. Given that the network comprises both terrestrial and marine protected areas, the link between marine and terrestrial protection is self-evident. Networks are also a means to ensure resilience of biodiversity in a changing climate. Global environmental change creates new challenges for protected species and habitats, as climate variations are one of the key factors in changing the abundance and distribution of species and reduce the amount of suitable habitat for protected species. Isolated MPAs are therefore of little usefulness in the context of climate change, and a move towards networks of MPAs to increase their connectivity and resilience is advocated in the scientific literature (see, for instance, McLeod et al, 2009).

Unfortunately, the Habitats Directive does not contain specific requirements related to the characteristics of the Natura 2000 network. Article 3(3) of the Directive states that 'where they consider it necessary, Member States shall endeavor to improve the ecological coherence of Natura 2000 by maintaining, and where appropriate developing, features of the landscape which are of major importance for wild fauna and flora, as referred to in Article 10'. Article 10 states that 'Member States shall endeavor, where they consider it necessary, in their land-use planning and development policies and, in particular, with a view to improving the ecological coherence of the Natura 2000 network, to encourage the management of features of the landscape which are of major importance for wild fauna and flora'. Neither Article 3(3) nor Article 10 uses mandatory language, leaving it at the discretion of member states to decide whether and how to improve the coherence of the network. However, the fact that improving the coherence is not mandatory does not contribute towards an integrated view of the environment. The weaknesses of these provisions are especially problematic in relation to climate change. Indeed, the Habitats Directive has received strong criticism from academics for its inadequate provisions to ensure the resilience of the network in the context of climate change, for being too site-centred and for the weak provisions of Article 3(3) and Article 10 (see, for example, Cliquet et al, 2009).

However, a less restrictive reading of the Habitats Directive proposed by some scholars shows that a creative interpretation of Articles 3(3) and 10, read in conjunction with other relevant provisions of the Directive (that is, Article 6, discussed next), provides for the flexibility necessary to enable biodiversity to cope with climate change (Verschuuren, 2015). In *European Commission v Kingdom of Spain* [2011], the CJEU concluded that mining projects in the Castilla y León region (Spain) within a Natura 2000 site breached Article 6(2) because they created the risk of closure of a corridor between two reproduction areas of the brown bear and the cutting of a corridor between two subpopulations of capercaillie, one of which was located outside the site. The case was concerned with connectivity measures within a protected site, rather than between protected areas. Nevertheless, it can be inferred that similar reasoning will apply when considering connectivity measures between protected areas. Also notable is *Commission of the European Communities v Republic of Austria* [2007] on the Birds Directive, in which the Court held that there is no need for conservation objectives to be specified for each species considered separately, thereby allowing a degree of flexibility and integration. The guidance of the European Commission on the Habitats Directive and climate change also pushes for adaptive management in conservation. However, this is only a guidance and there is yet to be seen case law on this issue.

Hence, the network provisions of the Habitats Directive are not strong enough to meet sustainability criterion 2. Decisions on network coherence are left to the member states, with no instructions regarding the involvement of third parties in decision making, hence not contributing toward sustainability criterion 3. As for sustainability criterion 1, Article 3(3) discusses only ecological coherence with the aim to maintain or develop landscape features of importance to wild flora and fauna, and again Article 10 focuses solely on ecological coherence, not social-ecological coherence.

The Habitats Directive and its sustainability scoring: a summary

To sum up, despite the fact that sustainability considerations are not absent from the Habitats Directive and cannot be absent once the Habitats Directive is placed within the wider context of the *aquis*, the approach to sustainability in the Habitats Directive does not satisfy the three sustainability criteria identified in this chapter, and more generally the holistic aspirations of Agenda 2030.

In relation to sustainability criterion 3, inclusive participation is not a priority, given that the Habitats Directive is technocratic in character and science led, offering very few opportunities for participation.[2] This is most visible at the designation stage, given that only environmental criteria are to be accounted for and there are no requirements for public consultation at the designation stage. This has resulted in protests in some countries, requiring a revision of the designation approach to make it more participatory (Paavola, 2004). The situation only slightly improves at the management stage. Under Article 6(3) the opinion of the general public may be obtained 'if appropriate' in decisions whether to approve a plan or project that has undergone an appropriate assessment. The appropriate assessment is to be based on the best scientific knowledge, closing down the possibility to open up to other epistemologies. Also, in the event in which Article 6(4) is triggered, deciding what counts as 'overriding public interest', or what compensatory measures should entail, is not to be decided collectively. The Directive requires only that the Commission is notified of such measures. As for the opinions of the Commission on other imperative reasons of overriding public interest under Article 6(4), there are no formal avenues for third-party involvement. The recently concluded Fitness Check (European Commission, 2016) of the Birds and Habitats Directives has deemed the Directives fit for purpose but has identified some areas that need improving. It is not surprising that knowledge gaps and stakeholder engagement are among the most significant gaps identified by the Fitness Check. The Fitness Check frames these 'implementation challenges', but it could be argued that if stronger procedures for participation and integration of different knowledges at different scales in the Habitats Directive would be available, as is the case in other sectors of environmental law (for example, Directive 2010/75/EU on Industrial Emissions),[3] these challenges would not arise at the implementation stage. For example, although partnerships are identified in the Fitness Check as instrumental to improve surveying, monitoring and management, the Directive itself neither requires nor mentions them, leaving the rise of partnerships an ad hoc occurrence.

In relation to sustainability criterion 1, socio-economic interests are portrayed as detached from the environmental ones, and also the jurisprudence of the CJEU reinforces such a dichotomy. This is so not only in relation to the designation of protected areas as environmental interests are the only ones to be taken into account, but also at the management stage with the strong precautionary logic applied to Article 6(3) and by confining discussions on compensatory measures to the derogation clause of Article 6(4). The Habitats Directive and the CJEU do not allow for the integration of environmental and socio-economic considerations at earlier stages, for example, in project planning. If the CJEU's strong precautionary approach is to be applauded from an environmental view-point, from a sustainability view-point it reinforces an approach to sustainability as a trade-off, not an integration between socio-economic and environmental considerations.

Finally, in relation to criterion 2, although the Habitats Directive is written primarily from the perspective of conservation of selected species and habitats in situ, network considerations are present, facilitating both links with terrestrial protection and potentially adaptation measures in the context of global environmental change. However, there are no obligations regarding the improvement of the coherence of the network, and the meaning of coherence is not clear cut, thereby falling short of meeting sustainability criterion 2 (see Catchpole, 2012). It can therefore be concluded that the Habitats Directive does not meet the sustainability criteria identified in this chapter, presenting a weak version of sustainability.

Conclusion

This chapter has discussed the meaning of sustainability in the context of marine conservation law and, more specifically, MPAs governance at the EU level. Starting from a purposive and theoretically informed reading of SDG 14.5, it has been argued that marine conservation within the framework of sustainability requires more than the achievement of a quantified target of protected seas (10%) through the establishment of MPAs and requires more than trade-off between pillars. Indeed, taking seriously the holistic, integrated and inclusive approach of Agenda 2030 means that marine conservation should attend to the relational entanglements between nature and society via inter-pillar integration, unpack the meaning of the environment beyond a monolithic view exploring intra-pillar relationships and expand the number and type of those who can provide insights into the meaning of conservation and make decisions to foster procedural inclusivity. These are the sustainability criteria that have been identified in this chapter, drawing on the purposive and theoretically informed reading of Agenda 2030. The sustainability criteria are all in line with the theoretical points made in Chapter 1 of this book, regarding the necessity to overcome unhelpful monolithic representations of sustainability and dichotomous representations of nature and society and to move towards a relational ontology and a pluralisation of sustainability via inclusive decision making.

These three sustainability criteria have been used to assess MPAs governance under the Habitats Directive. The assessment has produced negative results, as the Habitats Directive is entrenched in a technocratic paradigm, it proposes a narrow understanding of the environment worth of conservation and a dichotomous and oppositional view of environmental and socio-economic issues. Although sustainable development is explicitly mentioned in the Habitats Directive, a simplified, environmentally focused version of sustainability is presented in the text and in the interpretations of the courts. This is quite problematic, considering that the Habitats Directive is a key instrument under EU law for achieving SDG 14.5. The Habitats Directive can be a useful example to make broader reflections on the potential mismatch between the holistic and inclusive aspirations of Agenda 2030 and the current legal tools used for its implementation. To what extent can the pluralisation of sustainability occur if we are locked in a legal paradigm rooted in modernist assumptions?

Notes

1. Ecosystem services are defined in the Millennium Ecosystem Assessment (2005) as 'the benefits people obtain from ecosystems' and are divided into supporting services, provisioning services, regulating services and cultural services.
2. On who holds decision-making power under the Habitats Directive, see also Lee (2016).
3. The Industrial Emission Directive follows an integrated approach so that permits for industrial pollution must consider the whole environmental performance of the plant and, even more crucially, requires that the permit conditions, including emission limit values, are based on 'Best Available Techniques', defined through an exchange of information between the Commission and experts from member states, industry and environmental organisations.

References

Case C-371/98 *The Queen v Secretary of State for the Environment, Transport and the Regions, ex parte First Corporate Shipping Ltd, interveners: World Wide Fund for Nature UK (WWF) and Avon Wildlife Trust* [2000] ECR I-09235, ECLI:EU:C:2000:600.

Case C-127/02 *Landelijke Vereniging tot Behoud van de Waddenzee, Nederlandse Vereniging tot Bescherming van Vogels v Staatssecretaris Van Landbouw, Natuurbeheer en Visserij* [2004] ECR I-07405, ECLI:EU:C:2004:482 (*Waddenzee*).

Case C-507/04 *Commission of the European Communities v Republic of Austria* [2007] ECR I-05939, ECLI:EU:C:2007:427.

Case C-404/09 *European Commission v Kingdom of Spain* [2011] ECR I-11853, ECLI:EU:C:2011:768.

Case C-2/10 *Azienda Agro-Zootecnica Franchini sarl and Eolica di Altamura Srl v Regione Puglia* [2011] ECR I-06561, ECLI:EU:C:2011:502.

Case C-182/10 *Marie-Noëlle Solvay and Others v Région Wallonne* [2012] ECLI:EU:C:2012:82.

Case C-258/11, *Peter Sweetman and Others v An Bord Pleanála* [2013] ECLI:EU:C:2013:220.

Case C-521/12, *T.C. Briels and Others v Minister van Infrastructuur en Milieu* [2014] ECLI:EU:C:2014:330.

Case C-301/12 *Cascina Tre Pini Ss v Ministero dell'Ambiente e della Tutela del Territorio e del Mare and Others* [2014] ECLI:EU:C:2014:214.

Joined Cases C-387/15 and 388/15, *Hilde Orleans and Others v Vlaams Gewest* [2016] ECLI:EU:C:2016:583 (*Orleans*).

Case C-461/14 *European Commission v Kingdom of Spain* [2016] ECLI:EU:C:2016:895.

Case C-488/15 *European Commission v Republic of Bulgaria* [2017] ECLI:EU:C:2017:267.

Case C-142/16 *European Commission v Federal Republic of Germany* [2017] ECLI:EU:C:2017:301.

Case C-323/17 *People Over Wind and Peter Sweetman v Coillte Teoranta* [2018] ECLI:EU:C:2018:244.

Catchpole, R. (2012) *Ecological Coherence Definitions in Policy and Practice-Final Report*, Contract Report to Scottish Natural Heritage, No 41102. Available at: www.nature.scot/sites/default/files/2018-02/Ecological%20Coherence%20Definitions%20in%20Policy%20and%20Practice.pdf

Cliquet, A., Backes, C.W., Harris, J. and Howsam, P. (2009) 'Adaptation to climate change: legal challenges for protected areas', *Utrecht Law Review* 5: 158–75.

Council Directive 92/43/EEC of 21 May 1992 on the Conservation of Natural Habitats and of Wild Fauna and Flora, OJ L 206/7.

De Lucia, V. (2017) 'Beyond anthropocentrism and ecocentrism: a biopolitical reading of environmental law', *Journal of Human Rights and the Environment* 8(2): 181–202.

Directive 2009/147/EC of the European Parliament and of the Council on the Conservation of Wild Birds, OJ L 20/7.

Directive 2010/75/EU of the European Parliament and of the Council of 24 November 2010 on Industrial Emissions (integrated pollution prevention and control), OJ L 334/17.

Dudley, N. (2008) *Guidelines for Applying Protected Area Management Categories*, Gland, Switzerland: IUCN.

European Commission (nd) *Strategy, Sustainable Development Goals, EU Policies and Actions, SDG 14*. Available at: https://ec.europa.eu/sustainable-development/goal14_en

European Commission (2011) *EC Guidance on the implementation of the EU nature legislation in estuaries and coastal zones. The Implementation of the Birds and Habitats Directives in estuaries and coastal zones with particular attention to port development and dredging*. Available at: http://ec.europa.eu/environment/nature/natura2000/management/docs/guidance_doc.pdf

European Commission (2013) *Guidelines on Climate Change and Natura 2000: Dealing with the impact of climate change on the management of the Natura 2000 Network of areas of high biodiversity value*, Technical Report-2013-068. Available at: http://ec.europa.eu/environment/nature/climatechange/pdf/Guidance%20document.pdf

European Commission (2016). *FITNESS CHECK of the EU Nature Legislation (Birds and Habitats Directives)*. Brussels, 16.12.2016 SWD(2016) 472 final.

European Commission (2018) *Commission notice 'Managing Natura 2000 sites- The provisions of Article 6 of the "Habitats" Directive 92/43/EEC'* C(2018) 7621 final. Available at: http://ec.europa.eu/environment/nature/natura2000/management/docs/art6/Provisions_Art_._nov_2018_endocx.pdf

Garcia-Ureta, A. and Lazkano, I. (2015) 'Instruments for active site management under Natura 2000: balancing between stakeholders and nature conservation?', in C.H. Born, A. Cliquet, H. Schoukens, D. Misonne, and G. Van Hoorick (eds), *The Habitats Directive in its EU Environmental Law Context: European Nature's Best Hope?* Abingdon: Routledge, pp 71–92.

Grear, A. (2015) 'Deconstructing anthropos: a critical legal reflection on "anthropocentric" law and anthropocene "humanity"', *Law and Critique* 26(3): 225–49.

Hardin, G. (1968) 'The tragedy of the commons', *Science* 162 (3859): 1243–48.

International Union for the Conservation of Nature, *Protected Areas Categories*. Available at: www.iucn.org/theme/protected-areas/about/protected-area-categories

Kotze, L.J. and French, D. (2018) 'The anthropocentric ontology of international environmental law and the sustainable development goals: towards an ecocentric rule of law in the anthropocene', *Global Journal of Comparative Law* 7(1): 5–36.

Le Blanc, D., Freire, C. and Vierros, M. (2017) 'Mapping the linkages between oceans and other Sustainable Development Goals: a preliminary exploration', Department of Economic & Social Affairs Working Paper No 149 ST/ESA/2017/DWP/149. Available at: https://sustainabledevelopment.un.org/content/documents/12468DESA_WP149_E.pdf

Lee, E. (2016) 'Allocation of decision-making power under the Habitats Directive', *Journal of Environmental Law* 28(2): 191–219.

McGillivray, D. (2012) 'Compensating biodiversity loss: the EU Commission's approach to compensation under Article 6 of the Habitats Directive', *Journal of Environmental Law* 24(3): 417–50.

McLeod E., Rodney, S., Green, A. and Almany, J. (2009) 'Designing marine protected areas networks to address the impacts of climate change', *Frontiers in Ecology and the Environment* 7(7): 362–70.

Millennium Ecosystem Assessment (2005) *Ecosystems and Human Well-being: Synthesis*, Washington, DC: Island Press.

Ntona, M. and Morgera, E. (2018) 'Connecting SDG 14 with the other Sustainable Development Goals through marine spatial planning', *Marine Policy* 93: 214–22.

Ostrom, E., Gardner, R. and Walker, J. (1994) *Rules, Games and Common-Pool Resources*, Ann Arbor, MI: University of Michigan Press.

Paavola, J. (2004) 'Protected Areas governance and justice: theory and the European Union's Habitats Directive', *Environmental Sciences* 1(1): 59–77.

Peterson, C.H. and Lubchenco, J. (2003), 'Marine ecosystem services', in D.E. Lorey (ed), *Global Environmental Challenges of the Twenty-First Century: Resources, Consumption and Sustainable Solutions*, Wilmington: Scholarly Resources, pp 233–50.

Rees, S.E., Foster, N.L., Langmead, O., Pittman, S. and Johnson, D.E. (2018) 'Defining the qualitative elements of Aichi Biodiversity Target 11 with regard to the marine and coastal environment in order to strengthen global efforts for marine biodiversity conservation outlined in the United Nations Sustainable Development Goal 14', *Marine Policy* 93: 241–50.

Secretariat of the Convention on Biological Diversity (2010) *Strategic Plan for Biodiversity 2011–2020, Including Aichi Biodiversity Targets*. Available at: www.cbd.int/doc/strategic-plan/2011–2020/Aichi-Targets-EN.pdf

The Treaty on European Union (Maastricht) 7 February 1992, in force 1 November 1993 (Maastricht Treaty).

Treaty on the Functioning of the European Union, OJ L 326/47 (Treaty of the Functioning of the European Union), (Lisbon) 13 December 2007, in force 1 December 2009.

UN (United Nations) (1992) *Agenda 21: Programme of Action for Sustainable Development*, UN Doc A/Conf.151/26.

UN (2002) *Plan of Implementation of the World Summit on Sustainable Development*, A/CONF.199/20. Available at: www.un-documents.net/jburgpln.htm

UN (2012) *Rio+20 Summit. The Future We Want*, UNGA Res/66/288. Available at: www.un.org/ga/search/view_doc.asp?symbol=A/RES/66/288&Lang=E

UN (2017) *Our Ocean, Our Future: Call for Action*, A/RES/71/312.

UNEP (United Nations Environment Programme) (2004) *Decision adopted by the Conference of the Parties to the Convention on Biological Diversity at its Seventh Meeting,* UNEP/CBD/COP/DEC/VII/5. Available at: www.icriforum.org/sites/default/files/cop-07-dec-05-en.pdf

UNEP (2011) *Report of the Tenth Meeting of the Conference of the Parties to the Convention on Biological Diversity*, UNEP/CBD/COP/10/27. Available at: www.cbd.int/kb/record/meetingDocument/75996?Event=COP-10

Verschuuren, J. (2015) 'Connectivity: is Natura 2000 only an ecological network on paper?', in C.H. Born, A. Cliquet, H. Schoukens, D. Misonne, and G. Van Hoorick (eds), *The Habitats Directive in its EU Environmental Law Context: European Nature's Best Hope?* Abingdon: Routledge, pp 285–302.

Index

F

I

J

K

L

T

U